917.94
S182

MOTORCYCLE JOURNEYS THROUGH

CALIFORNIA

W9-BYZ-154

CLEMENT SALVADORI

Whitehorse Press books are also available at discounts in bulk quantity for sales and promotional use. For details about special sales or for a catalog of motorcycling books and videos, write to the Publisher:
Whitehorse Press
P.O. Box 60
North Conway, New Hampshire 03860-0060
Phone: 603-356-6556 or 800-531-1133
Fax: 603-356-6590
E-mail: CustomerService@WhitehorsePress.com
Web site: www.WhitehorsePress.com

ISBN 1-884313-18-3

5 4 3 2 1

Printed in Hong Kong

This book is dedicated to my mother, Joyce Woodforde Salvadori (née Pawle), who never thought she would give birth to a motorcyclist, but bore up well, nevertheless.

Acknowledgments

A great many people helped in the preparation of this book, from my long-suffering wife to the CHP officer who stopped in the Mojave Desert to see if I were alright . . . I was, but the motorcycle had a flat tire.

Some of these people gave me advice and information (good and bad), others provided a meal, or a place to stay. Some took photographs, others recorded mileages, kept me company on a ride, or loaned me a motorcycle; a few suggested I get a real job.

I did enjoy a truly excellent year doing research for this book, and I rode some roads in the Golden State that are on par with good motorcycling roads anywhere else on this planet.

In alphabetical order, I thank: Joe Anastasio, Bruce Armstrong, Geraldine August, Steve Bergren, Terry Bowen, Jeff Brodie, Buzz Buzzelli, Rich Cox, Craig Erion, David Fairchild, Kurt Grife, John Hermann, Larry Kahn, Reg Kittrelle, Clea Kore, Steve Posson, Jim Quaintance, Tod Rafferty, Bob & Jan Reichenberg, Ted Simon, Craig Stein, Calif Tervo, Mark Tuttle Jr., Bruce & Joan Webster, David Wells . . . and a lot of others whose names escape me at the moment.

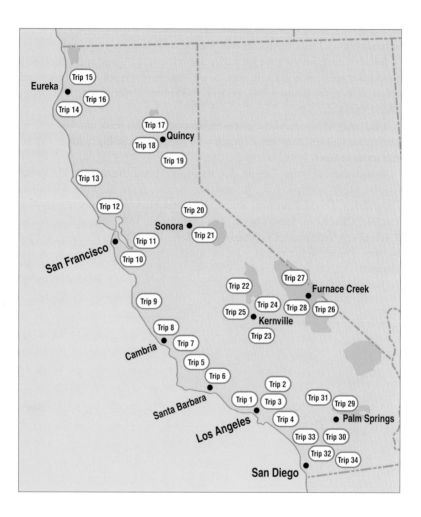

Table of Contents

Introduction

Welcome to California. This place, in my own rather less than humble estimation, offers the best motorcycle riding in the world.

Some of you will exclaim, "What does he know? What about the Swiss Alps! What about the Colorado Rockies!" I have been to the Alps many times, and to the Rocky Mountains, but in each case, you must trade in your motorcycle for skis when the inevitable snow comes. I am writing this in January in California's San Luis Obispo County, and I could go out today, get on my motorcycle, and have a blistering good ride up the Big Sur Highway.

There are great riding roads all over this country—all over this world. But there are more great motorcycle roads in this state than anywhere else on this planet, and many of them can be ridden 12 months out of the year.

Strong words. Most Californians aren't even aware of the full extent of their riding pleasure. Many riders from the south have never been north to CA 96, running along the Trinity and Klamath rivers, from Willow Creek to Yreka. And how many riders from the north have gone down to CA 94, running east from San Diego along the Mexican border to Mountain Springs Pass?

Some benightedly selfish California riders will curse me, saying that I am ruining their favorite roads by writing about them. So be it. For every curse, I imagine that I will get a thousand thanks—from a lot of Californians as well. And, I might add, a few intelligent riders who did not want me to describe their own little Racer Roads have since paid me off handsomely not to mention them.

This book is intended both for Californians and for foreigners, be they from Arizona, Austria, or Australia. Dozens of books have been written about California's roads, but this is specifically intended for the motorcyclists—be they on touring bikes, sport bikes, or even dual-purpose bikes.

Native Californians will accuse me of carpet-bagging. It is true, but though born in the East, my bag is well-traveled on the Golden State roads.

My biggest problem is always deciding: Where will I go today?

I first came to California in 1965, riding a Velocette Venom from Massachusetts. My entry-way to the state was from Mono Lake over Tioga Pass into Yosemite Valley. I went up to Bodega Bay and down to Big Sur. I was hooked. I came back two years later, with a Triumph TR6, ostensibly to get a master's degree at the Monterey Institute of International Studies, but really to ride the Big Sur. I was back in 1975 for a few months. Again in 1977. In 1980, I moved here for good and I've had no regrets. The Big Sur is my backyard. Death Valley is half a day away. The Lost Coast is 400 miles to the north. And the many gorgeous passes through the Sierra Nevada Mountains are to my east.

Out-of-staters should be aware that California is plagued by a disgustingly high cost of living, as well as earthquakes, hurricanes, forest fires, tidal waves, and other natural and un-natural disasters. Do come and visit, but don't plan to stay; we are crowded enough.

The carpet-bagger has spoken.

The Where of It All

As I write this, the state of the state of California is pretty good. The economy is healthy, the natural environment is reasonably well-looked after, and thanks to an overly zealous taxation program, the population is actually diminishing a little. Or at least not growing very fast.

California is one big place. From Crescent City in the north to El Centro in the south is some 800 crow-flying miles, and the width of the state averages about 200 miles across. All told, the Golden State encompasses more than 155,000 square miles, making it the third largest in these 50 United States. (If you don't know what the two biggest are, shame on you.)

On the west side of the state are more than a thousand miles of coastline, much of it bordered by California Highway 1, a truly scenic highway. From the Siskiyou Mountains in the north to the Jamul Mountains in the south, an irregular chain of low coastal mountains keep the seaside climate rather separate from the inland weather for the entire length of the state. We will be doing a lot of coastal riding.

In the middle of the state is the huge Central Valley, made up of the Sacramento Valley to the north and the San Joaquin Valley to the south. It is one of the

The inland valleys of the Central Coast are used for ranching, as well as growing grapes—and the roads can flood in the winter rains.

most fertile places in the nation, thanks to the taxpayers who pick up most of the tab for irrigating everything from cabbages to cotton. To be a farmer in that valley is to be rich. We shan't have much to do with the valley, because the roads are long and straight and rather boring.

Over to the east, coming down from Oregon, the Cascade Range of mountains turns into the Sierra Nevada Range around Lassen Volcanic National Park. These mountains run all the way south to the Tehachapi, San Gabriel, and San Bernardino Mountains, which provide superb riding for the Los Angeles area motorcyclists. Mountains are good, and we will see a great deal of them, from Mt. Shasta in the north, to Palomar Mountain and the Laguna Mountains in the south.

Down in the southeast of the state are the great Mojave Desert, which sits pretty high at 2,000 feet or more, and its cousin to the south, the Colorado Desert, a low desert. Choose the right roads and the riding in those wide-open spaces can be superb, as there is nobody else out there. I can tear up a set of tires in a hurry on those roads, much to the frustration of many a tire distributor who has been kind enough to offer me a set of rim protectors for "testing."

Tallest spot in the state, at 14,494 feet, is Mt. Whitney in the Sierra Nevadas (named in 1864 for one Prof. Josiah Dwight Whitney of the California State Geographical Survey); you can't ride up to the top, but you can get to Whitney Portal at 8,371 feet above sea level. And less than 150 road miles to the east-southeast is Badwater, in Death Valley, at 279 feet below sea level. So, in two to three hours of brisk riding you could go from one of the highest points to the lowest point in the state, which is sort of neat. I guess.

Criss-crossing California's vast geography are about 170,000 miles of roads—big roads like 12-lane freeways, and little roads that wander through the national forests. The California Department of Transportation (known affectionately as CalTrans) maintains a lot of these highways and byways, and keeps them in pretty good shape. The condition of the county-maintained roads varies a great deal, however, depending on how much money a county has, and where it is willing to spend it.

One interesting statistic is that fully 44 percent of the state is owned by us, the public. In addition to county, state, and national parks, there are thousands of square miles under the aegis of the National Forest Service (NFS) and the Bureau of Land Management (BLM), and most of these publicly-owned lands have few or no inhabitants.

Population of the state is some 33,000,000 souls, which would average out to more than 200 people per square mile. But who cares about averages? In Alpine County, 762 square miles consisting mainly of national forest, the 1,000 year-round inhabitants each average almost a square mile to play in. In contrast, the 46-square-mile San Francisco County is jam-packed with some 800,000 people. In fact, a third of all Californians are stuck in greater Los Angeles, another five million in the San Francisco Bay Area, and a few million more in San Diego,

Bakersfield, Sacramento, and some other cities—which leaves relatively few to clutter up the roads we like to ride. There are not many people living along CA 36 between Red Bluff and Fortuna, and not a single gas station between Santa Margarita and Buttonwillow on CA 58. Our megalopolises are mega in size, but you don't even have to go near them if you don't want to.

The economy of the state is worth about $5 trillion annually. If California were to secede from the union, as an appreciable minority of the population might wish, of the 195 or so countries in the world, it would rank about 7th in wealth. And tourism, which we happen to be addressing in this little book, is a contributing factor.

Most of the state's money comes from agriculture, followed by industry (including the sizable remnants of the military-industrial complex), a little oil, a lot of entertainment (Hollyweird), and the give-and-take of general commerce from the Halcyon General Store to Wal-Mart.

All business of which is taxed, of course, the revenue feeding both the federal and state bureaucracies. There's lots of bureaucracy in the Golden State, with 58 counties and hundreds of towns and cities all represented by b'crats striving desperately for womb-to-tomb financial security. Education also chews up a whole bunch of money, with California's public schools going all the way from kindergarten to post-Ph.D. programs.

The pre-history of the state is a bit vague. Some say that the first people strolled in from Asia via the Bering Straits some 10,000 years ago. We do know

Other than this unused railroad station, there is a lot of nothing around Kelso, which is in the middle of the Mojave Desert National Preserve; I, for one, love all the nothingness that the deserts have to offer.

Now, this is riding at its best—the Big Sur coast.

that a number of Indian tribes lived in the state before the Europeans came. Today many of these tribes are recognized as legal entities, which means they can build casinos on their land, much to the great irritation of the Nevada gambling types.

A Spanish explorer named Johnny Cabrillo made note of the coastline back in 1542, but the colonists didn't get around to building a permanent site until 1769, and that was in San Diego. No one knows precisely when the Spaniards first began calling this stretch of Pacific coastline California, but we do know the name came from a 16th-century Spanish novel, *The Adventures of Esplandian,* in which the hero finds an island of beautiful women run by Queen Calafia. The northern part of the west coast was called Alta California, to distinguish it from Baja California, which is now part of Mexico.

The Mexicans threw out the Spaniards in 1821, and in an effort to populate Alta California, they allowed foreigners to come in and settle. Unfortunately for Mexico, most of these ingrates thought they would be better off as American, rather than Mexican, citizens. The U.S. government, feeling the need to create its own destiny, threw the Mexican government out of Alta California in 1847.

The next year, a fellow named John Marshall found gold up at Sutter's Mill in the Sierra foothills. By 1849 the Gold Rush had begun, and the highway that connects many of the old mining camps is called, appropriately, CA 49.

After the gold madness subsided, while the East and Midwest developed factories, California stuck with cattle ranching, lumbering, and a lot of farming. In the early 1900s, an unscrupulous developer by the name of William Mulholland figured he could make a fortune selling land in the greater Los Angeles area if he could guarantee a steady supply of water. He consequently built an aqueduct to drain the huge Owens Valley on the east side of the Sierras and bring the water 400 miles to the southwest. As a result, Bill got very rich, but his family life was very dysfunctional.

Then the Great Depression arrived, and many people starved out of their livelihood in the Dust Bowl headed for the promised land of California, as characterized in John Steinbeck's novel, *The Grapes of Wrath.* (For more on that, visit the Steinbeck museum in Salinas.) World War II ended the Depression and boosted the population of southern California, as the numerous industries which set up to do war work needed laborers.

Since then, California has been on a roll: business has boomed, population has soared, and CalTrans, that aforementioned governmental agency responsible for many of the state's excellent roads, has constructed and maintained a lot of fine byways in the more remote parts of the state. To my admittedly selfish way of thinking, the money that goes into maintaining the Big Sur Highway or Feather River Canyon Road is money well spent.

Conversely, the police forces, from county deputy sheriffs to California Highway Patrol officers, create a lot of revenue for local coffers by ticketing (presumed) speeders. But there are a lot of little-used roads with minimal surveillance, and those are the ones I tend to like to ride.

I've got a good mix of roads in this book, from the touristy, like the Big Sur Highway and Tioga Pass Road in Yosemite National Park, to the little-trafficked, like the Lost Coast loop or the Cecilville Road.

But they are all great roads to ride.

All sorts of surprises will greet you along California's highways, such as this fossilized (concretized?) T-Rex at Cabazon, along I-10 between Palm Springs and Riverside.

How This Book Works

This is a book written for road-going motorcyclists, be they riders who like twisty roads along the coast and in the mountains, and flat-out-hauling roads in the deserts, or riders who like to take their time and smell the roses, or the orange blossoms—or whatever flowers are lining their particular stretch of road.

Since the speed of a motorcycle on any road is determined by the rider's right hand, any road that can be ridden fast can also be ridden slow, so I am appealing to both ends of the speed spectrum. I am not advocating excessive velocities, but there are some far-off roads in California which certainly do appeal to the sporting sense of many riders.

I could fill up a huge appendix with the titles of books about California highways and byways. A few are good, but most are pretty ho-hum. But there has never been a book quite like this one. The focus of this book is on the road, on the ride. Getting there is far more important than being there—wherever "there" might be. Add some spectacular scenery and interesting history, along with a few places to eat well and sleep soundly, and you should have a motorcyclist's travel guide for California.

I spent much of 1999 riding around the state, covering more than 40,000 miles of pavement, riding every road you will read about—and this was backed up by more than 20 years of living and riding in California. In the past year alone, I saw bear, cougar, lynx, elk, antelope, deer, fox, coyote, and other undomesticated animals, which shows that there are a great many more rural miles yet to be explored.

Wandering down back roads can be fun, but be prepared for the occasional water-crossing or cougar-crossing.

The whole purpose of this exercise is to get you on great roads. Do Disneyland if you want, go to the Palace of the Legion of Honor in San Francisco, San Diego's Seaworld, or Sacramento's Old Town, but dealing with those tourist hot spots is not really within the purview of this little tome. For that, you can buy any of a hundred California guidebooks variously dedicated to the fly-and-rent-a-Taurus crowd, the motorhomers, and the like. This book is for motorcyclists. Or people with sporty cars who like going around curves. Yes, I do think the Sports Car Club of America should get a copy.

This book should be read before you go to sleep at night, so dreams of high mountain passes and curling coastal byways will pleasure your night away. Then, stuff it in your tankbag, read about a Trip at breakfast, finish the coffee, and take off for an excellent day's ride.

Maps

Since we are covering a rather large area in relatively few pages, I will explain how I'm going to do it. To create your own perfect journey, you will also need to use your own imagination and get a good map(s). Any decent commercial map of the whole state of California should have 99 percent of the roads that I mention; if the scale is 15 miles to the inch or more, you will be in good shape. Of course, regional and county maps are even better, and if you are a AAA member, note that the California offices have some excellent cartographic renditions of the roads I will describe.

Some people swear by those DeLorme books, with the whole state covered in page after page of detailed topographic rendering. I do use them, but they are a bit large (11"x15") for tankbag work, and the scale is such that I am always having to turn to another page. I far prefer an easy-to-read folding map on which I can plot my route with a Magic Marker.

Yes, the author must occasionally recourse to a map . . . although by then he is usually so lost that only a GPS will help.

In addition to great roads, California also has great motorcycle racing venues, such as the Laguna Seca Raceway near Monterey.

Chapters

For the purposes of this book, I have broken California into 13 general areas, each with its own chapter. These 13 chapters are spread pretty much around the periphery of the state, so that you can easily go from one to another. In addition, there is a 14th chapter which covers the whole state at one whack. The "Been-There, Done-That" riders can go straight to that section, make the loop, and then go home and boast that they've seen all of California. Which, of course, they haven't.

Two of the 14 chapters describe linear routes. The first of these runs up CA 1 along the Pacific shoreline from the Golden Gate Bridge to the Lost Coast; the second takes you along the Western Divide Highway, through Kings Canyon and Sequoia National Parks in the western Sierra Nevadas. These are great roads which lend themselves to straightish shots, but I also include some excursions, places to stay, et cetera.

The remaining chapters each have a Headquarters, a town or city which offers at least two days of good riding within its own area, such as Eureka in the north, and Julian in the south. When I travel, I like to unload the bike at a hotel and then spend a day or two riding without benefit of saddlebags. At each of the Headquarters I will recommend a couple of motels, hotels, and B&Bs, but I will also suggest lodging in other places that I cover on each separate trip. For example, in the Central Coast section I suggest you bed down in Cambria. But some might want to go up to the Monterey Peninsula, which is perfectly fine, if a bit overly touristed, so I have included comments on what Monterey has to offer.

Trips

From each of the Headquarters I will take you on two or three Trips, loops which will bring you back to your toothbrush. The Trips all have mile-by-mile directions, and I throw in a bit of history, and where to find a great burger or a plate of the freshest seafood.

Some feckless types might complain that in some chapters they have to use up part of a Trip just to get to the Headquarters. In that case, to avoid confusion, I recommend they hire a helicopter to pop them right into the motel parking lot at any given Headquarters, so they won't have to fret about it. Of course there is some occasional road-repetition, but you will notice that when I do lead you over the same road twice, I try to do it from either direction. Capable, imaginative riders should be able to make their own minor adjustments to my programs.

Roads and Navigation

Roads are denoted as Interstates (I-5), U.S. routes (US 395), state highways (CA 168), or county roads (S2). Some roads have no numbering, just a name (Santa Rosa Creek Road).

I will include a *few* bits of gravel and dirt, but 99.9 percent of the roads I cover are paved. The text will have big WARNING signs if I'm about to put you on gravel, and I will evaluate the harshness of any non-paved stretch. In dry weather, all of them should be Wingable. If you are one of those riders who suf-

When you're wandering through the California deserts, and you think that little side-road off the asphalt looks good, be prepared for the worst.

The California Highway Patrol are your friends; this patrolwoman stopped to see if I were okay as I was contemplating a flat tire. Of course, they occasionally feel compelled to write speeding tickets as well.

fer a paralyzing phobia in the absence of pavement, however, you can just steer clear of such roads.

Each of the main Trips, loop or linear, will be well-explained, with mile-by-mile directions. These mileages are reasonably accurate, but not too precise—for good reason. First, if you and two friends went for a 100-mile ride, you might have three different readings on the tripmeters at the end. And second, I have found that a stretch of road on a map might be measured for one distance, the sign on the actual road might indicate another, and your odometer might show yet a third—Skyline Boulevard (CA 35) south of San Francisco between CA 92 and CA 9 being a case in point, in which the CalTrans (California Department of Transportation) sign reads 23 miles, the AAA map says 26, and a Harley trip-meter registered 26.3 miles.

Even with imperfect mileages, you shouldn't make a mistake with my directions; I will make it pretty obvious where you have to turn. Sometimes the text will list a Detour, which could be a more picturesque/interesting way to get from Point A to Point B than the main route. I also note Alternate Routes, which will veer you off in some other direction, but always with the same destination in mind. And connecting the trips are Connectors, routes you might consider to get from one chapter to another. A Connector might appear in mid-Trip, so if you want to head off to Death Valley from the town of Lee Vining, the book will tell you how to do it.

Accommodations and Food

Motels, hotels, and flea-bitten, low-life joints will be rated with their lowest prices. Pricing structures have become so complicated that a motel that charges $150 for a room on a weekend in high season can go for $50 on a Wednesday in low season. And some counties charge a 10% "hospitality" tax; others do not. However, the "low price" will give you a hint of what to expect, and you can call up and inquire further. I am covering very few of the hostelries that you will find along the road, and there will be lots of others to choose from; the local Chamber of Commerce/Tourist Bureau that I list in each chapter can send you a big packet of additional information in the mail.

In the Sequoia National Forest, not all fir trees are giants. (Photo by Craig Erion)

You will find that I have a weakness for rather old-fashioned, Fifties-era motels. The paint may be peeling, the faucet might drip, but I love them. Especially when each unit has its own little carport, and the place is a bit out of the way. And they're usually cheap. (I also like rather expensive places, for obvious reasons.)

Food will be where you find it, and out of the roughly 25,000 establishments which serve food in this state, from expensive lobster to a general-store sandwich, I list maybe a hundred. This is not a gastronomical guide, but I will try to keep you away from the fast-food chains. You can get precisely the same Whopper in both your hometown and mine (Atascadero), and that more or less defeats the basic notion of travel, which is to experience something different.

California's National Forests

In the chapters dealing with southern California (3, 4, 5, 14 & 15) I run Trips through four national forests, the Angeles, Los Padres, San Bernardino and Cleveland, and as you enter these forests you will be greeted by a sign alongside the road saying FEE AREA. This means that you, the public, should pay yourself a fee of $5 a day, or $30 a year, for using your own land. This bureaucratic idiocy, applicable to only those four forests, was established in 1997, but I have yet to purchase a Venture Pass, as the recreational fee is called. You only need pay the fee if you are going to stop and actually recreate in the forest; if you are just passing through, no need.

I'm sure that other things you'll see as you ride through California will perplex you on occasion; don't worry about it. Traveling should be enjoyable, and the best kind of travel is the simplest kind: point your front wheel in the direction you want to go, and let out the clutch. With this book in your tankbag, you can ride the best roads that California has to offer, with a minimum of the boring in-between stuff. Go forth, consume gasoline, wear out tires, and have a good time.

And remember, a journey without incident is a pretty dull trip indeed.

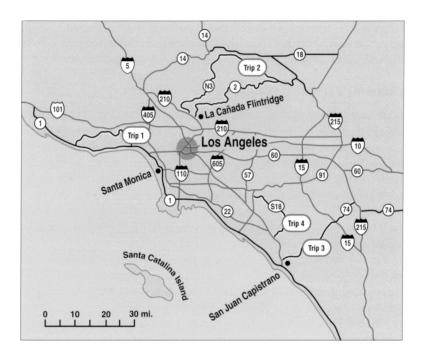

Los Angeles & Environs

3

Headquarters   *Somewhere in Greater Los Angeles*

Los Angeles Bureau of Tourism   *800-228-2252, 213-689-8822*

Best Time to Visit   *All year. Except during earthquake season. And the Crest Highway may be closed due to snow during the winter.*

Getting There   *If you can't figure that out for yourself, you will be in trouble; sell your bike and get a chauffeured limo. But just for the record, Interstate 5 is the main north-south route, with I-10 coming in from the east. Or you could arrive by plane (ship, car, bicycle, hitchhike) and rent a bike (see Appendix B).*

Ground Zero   *There is none—can't be one, for the whole place. However, directions for the four trips I have planned for you will begin on one of the major highways that cuts through Los Angeles, and with the help of a decent map you can figure your way around.*

I'm going to start the riding tour of California here, despite some minor misgivings on my part. Cities do not provide the best of riding venues, unless one is of the hooligan variety, but our geographic focus on a place often starts with a city, and spreads out from there.

I had thought of beginning the book in Death Valley, a place unlike any other place in the world. But, in the end, I decided that this urban environment would give readers a proper appreciation for the realities of the Big Angel. Besides, most out-of-staters would consider Los Angeles a place they would like to see, though they usually have no idea what it is they want to see in it.

Believe it or not, a lot of people who have never been out here actually doubt that there is some superb riding within an hour of LA City Hall. Yet the Los Angeles basin has got the very rugged San Gabriel Mountains to the north, the Santa Monica Mountains to the west, and the Santa Ana Mountains to the south—and each of these hilly places has great roads.

Los Angeles is a very interesting city, a place unlike any other place, a vast collection of small urban enclaves which tries to function as a unit. Its name has been substantially abbreviated from the original 18th-century **Nuestra Senora la Reina de Los Angeles** (Our Lady Queen of the Angels), when a one-legged man could get from one side of town to the other in half an hour. Today you must have your own transportation. Back in 1980, recently moved to the area, I thought I would drop my bike off for some repair work and take a bus home. It took me 20 minutes to ride to the dealer, and four and a half hours to get back to where I lived. And things have gotten worse since then.

CHAPTER

3

The muralists down in Venice have done a lot to pretty up some otherwise bleak views.

Here we are, in the **biggest city in the U. S. of A.;** those Big Apple guys might throw a fit, but if you take into account the population of Greater Los Angeles, and the amount of acreage covered, this is one helluva sizable town. About ten million people live in Los Angeles County, most of them legal. Attach Orange County, which is really just a suburb of LA, and maybe some little bits of adjacent Riverside County, and you have a big land mass with a lot of people.

Do get a map of Los Angeles County, not just the city. The whole place is based on **freeways, or Interstates, or super-slabs**—whatever you want to call those big highways that divide and re-divide the city. I-5 and I-405 are the major north-south routes, but you must not forget I-110 or I-710 or I-605 or CA 55 or CA 57. East-west roads include I-10, I-105, I-210, along with CA 22 and CA 60 and CA 91. Then there is US 101 which plunges right into the heart of LA—and disappears. Of non-freeway roads, the only one I'll slip in here is CA 1, running more or less along the coast from Dana Point to Malibu. Taking fast freeways I could do those 80 miles in a little over an hour; taking scenic CA 1, I'd figure four hours.

There is no conventional "downtown" to LA. **City Hall** is roughly where I-5 and I-10 cross over each other in a gloriously complicated intersection. Another clump of high-rise structures can be found over in **Century City,** about ten miles to the west, just south of Beverly Hills. The rest of the city just sprawls, thanks to the automobile, mostly in bungalows and two-story apartment buildings. Los Angeles has always been a car-conscious place, and the **Automobile Club of Southern California** was founded there in 1900. In 1915, LA had 55,000 registered cars; no mention of motorcycles, but I bet there were a bunch.

Where to stay? Not easy. If you want a cheap motel, try around Los Angeles International Airport, or Disneyland in Anaheim in Orange County. Figure out your favorite hotel chain, be it Motel 6 or Radisson, call up their 800 number, and see if they have some suitable digs somewhere you want to be.

For my recommendations, with safe motorcycle parking, try the following: for old-fashioned high class, the **Chateau Marmont** at 8221 Sunset Blvd. in Hollywood, offers 63 rooms and bungalows with prices ranging from a modest $210 to staggering $1,800 (800-242-8328). The Marmont opened in 1929 as a very sophisticated place where movie stars could live and be indiscreet, and its reputation holds. Another Tinseltown dormitory is the **Hollywood Roosevelt Hotel,** at 7000 Hollywood Blvd., right opposite Mann's Chinese Theater, with 320 rooms going from $100 to $1,000 a night (213-466-7000; 800-950-7667).

Mann's Chinese Theater on Hollywood Boulevard, along the Walk of Fame, attracts tourists from all corners of the globe.

Down in **Venice,** where watching buff bodies is at its best, try the **Marina Pacifica Hotel** at Pacific Avenue and 17th Street, which is right in the very heart of Venice, a half-block off the **Boardwalk**—which is really made of asphalt, not wood, but the pedestrians and roller-bladers are definitely worth seeing. The place is less than five minutes' walk from **Restaurant Row** on Main Street; the hotel has 92 rooms and rates go up from $130 (800-421-8151; 310-452-1111). If you wonder why there are no longer any canals in Venice—there were when Venice was created in 1904—it is because California's mad passion for the automobile caused them to be filled in and paved over 25 years later.

For a really nice spot a little outside of mainstream LA, try one of the 47 rooms at the **Malibu Beach Inn,** on the beach smack dab in the middle of Malibu town, priced from $150 to $325 (22878 Pacific Coast Highway, 800-4-MALIBU; 310-456-6444).

There are ten thousand things of interest in LA, whether it is the **Los Angeles County Museum of Art,** or the **Petersen Automotive Museum** for fine motorcycles. But if I were to start getting into "city sights," we would never get out to the good riding. I should mention that the primary cultural attraction in the area, the new **Getty Center,** is motorcycle friendly; just ride up along I-405, and between the I-10 interchange and the US 101 interchange is the Getty exit. For automobiles, the Getty's limited parking has a reservation list weeks long, but for motorcycles there is no waiting, and the parking in the museum's garage is also

Down in Venice, you could sit at an outdoor cafe and cheerfully watch people all day long; in this case, Bob Reichenberg is the fellow being watched.

The Rock Store on Mulholland Highway, a semi-sacred shrine for Los Angeles-area riders, is a very worthwhile Sunday destination for anyone visiting on two wheels.

free. The good, decent people who run this outfit understand that we take up little space.

LA is noted for its "weekend motorcycle venues," and I will include the three most notorious in this chapter, the Rock Store, the Crest, and the Ortega—plus a short jaunt out Santiago Canyon to Cooks Corner. During the week, hardly a bike is to be seen on these roads, unless it is ridden by some moto-mag editor flogging the latest and fastest, but come Saturday morning, the picture changes, as $40,000 Titans and $400 junkers tear off to the rendezvous of choice.

Curiously, in California, and especially in SoCal (as southern California is abbreviated) where the weather is generally sunny, relatively few of the half-million motorcyclists appear to commute on their machines. Maybe when gas hits $3 a gallon that will change.

Trip 1 The Rock Store

Distance *64 miles*

Highlights *This is Profiling Paradise. On a sunny Sunday morning you will see the rich and famous, the poor and infamous, and everybody in between up there in the Santa Monica Mountains above Malibu.*

The Rock Store itself is a defunct gas station and country grocery store on Mulholland Drive to the west of the village of Cornell. Its still-functioning cafe is the destination of a thousand motorcyclists every weekend. Although there is plenty of good riding in these mountains, the purpose of most attendees is just to see and be seen, and discuss the latest carbon fiber license-plate holder or chromed brake disc. And to check out the celebrities.

Ground Zero for this trip will be on CA 1 between Santa Monica and Malibu, right at Topanga State Beach—which is just six miles west of where I-10 turns into CA 1, a mile or so west of where Sunset Boulevard runs into the sunset at the ocean's edge. Between Sunset and Topanga you will pass from the LA city limits into LA County.

0 Miles Traffic light—turn right onto Topanga Canyon Blvd., a/k/a CA 27. Forty years ago this place was rustic; today it is high priced. A few elderly hippies are still trying to hang on, but the two-lane road is now mostly jammed with new SUVs.

4+ Miles Turn left, going across bridge, onto Old Topanga Canyon Road. On your left you will have just passed the **Willows Restaurant,** the Topanga General Store, and the Topanga Post Office; right opposite the turn, on the right, will be the Topanga Central Auto Service.

   Old Topanga Canyon Road twists and turns a bit, past the **Mill Creek Dressage & Equestrian Center** and other signs that the earth people are on the losing end of possession.

Headed for the Rock Store, a couple of scratchers are coming up Latigo Canyon, the Harley hot on the heels of the BMW.

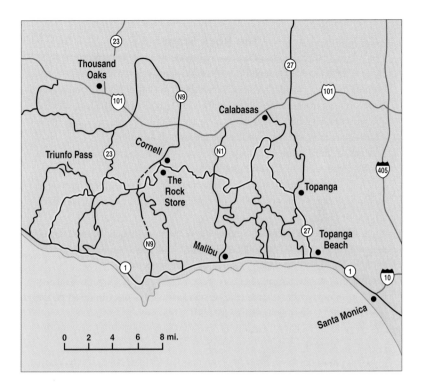

12 Miles STOP sign—turn left onto Mulholland Highway. You will have gone up a thousand feet since leaving the beach and are now actually in the suburbs of the "rapidly growing" (an understatement) town of **Calabasas.** Curiously, you are also in the **Santa Monica Mountains National Recreation Area,** and the government and the property owners go toe to toe. At more than 35 percent, the amount of open, publicly-owned land within the 4,000 square miles of Los Angeles County is quite impressive.

16 Miles Off to the left goes Stunt Road, which leads to Saddle Peak Road, Tuna Canyon Road, and other roads where the weekend morning riders like to test their lean angles. Mulholland itself will be a trifle on the tame side, however, as it is regularly cruised by the sheriff and the CHP.

17 Miles Cold Canyon Road goes off to the left, down to **Monte Nido** and Piuma Road and La Flores Canyon Road. But for my money and pleasure, the better canyon riding is in the western part of the Santa Monica Mountains, so I recommend you go straight along Mulholland Highway. For the geologically curious, these mountains got tossed up out of primeval ooze less than two billion years ago, in Precambrian times.

20 Miles Traffic light—go straight, crossing over Las Virgenes Rd./Malibu Canyon Rd. (a/k/a County Road N1) and enter **Malibu Creek State Park.**

CHAPTER

3

The Rock Store

The original store, not surprisingly, was made of rock. Outside sit two gas pumps which have not pumped gas for a good many years. The Rock Store has become the most singularly focused destination in California—all you see are motorcyclists, from all rides in life, be they Jay Leno on a Black Shadow or the average stud or studette on what he or she can afford. The motorcycling life is a great equalizer, and while at The Rock Store, all are equal.

Back in the Fifties, the Rock Store was simply a store that served the nearby community of **Cornell** and the venturesome types coming out from Los Angeles for a day in the mountains. This, of course, included groups of motorcycle riders who would stop, sit in the shade of the trees, and knock back a Pabst or NuGrape.

In 1961, **Ed** and **Veronica Savko** bought the store, which the local tax assessor lists at 30354 Mulholland Highway, and life continued pleasantly enough. Thanks to the Japanese invasion, the number of motorcycles in the Los Angeles area began growing considerably, and this place was an ideal destination for a day ride. A little cafe was added, and business boomed on the weekends. Ed soon stopped selling gas, as it was more of a convenience for his customers than a means for profit; his decision was helped along one fine day soon after his tanker truck lost its brakes when he was at the wheel.

Then the store became less important, as Cornellians could just as easily buy from the malls along the burgeoning US 101 corridor in the **San Fernando Valley,** just three miles to the north. Catering to the increasing motorcycle crowd became the way to do business. The cafe expanded, and Ed

The genial Ed Savko runs the Rock Store with a benign hand.

added a patio with an outdoor grill. The food that the Rock Store serves, from eggs and bacon to double cheeseburgers, is not *haute cuisine,* but rather good, solid stuff. The coffee is hot, and the sodas are cold.

As a sideline, the Savkos rent the Rock Store to movie companies for location shots. Hollywood usually wants the place during the week, and the motorcyclists come on the weekends, so for the last ten years the cafe has operated on Fridays from 11 o'clock, and on Saturdays and Sundays from seven o'clock, generally closing after dusk. Try calling 818-889-1311 to check on things—or better yet, just show up. ✹

Just west of the Rock Store, at a lookout above a sweeping 180-degree turn, blood-sport enthusiasts gather to watch the squids scrape metal, plastic—and sometimes leather.

23 Miles STOP sign—go straight, crossing over Cornell Rd./Lake Vista Dr.— and watch it, as cross-traffic does not stop.

25 Miles The Rock Store, will appear on your right. On any sunny Saturday or Sunday morning, there will be several hundred motorcycles in front (see The Rock Store sidebar).

26 Miles The road will wind away from the Rock Store, climbing to a sweeping left-hand, uphill turn—and a pull-off spot to the left that is the official **Volcanic Landscape Lookout of the Mulholland Scenic Corridor**—or at least that is what the sign says. Mostly it is referred to as the **Squid Spotting Place,** because a lot of overly zealous riders come tearing along Mulholland, realize that ten to a hundred people are looking at them, and stage fright freezes them at an inopportune moment. Whenever a TV crew wants to do some blood 'n' gore shots, they set up a camera here, and the squids will come out in force and oblige them by tearing up a lot of expensive bodywork.

29 Miles STOP sign—go straight across Kanan Rd./N9.

30 Miles Angle right, staying on Mulholland, as Encinal Canyon Road drops off to the left; Encinal is a good ride, and would take you back to the coast in a most curvaceous manner.

32 Miles STOP sign—turn left onto Decker Rd./CA 23, which also serves as Mulholland.

34 Miles STOP sign (three-way)—turn right on Mulholland, as Decker goes straight.

34+ Miles A barely noticeable road, Yerba Buena, goes off to the right, a rather rough stretch of pavement that will take you down to the coast in 11 miles, over **Triunfo Pass.** At 2,777 feet, it is the highest paved road in the Santa Monica Mountains.

Mulholland itself will be dropping fast, down through **Arroyo Sequit;** those huge dishes off to the right belong to AT&T. Do not get cocky as the road nears the sea, as there are a couple of turns which regularly catch a silly rider, possibly causing grievous damage to bike, body, and spirit.

41 Miles STOP sign—turn left; you will be at CA 1 at **Leo Carrillo State Beach.** Be aware as you breeze along, mountains to your left, ocean to your right, that it took a lot of work to build this road along the shore. It was begun in 1921, finished in 1929, and still manages to get regularly closed down by mudslides when there is a very heavy rain.

If you are looking for properly cooked fresh fish, take a right at the previous STOP sign, head up the coast, and in a mile you will come to **Neptune's Net,** a surfing and motorcycling hangout that serves up excellent seafood and has superb views of the surfing and wind-surfing action across the road.

44 Miles As you go east on PCH, Decker Rd./CA 23 goes off to the left.

Neptune's Net, a roadhouse along the Pacific Coast Highway/CA 1, just west of where Mulholland Highway ends, is a nice spot to hang out and enjoy the surfing and windsurfing action across the road.

45 Miles To the left is Encinal Canyon Road, a very fine way to get back to Mulholland.

48 Miles **Zuma Beach** will be off to your right, where, for a fee, you could park your bike, eat beach food, and stare at out-of-shape humans in skimpy bathing suits. Have you ever stopped to consider how absurd the term "suit" is when applied to what we wear when going for a swim?

50 Miles At a traffic light, Kanan-Dume Rd./N9 goes off to the left, while CA 1 becomes a four-laner.

53 Miles **Latigo Canyon** will be up to the left, another marvelous way to return to Mulholland.

Malibu Colony

In 1927, some movie types wanted to get away from the hustle and bustle of Hollywood, and the newly opened road gave them access to this remote stretch of beach. A small colony grew, with severe gate-guards to keep the hoi polloi away. Malibu Colony has since grown to cover more than a mile of coastline, and though anybody can use the low-tide beach, it takes some walking from either **Malibu Lagoon State Beach** to the east, or **Amarillo Beach** to the west. It would be much easier if you knew somebody famous (or merely rich) who could let you in through the gate, so you could watch the sun set from some of the most expensive real estate on earth. ✳

56+ Miles You will pass the well-manicured campus of **Pepperdine University,** where Clinton's nemesis, Ken Starr, was offered a deanship, and continue past Malibu Canyon Rd./N1, dropping down a long hill, at the bottom of which is a traffic light. To the right will be the **Malibu of Movie Legend.** The city actually stretches for more than 25 miles along the coast, but here, right off Webb Way, is Malibu Road, which leads to the **Malibu Colony** (see Malibu sidebar).

57 Miles After crossing over **Malibu Creek,** you will be in the main part of the Malibu business district, with the **Malibu Inn** serving up very good food, and the Malibu Pier a good place to walk off the lunch. The aforementioned **Malibu Beach Inn** is not far from the pier, if you are so taken with the scene that you wish to spend the night.

60 Miles **Las Flores Canyon** will be off to the left, leading up to Mulholland through a maze of other roads; don't worry about getting lost, as eventually you will be back at either Mulholland or CA 1.

63 Miles Tuna Canyon comes down to meet CA 1—in recent years it was made one-way down to the sea, rumor having it that local residents objected to snarling bikes going up the hill.

64 Miles Arrive back at **Topanga Beach.**

Trip 2 The Crest Highway & Newcombs Ranch

Distance *123 miles*

Highlights *This loop can be ridden slowly by the touring type with trailer in tow, but it is best enjoyed by a serious sporting rider, as it is a superb and occasionally tricky loop that starts down in the valley, goes up to nearly 8,000 feet, swings along the south side of the Mojave Desert, then returns via low canyons through the mountains.*

The starting point will be where the northern segment of CA 2 and I-210 meet in La Cañada Flintridge, just north of Pasadena; the exit sign reads CREST HIGHWAY. You will be at about 1,300 feet above sea level here, the Santa Monica beaches a mere 25 miles away. Technically CA 2 starts in Santa Monica, but unless you really love crawling along with urban traffic through numerous traffic lights, you should freeway over to La Cañada Flintridge.

Ground zero for this trip will be where CA 2 starts north from Foothill Boulevard, which parallels I-210 on the south side. Right there is the Hill Street Cafe, a meeting place for riders who want to fortify themselves before heading up the mountain.

0 Miles Start at the intersection of Foothill Boulevard and Angeles Crest Highway, with a 76 Station on your left, Shell on your right; next gas, 60 miles. If you wish—and many a sport-rider does—you could do those 60 miles in less than an hour, which would cause adrenaline to course through your veins like the oil passing through the pump in your engine.

Arriving at Newcombs Ranch, on the Crest Highway, on a cold December Friday, I found nought but hot coffee and good steak and eggs; on a warm weekend there would be a hundred bikes here.

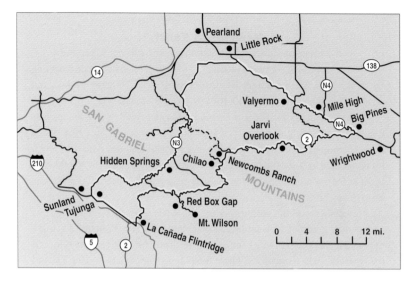

First-timers be wary, however. There are some deceptive curves on this road, and an error in judgement just might have you running off a mountain-side with nothing to stop you for the next 2,000 feet.

Crossing over I-210, heading up the hill, the road will be four-lanes for two miles, running through suburbia and past the country club. When all signs of dwellings stop, the road narrows to two lanes, and you will be in the **Angeles National Forest,** climbing up through the **San Gabriel Mountains,** passing a ranger station, Slide Canyon, and Dark Canyon—twisting higher and higher. This is a serious road, and all the black tar stripes that CalTrans puts in the cracks (or snakes, as these are unaffectionately called), can put your lean angle on alert.

9 Miles Go straight at the Clear Creek intersection, staying on CA 2. N3, a/k/a the Angeles Forest Highway, goes off to the left; you will be on the northern end of that road in about 80 miles.

14 Miles Go straight at the Mt. Wilson intersection, or **Red Box Gap** as it is of-ficially called. If you want a really, really, twisty nine-mile (up and back) side trip excursion, go up to **Mt. Wilson Skyline Park** and the observatory. The observatory tends to be open only on the weekends, but the ride up, and the view from the top, amidst a huge antenna field, are stupendous. I might add that skate-boarders like this little stretch, sometimes outfoxing the rangers to come slithering down at outrageous speeds—sans brakes.

18 Miles Go straight on CA 2 as Upper Big Tujunga Canyon Road goes down to the left. If you have very limited time, or are suffering from vertigo, take Upper Big Tujunga and in nine miles you will loop back down to the Angeles Forest Highway.

CHAPTER

3

Newcombs Ranch

On a sunny weekend, upwards of a hundred bikes will be parked out front, their riders outside tire-kicking or inside eating. Still others will be screaming by on the road. The restaurant is open all week in the summer, Fridays and weekends in the winter (626-440-1001, if you wish to check).

As I said before, this is a serious road, and riders tend to take themselves quite seriously, with all the go-fast stuff that can be bolted on a bike. They dress accordingly, too, with expensive and colorful leathers. And then feel a bit humiliated as some old codger on an aged 750 Nighthawk stays right with them as they continue up the mountain at great rates of speed. Experience is the real key here.

I remember well the morning years ago, when video was relatively new, and a small group of us went up the mountain with **Jim Wolcott,** a camera mounted on his seat pointing backwards. We chased him up the mountain, and then back down to Newcombs, where Jim plugged the camera into the TV, and we all sat, ate breakfast, and watched what we had just done. Everybody else came in from outside to watch, as well. There we were, all watching what we had just done. Then we went out and did it all again. Motorcyclists are a strange breed—as any golf addict will attest. ✸

20 Miles At 5,000 feet, the views of the Los Angeles Valley will be receding as you enter the middle of the mountain range, going past **Charlton Flats,** and climbing into the forest. Although much of the road is open, some of it is wooded, and the transfer from bright sun to shade can be a trifle unnerving.

26 Miles Pass the turn-off to **Chilao. Newcombs Ranch** will appear on your left (see Newcombs Ranch sidebar).

31 Miles You will be coming up to the **Waterman Ski Area** and **Cloudburst Summit** (7,018 feet)—and you are barely an hour from the beach. (This is one reason why SoCal is as close to being a motorcyclist's paradise as you can reasonably hope to find.) Past the **Krakta Ridge Ski Area,** the road will be high and open, and can be ridden exceedingly fast. You will be paralleling the **Pacific Crest Trail** for a few miles, should you care to park your bike and take a hike.

37 Miles You'll see a short, straight tunnel ahead of you, which turns out to be two short, straight tunnels. Be cautious. There is a slight curve at the far end, and if you have just whacked it up to 120 mph, you could be in for a surprise.

Do stop at the **Jarvi Overlook** just beyond the tunnels, to admire the view and contemplate your mortality. Mr. Jarvi was a U.S. Forest Service manager who did a superb job keeping this place just as we motorcyclists love it to be.

From this point, you will be getting huge views of the **Mojave Desert** off to the left. After going up and over **Dawson Saddle** (7,901 feet, the high point on the road), you can see **Mt. Baldy** (a/k/a Mt. San Antonio) off to the right, more than 10,000 above sea level. Then it is up to **Blue Ridge Summit** (7,386 feet), followed by a steady descent which will take you down to a wide spot in the road called Big Pines.

56 Miles Turn sharp left onto N4, marked PALMDALE, JACKSON LAKE on the sign. Not much in **Big Pines,** but there is a stone tower and a ranger station, and if you have passed them, you have missed your N4 turn and will soon be in **Wrightwood** (see Wrightwood sidebar).

Back at Big Pines, angle right, heading northwest, downhill, on N4, a/k/a Big Pines Highway, with that aforementioned sign reading PALMDALE, JACKSON LAKE. Nice road, as it curves down through the foothills, past Jackson Lake.

62 Miles Go straight on Big Pines Highway, while N4 cuts sharp right. At the corner is the **Mile High Cafe,** open every day except Wednesday, open for breakfast from eight o'clock Friday through Sunday, 11 a.m. the rest of the time.

As you whizz along Shoemaker Canyon, **Pinyon Ridge** will be to your left, while the **Mojave Desert** is becoming more apparent on your right.

Wrightwood

Four miles beyond Big Pines on CA 2, past the Mountain High Ski Area, is the mountain community (6,000 feet) of the Wright brothers' wood, a family who ranched up here about a hundred years ago. Arco and Shell both sell gas.

A lot of motorcyclists come here to eat, though the number of eateries is limited. On Park Street, the main street in town, at right angles to CA 2, is **Lyle's Pine Manor & Saloon,** serving a large breakfast daily. Opposite Lyle's is the **Yodeler,** but that is not open until lunch. The **Crystal Island,** on Cedar Street (paralleling Park) has brunch on the weekends. **Cinnamon's Bakery,** on CA 2, is open at 5 a.m. every day, but that is a bit early, even in June, for a dedicated motorcyclist to arrive. If you want to inquire about taking motorcycle trips to Australia or Zimbabwe, **Tri-Community Travel,** on CA 2 opposite Park Street, is the official U.S. representative for Edelweiss Tours (800-582-2263); As both a motorcyclist and skier, the owner, **Mary Etta Horne,** has the best of both worlds up here.

If you are so taken with the place that you wish to stay, the **Mountain View Motel** on CA 2 offers an assortment of rooms, some with jacuzzis ($60+; 760-249-3553). ✱

67 Miles Stay straight as Big Pines Highway becomes Valyermo Road, and Big Rock Creek Road goes off to the left.

67+ Miles Stay left on Valyermo Road, going over a bridge, while Bobs Gap Road goes off to the right.

71 Miles Turn left at the sign reading LITTLE ROCK DAM 11, onto Pallet Creek Road—and a hundred yards along turn right onto Fort Tejon Road. This good asphalt will whistle you along through the foothills at a great rate.

78 Miles Turn left where the sign reads ANGELES FOREST HWY 10, LITTLE ROCK DAM.

81 Miles STOP sign at a four-way intersection out in the middle of nowhere; the other traffic, running between **Pearland** and **Little Rock Reservoir,** does *not* stop. Continue straight, and you will be on Mt. Emma Road, circling the northwesterly portion of **Mt. Emma Ridge.**

88 Miles STOP sign—turn left onto Angeles Forest Highway (N3), where the sign says HWY 2 21. Pointing to the right, the sign reads PALMDALE 10.

Hidden Springs Cafe, along the Angeles Forest Highway, is open every day; Otis the Chef was kind enough to take my picture.

90 Miles To the right goes Aliso Canyon Road, which runs into **Soledad Canyon**—yet another way out of these mountains.

93 Miles You will be up on **Mill Creek Summit** (4,910 feet) at a small intersection, the right turn going to **Mt. Gleason,** the left back up to **Chilao** on a dirt road.

99 Miles To your left will be the well-marked turn to Upper Tujunga Canyon Road, which can take you back to CA 2 in nine miles.

100 Miles **Hidden Springs Cafe** is on your right, open from roughly 10 a.m. until roughly dark, with the Lewis family running the operation; Otis is often at the griddle, and he turns out a fine hamburger.

104 Miles Turn right onto Big Tujunga Canyon Road, leading to Sunland. You could go straight, hit CA 2 in four miles, and backtrack to La Cañada Flintridge, but this will be more fun.

   The Big Tujunga Canyon Road will make a steep descent into **Big Tujunga Canyon,** over several old concrete bridges, before flattening out to run alongside the river; it is generally dry, but when winter rains come, the river can fill up in a hurry and the road can be closed.

115 Miles Enter **Sunland** from the north and go through several STOP signs, always following your nose.

116 Miles Traffic light—turn left at the intersection with Foothill Boulevard, to go seven miles east on Foothill. Or pick up I-210, if that is in your plans.

123 Miles Arrive back at the **Hill Street Cafe** and the start to Angeles Crest Highway.

Trip 3 The Ortega Hwy & The Lookout Roadhouse

Distance *44 miles (if you just go up to the Lookout and come back)*

Highlights *This is not really a loop, as more than 90 percent of the riders who go up the Ortega Highway come back the same way. CA 74 is a good road and it has superb views—on a clear day. And the destination, The Lookout Roadhouse, always has a bunch of motorcyclists eating breakfast, drinking coffee, kicking tires, and exaggerating the truth.*

When I first went up the Ortega in May of 1980, I thought this was one out-landishly great ride, and it began just ten miles from where I was living in Laguna Beach. Life couldn't get much better. Then, long after I had moved from Laguna to Atascadero, the county made the highway a "double-fine" zone. If you adhere to the speed limits, you will have no worries. Unfortunately, this Orange County Racer Road is becoming a tad too civilized for a lot of riders.

To get there, come south down I-5 past El Toro and Mission Viejo to San Juan Capistrano.

Ground zero for this trip is at the ORTEGA HWY, CA 74 exit.

0 Miles Turn left at traffic light after exiting I-5 at Ortega Hwy./CA 74 exit, crossing over I-5, heading east. Several gas stations will be there to do your bidding (see San Juan Capistrano sidebar).

The Lookout Roadhouse, on the Ortega Highway/CA 74, is the destination for Orange County motorcyclists on any Sunday. (Photo by Bob Reichenberg)

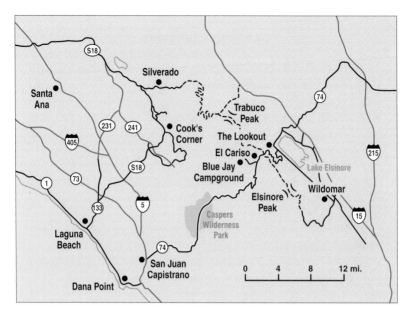

1 Mile If you are historically curious, note the **Parra Adobe & Harrison House** site on your right, now in the middle of San Juan suburbs; these are two of the oldest buildings in the county, though there is nothing of great visual appeal to recommend them unless you are a student of 19th-century California architecture.

3 Miles Beyond the San Juan city limits, cross over **San Juan Creek** and pass through a tid-bit of the fast-vanishing cropland in Orange County, and through the traffic light where Antonio Parkway goes off to the left, La Pata Avenue to the right. From this point, the road will become pleasant, sliding over low hills and down into dales, the San Juan Creek off to your left a-ways.

8 Miles The entrance to **Caspers Wilderness Park** will be to your left. This is a county park, some 7,600 acres, and it can be wild. And the fact that it is just a few minutes from gross over-population makes it even more astonishing. Every few years somebody gets mauled by a mountain lion here—which just makes it all the more exciting. Day use is $2, camping is $12.

10 Miles You will have a long straightaway out in the middle of absolutely nowhere, and halfway along will be a traffic light which marks the entrance to the **Nichols Institute,** some sort of bio-medical research outfit. How the place got permission to build out here in the middle of the wilderness beats me. I'd like to think that they do top-secret work for the government, handling potentially dangerous biological and extraterrestrial stuff. Though I doubt it.

San Juan Capistrano

If you wish to soak up a bit of California history, turn right at the traffic light at Mile 0, and after 300 yards you will be in front of the old **Mission San Juan Capistrano.** Construction on this mission began in 1776 and was completed some 15 years later. A few years went by and the padres decided that an even bigger church was needed to glorify the Almighty. Nine years were then spent building a more noble edifice—which an earthquake knocked down in 1812; God does work in wondrous and mysterious ways.

After the Mexican revolution of 1821, in which the Catholic church had sided with the Spanish losers, the mission and its property were secularized by the new government. President Lincoln gave it back to the church in 1865, however.

The town of San Juan Capistrano *is* a tourist trap, but a nice one. **Sarducci's Cafe,** on Camino Capistrano on the west side of the mission, serves good food all day. If you want a place to stay down in these parts, you could do worse than the **Best Western Capistrano Inn,** on the east side of I-5, which is within walking distance to all the sights and sites ($75+; 27174 Ortega Hwy.; 800-441-9438; 949-493-5661). From there you could get an early start on the Ortega.　　　　　　　　　　　　　　　　　❋

12 Miles　The road winds along past the **San Juan Hot Springs,** which was a hedonistic hangout until it burned down in the early Nineties; the county is going to reopen the place as a campground later in 1999. Beyond a little bridge, a small road on the left leads to a church-sponsored camp called the **Lazy W Ranch.** After you pass the forest service fire station, you will be in the **Cleveland National Forest,** where the good part of the Ortega starts.

For the next 12 miles you will be climbing up the **Santa Ana Mountains,** which divide the super-heated inner valleys from the cool coast. When you hear someone saying that "the Santa Anas are blowing," it means a hot wind is coming from the east, and this is the time of year (usually the fall) that keeps the fire-fighters well employed.

The road runs along the south side of **San Juan Canyon,** with a lot of curves and bends that should be ridden with caution. If you happen to arrive an hour after dawn on a weekend morning, you will find brightly-leathered boys and girls dashing up and down on their R-bikes. After you cross into **Riverside County** and pass a picnic area and a campground, you will come around a 180-degree sweeper and up a hill to . . .

18 Miles　. . . the **Ortega General Store & Old Candy Shop,** on your right, with a small commercial campground. Not much of a motorcycling hangout.

Then dash down the hill a bit, crossing **Decker Canyon,** and a superbly fast "S" will run you up high; this road was reconstructed about 1990, and whoever engineered the place had to have had a racetrack in mind. The road straightens a bit as it goes past the turn to **Los Pinos Camp** (for wayward youth) and the **Blue Jay Campground.** After this, you could take a left onto a long, rough dirt road that goes past **Trabuco Peak** (4,604 feet) and eventually drops down to **Silverado Canyon** (see Trip 4), or you could stay on the rough pavement as it curves back to the Ortega.

21 Miles Come into **El Cariso,** a small mountain community with the **El Cariso General Store** on the right side; the **Eagle's Nest,** on the left, was an afternoon gathering spot for the cruiser types, but it had a FOR SALE sign on the door in January 2000.

Past the forest service fire station, you'll find an intersection, with pavement leading off to the left and right. The left road connects with Blue Jay and Trabuco Peak, while to the right the road runs past some upscale housing, then turns to dirt as it goes by **Elsinore Peak** and drops down to **Wildomar.**

21+ Miles As you crest the highway, you'll be about 2,600 feet above the Pacific that lies just 21 condor-flying miles away. Swing down a couple of bends, curve right—and the whole of **Lake Elsinore** and the surrounding valley will be 1,500 feet below.

22 Miles The **Lookout Roadhouse** will be on your left; if you want to see the view beforehand, surf on over to www.LookoutRoadhouse.com. On a weekend, there will be many, many motorcycles parked in the lot. Lots of riders

The Lookout Roadhouse attracts the fast crowd early in the morning, while the Harleys and Gold Wings come later. (Photo by Bob Reichenberg)

come here just to fraternize, compare notes on the latest sticky tires, and discuss the latest ups and downs of H-D stock. The knee-grinders are here from dawn 'til nine or ten, followed by the more laid-back types throughout the rest of the day. The Lookout has been in business since 1945, and was bought by **Barbara Sheahan** in 1968; this delightful woman keeps the place open from eight in the morning to seven in the evening, seven days a week, and she serves up a rib-coating breakfast.

28 Miles You have just looped down and down the mountain to the STOP sign at the intersection with Grand Avenue. Taking a left would keep you on CA 74, which, as I said at the beginning, will run you over the next set of moun-

Barbara Sheahan owns The Lookout Roadhouse on the Ortega Highway, and her sausage and eggs are as good as her smile.

tains and down to **Palm Springs;** a right would run you south down to Palomar Mountain, or a windy trip through the **Walker Basin** via De Luz to Fallbrook. Or you could return from whence you came; as I have always maintained, no road has been ridden properly until it has been ridden in both directions.

Connector

The Ortega does provide a great connection to other motorcycling venues, such as the **San Jacinto Mountains** above Palm Springs (just follow CA 74), or **Palomar Mountain** down in San Diego County (see Chapter 15). ✸

Trip 4 Santiago Canyon & Cook's Corner

Distance *27 miles (freeway-to-Interstate distance)*

Highlights *This is a short half-loop, running up along the edge of the Santa Ana Mountains, with a couple of possible excursions into little canyons.*
   Ground zero is in northeastern Orange County about 6 miles east of Disneyland, at the intersection of the CA 55 freeway and Katella Avenue. Katella going east will soon turn into County Road S18.

0 Miles Head east from CA 55 on Katella Avenue, into Villa Park. S18 becomes Santiago Canyon Road, and curves south, past housing developments.

5 Miles Traffic light—turn right, following S18. If you went left, you would end up in **Irvine Regional Park,** a destination for the urban hordes who flee their habitats on the weekends. Go just a couple hundred yards and you will find another . . .

5+ Miles . . . Traffic light—turn left, following S18/Santiago Canyon Rd. over the 231/161 Payways. (Toll roads are the rage of the late Nineties in Orange County, and it is best to stay in the center lane so as not to find yourself at some tollbooth where they want $252.20). The bucolic scenery will roll past **Irvine Lake** and through **Limestone Canyon.**

On a pleasant Sunday, several hundred motorcycles will show up at Cook's Corner, in eastern Orange County.

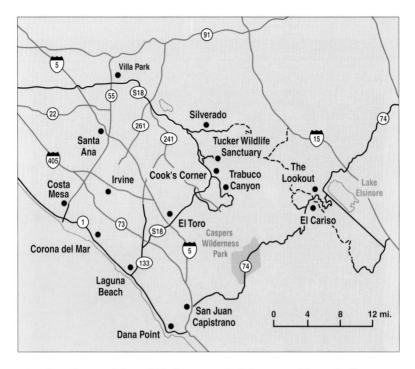

12 Miles Stay straight on S18; the turn to the left goes up **Silverado Canyon,** a dead-end, unless the gate is open to climb a rough dirt road up to **Santiago Peak** and on to the **Ortega Highway** (a dual-purpose bike is highly recommended). If you have the time, the side trip to the end of the canyon is only ten miles. The **Silverado Cafe,** on your right, is where the locals eat breakfast, lunch, and early suppers.

From here, S18 moves along **Santiago Creek,** which is presently a rather under-populated part of Orange County.

15 Miles To the left will be the turn to **Modjeska Canyon,** named for an actress who retired there in the 1890s. For the ornithologists among us, the **Tucker Wildlife Sanctuary** at the end of the canyon, just three miles off S18, offers good bird counting. A mile up the canyon, the **Modjeska Country Store** has a small stock of essentials.

S18 will cross over **Santiago Creek** (which runs into Modjeska Canyon), go over a rise, and start a gentle descent.

17 Miles To your left, you will see an alternative and much more enjoyable (i.e. twisty) approach to Modjeska Canyon. Housing developments are beginning to pop up alongside S18.

18 Miles **Cook's Corner** will be on your left, where Live Oak Canyon Road butts into S18. Signs indicate MISSION VIEJO 1 straight ahead on S18, with

49

On weekend afternoons, the motorcyclists gather at Cook's Corner, on Orange County Road S18 east of El Toro. (Photo by Bob Reichenberg)

Cook's Corner

On any weekend short of a rainy one, a hundred or more bikes will be pulled up—mostly Harleys, but everything else will be represented, too.

Cook's, a bar and grill, has been around in roughly the same state of disrepair since 1947. It used to be a reasonably rural hangout when I began going there in 1980, when the mainstay of the business consisted of locals who lived in the hills, and bikers. A number of patch-holders (1%-ers) used to show up, but the then-bartender, **Big Mac,** was large enough to maintain the peace. As we end the century, the clientele has changed somewhat, but though the sawdust on the floor is now imported, the place still has its charm. Cook's opens at seven o'clock for the breakfast, and continues on well into the night, 365 days a year. Beer and booze are the money-makers; the food is just a convenience so serious drinkers don't have to go home.

18 Miles **Cook's Corner** will be on your left, where Live Oak Canyon Road butts into S18. Signs indicate MISSION VIEJO 1 straight ahead on S18, with O'NEILL REGIONAL PARK 3, TRABUCO OAKS 4 going to the left (see sidebars on Cook's Corner and Trabuco Canyon).

Back at Cook's, continue on S18, which will become El Toro Road.

21 Miles Traffic light at the Santa Margarita Parkway—go straight. You will be in **El Toro,** with a straight, broad road in front of you and lots of traffic and shopping malls on either side.

27 Miles At I-5, you must figure out the next move for yourself. Straight on S18 would take you to **Laguna Beach,** which is not a bad place if you don't mind crowds. North on I-5 goes to **Disneyland** and LA, and back to CA 57. South goes to San Juan Capistrano and San Diego.

Trabuco Canyon

From Cook's you could take a left onto S19 and go along Live Oak Canyon Road, which has a lovely awning of trees as it drops down into **Trabuco Canyon** and becomes Trabuco Canyon Road. In the small community of Trabuco Canyon, the **Trabuco Oaks Restaurant,** right behind the general store, prides itself on cutting off the neckties of presumptuous clients, and serving excellent red meat. From there, you could continue along Trabuco Canyon Road, go over **Trabuco Creek,** and climb a short twisty bit to crest a hill and find a gigantic housing development.

The sensible/faint of heart will then turn around and go back. The intrepid will continue straight along **Plano Trabuco** to the Santa Margarita Parkway; from there you would go right (north) and then turn left at El Toro Road. ✳

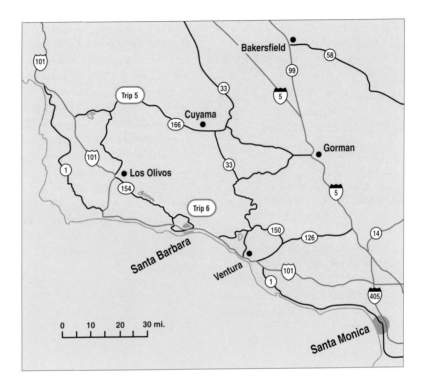

Santa Barbara County

Headquarters *Santa Barbara*

Chamber of Commerce/Visitor Center *805-965-3021 or 805-568-1811*

Best Time to Visit *All year*

Getting There *US 101 is not only the road of choice—it is virtually the only road. It is a freeway, so you will have to choose your exit. If you are coming from Los Angeles and want a peaceful seaside approach, take the Cabrillo Blvd. exit and ride in along the beachfront. You will pass right by the Visitor Center, at the corner of Garden Street, should you want to collect an armful of literature and maps. If you want to go downtown, take the Garden Street exit to stay on the inland side of US 101.*

Ground Zero *This will be where State Street butts into Cabrillo Boulevard at Stearns Wharf. If you are coming north (west, really) on US 101, you could take the above-mentioned Cabrillo Blvd. exit, or, from either direction, you could take the Garden Street exit and head for the shore, just a quarter-mile away. That will put you on Cabrillo; turn right, and a block down will be State Street.*

Santa Barbara is easily accessed from the City of Lost Angels, just a hundred miles away, but it has an entirely different atmosphere. Civilization, such that it is, is wedged in along a narrow coastal strip. Thanks to the presence of the **Los Padres National Forest,** however, everything else in the county is close to the 21st-century definition of wilderness (no houses and a lot of trees). And the area does provide two good loops, one big, the other small.

Very nice city, the city of Saint Barbara. Charming. Almost too charming, especially since the City Fathers chased out most of the homeless children. I think they gave them all bus tickets to Ventura.

The town of Saint Barbara occupies a narrow east-west strip of land backed by the **Santa Ynez Mountains** and fronted by the **Pacific Ocean.** A lot of expensive people live here, most of them discreetly tucked into the hills above the city; they know that the tourists throng to the coast, and prefer to keep their distance.

It takes a bit of figuring to get geographically oriented in this town. Central Santa Barbara has been built on a grid pattern with a lot of one-way streets, so circling a block or two will usually get you to where you want to go. The main street is **State Street,** which runs west from Stearns Wharf, under US 101, for about four miles, only to meet up with US 101 farther along. This was the old 101, and the west end has a lot of older (inexpensive) motels. Ten downtown blocks of State Street have been turned into a strolling paradise, with sidewalk

Santa Barbara became an active mission in 1786, but the building you see today was completed in 1820, after the original was destroyed in an earthquake.

cafes, restaurants, bookstores—all the ways to spend money. One lane of traffic still moves along in each direction, but there is no parking on those blocks; there are lots of spaces and garages on the side streets, however. On Tuesday afternoon, two blocks are closed off for a farmers' market.

The city has several key tourist destinations, the primary one being **Stearns Wharf** (where, by the way, you can ride out and park your motorcycle *for free*—cars pay), the **Mission Santa Barbara,** founded in 1776, and the **Presidio,** the old Spanish military headquarters.

Where you stay is up to you and your budget. The **first Motel 6 in the country** is a two-minute walk from **East Beach,** at the east end of Cabrillo Boulevard, and you will notice that the company down-sized the rooms after building this one ($55+; 51 rooms; 443 Corona del Mar; 805-564-1392; 800-466-8356); note that this is one of five M6s in the area, so make sure you know which one you want. Smack dab in front of the Motel 6 is the **Radisson Hotel Santa Barbara,** at 901 East Cabrillo Blvd., which is a bit bigger and pricier, with 174 rooms available at $120 to $260 per night (805-966-2285). If you want to stay right by Stearns Wharf, the **Harbor View Inn** has 80 rooms, ranging from a "non-view" for $150 to a "luxury ocean view" for $350.

For a slightly different and more elegant approach, try the **Montecito Inn,** built in 1928, some 35 years before the US 101 freeway separated it from the sea. Legend has it that **Charlie Chaplin** was involved in its construction, and this

That, dear reader, is the first Motel 6 ever built, just a hundred yards from the Santa Barbara beaches; the rooms were a little bigger back then.

connection is made known in the establishment. The 60 rooms are priced from $185 on up (1295 Coast Village Rd.; 805-969-7854; 800-843-2017).

Sustenance. Like any good tourist, you could stroll out on Stearn's Wharf, which has several restaurants and cafes, and have a meal in which where you eat is more important than what you eat. You'll find perfectly adequate, but uninspired fare; I have been told that at one well-advertised restaurant, the clam chowder comes right out of a can. More interesting and generally less expensive food can be found among the shops at the marina, less than a mile west of the wharf.

For more rewarding gastronomical experiences, I would recommend **Esau's Coffee Shop** at 403 State, near the intersection with Gutierrez Avenue, bracketed by a liquor store and a porn shop (their breakfast is excellent). Or go up State for 13 blocks to 1701, which has the nicest **IHOP** I have ever eaten at, with patio dining. For lunch, go to **Fresco!** at the west end of State Street, in the Five Points Plaza at the intersection with La Cumbre Road; the gorgonzola and walnut salad is delightful, as are the calzones. For dinner, the **Montecito Cafe** at the Montecito Inn does itself proud, or you might check out **Chad's,** at 625 Chapala (parallel to State).

Trip 5 The Big Loop

Distance *207 miles*

Highlights *This loop covers some territory, going east from Santa Barbara to Ojai, north over Pine Mountain Summit to Cuyama, west on CA 166 along the Cuyama River, south on Tepusquet and Foxen Canyon roads, and then east on CA 154 over San Marcos Pass.*

0 Miles Head east on CA 225/Cabrillo Blvd., going past the **Tourist Information Office** at the corner of Garden Street.

2+ Miles Turn right to access US 101 South/Los Angeles, though technically this runs in an easterly direction, passing through **Montecito and Summerland,** passing the **Santa Barbara Polo Club,** and continuing on into **Carpinteria.**

14 Miles Exit right at CA 150, OJAI sign, and turn left, heading for Ojai. After a little more than a mile, you will pass the east end of CA 192, which was Foothill Road in Santa Barbara, Casitas Pass Road in Carpinteria.

21 Miles Cross over **East Casitas Pass** at 1,143 feet and come down by **Lake Casitas.** This stretch is all rather uncluttered, and it has a nice curvy highway, quite suitable for a recreation area, although the police might object to a motorcyclist's definition of "recreation." As you drop out of the hills and into

Along CA 54, Lake Cachuma, a mighty reservoir fed by the Santa Ynez River, caters to boaters.

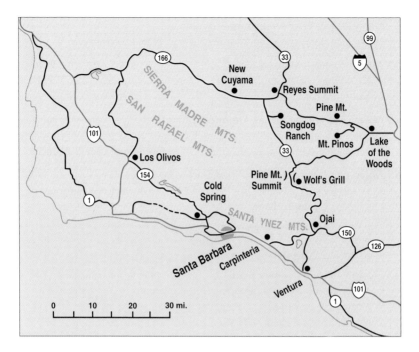

Ojai Valley, you can see the **Santa Ynez** and **Topatopa Mountains** off to the north, and a discerning eye can even spot the opening created by the **Ventura River.**

29 Miles Traffic light—turn left (on green light) onto CA 33/150.

31 Miles Traffic light—turn left, following CA 33, letting CA 150 run into Ojai. **Ojai** itself is a charmingly overpriced town with a lovely main street and many delightful places to spend money.

31+ Miles The 76 Station on your left will be the last gas for 65 miles.

32 Miles STOP sign—and continue straight on CA 33, through orchards, soon coming alongside the **Ventura River** (such that it is). Follow **Matalija Creek** through **Wheeler Gorge,** and the road will get seriously twisty.

38 Miles You will pass a shady watering hole, **The Wheel,** on your right, with food and drink.

39 Miles Pass through a blind tunnel (i.e. it has a curve in it so you can't see through it to the end), and then a quarter-mile beyond that two short, straight tunnels. *Beyond them is a slight left curve and there is often water on the road, which can freeze in cold weather.* You have been officially cautioned.

The road will ascend for several delicious curves, then drop back down into the valley of **Sespe Creek,** going through **Sespe Gorge** (very nice!) to follow the creek upriver for a good ten miles into a broadening valley. A lot of weekend motorcyclists come out here, as this is primo country.

59 Miles A small white-and-red house will be on your right, with WOLF'S GRILL on the sign. Its hours of operation are anybody's guess, but weekends are your best bet.

63 Miles You will be at **Pine Mountain Summit** at 5,084 feet—not bad considering you are a mere 20 miles from the ocean. Keep an eye out for sandy corners as you start to wiggle downhill to the **Ozena Forest Service Station.**

69 Miles Stay straight on CA 33, as Lockwood Valley Road goes off to the right (see Detour). This is a fast piece of asphalt which curves along the east bank of the **Cuyama River.**

Detour

Riding around **Mt. Pinos** will add an additional 44 miles to the route, but is well worth it. You begin by zipping up Lockwood Valley Road; after about 3.5 miles, a sign pointing to the right indicates CAMP SCHEIDECK a mile off the road, an old-fashioned resort with a good cafe. The road then goes over the 5,516-foot summit, into **Lockwood Valley,** and on to the STOP sign at **Lake of the Woods** (21 miles). Turn left and go five miles up Cuddy Valley Road, but take care not to miss the right turn to Pine Mountain (nothing to do with the previous Pine Mountain Summit)—otherwise you will dead-end up on top of Mt. Pinos. Head into the summering community of **Pine Mountain** on Potrero Road, which turns into Cerro Noroeste Road, and you will have a stunning run along the edge of the **San Joaquin Valley** to the intersection with CA 33/166 at **Point Reyes Summit** (2,968 feet). At the STOP sign, turn left on 33/166, and in 4.6 miles you will be at an intersection with CA 33, back on the main loop. ✳

---

71 Miles At a less-than-wide spot in the road, you will find two eateries. **Sagebrush Annie's** (805-766-2319), on the right, serves up excellent food. On the left is the **Halfway House Station,** better known for beer than burgers, although the person behind the bar might be willing to put a patty on the griddle.

81 Miles At another wide-ish spot in the road, **The Place Restaurant** will be on your left.

86 Miles Slow—look carefully—and you will see Ballinger Canyon Road and a sign reading SONGDOG RANCH (see Songdog Ranch sidebar).

90 Miles STOP sign—turn left onto CA 166.

95 Miles Cross over the Cuyama River and enter **Cuyama** (pop. 160), with the Old Cuyama Store as its focal point. You are now in **Cuyama Valley** proper, and will be following it for a good many miles.

99 Miles Arrive in **New Cuyama,** with about ten times the population of Cuyama. There is even the **Buckhorn Motel** ($50; 805-766-2591) and the **Buckhorn Saloon,** and the **Buckhorn Restaurant** (occasionally closed), and a hundred yards away you'll find a Mobil station and the **Burger Barn.**

After leaving town, you will have a delicious ride along the **Cuyama River** for the next 39 miles. However, in the recent past, this very rural section of two-lane highway has had a lot of accidents (mostly stupid drivers running off the road), and the CHP now patrols it quite heavily. With radar. The road slips and slides and curves along the river, and it is a beaut. You will hardly see a house until you get to the **Pine Canyon Forest Station,** where you should be prepared to slow.

138 Miles Turn left onto Tepusquet Road, which winds into **Buckhorn Canyon.** As of January 2000, the paved surface was a tad on the rough side, so either adjust your suspension or go slowly.

140 Miles Cross over **Buckhorn Creek** and begin a steep climb.

141 Miles From the summit, you will begin a long descent along the **Tepusquet Creek.**

Out at Songdog Ranch, Jim Reveley will make you feel right at home . . . and he'd be happy to sell you some of his Rev-Pack motorcycle luggage, as well.

Songdog Ranch

A mile up the road, you will find the palatial country estate of **Jim and Robyn Reveley.** Jim has been making his **Rev-Pack** motorcycle luggage for nearly 20 years, and has operated his motorcycle-friendly **Songdog Campground** for more than ten years (805-766-2454).

Stop in to say hello, or better yet, allow Jim to give you all the benefits of camping with none of the hassles. He will set up your campsite, complete with tent, air mattresses, and sleeping bags, lay on a superb dinner, and leave you to lie out under the stars and think that this here planet is pretty much okay. In the morning, he will provide the breakfast, as well—and you don't even have to fold your tent. ✴

59

153 Miles Stay left (straight) at the Y, right after the **Byron Vineyard.**

153+ Miles To cross over the **Sisquoc River,** you will need to traverse about a hundred feet of gravel. If it is flooded, as it might be in winter, you will have to backtrack to the Y, go right on Santa Maria Mesa Road to the STOP sign, turn left onto Foxen Canyon Road, and follow it to the far side of the Sisquoc River.

154 Miles STOP sign—turn left on Foxen Canyon Road, and soon the **Foxen Winery** will appear.

155 Miles The **Sisquoc Winery** and the church will be right ahead, while Foxen Canyon Road swings to the right.

On Foxen Canyon Road you will find ten wineries—but you should forego sampling all their wares if you are riding.

165 Miles You will be on top of **Zaca Mesa,** with wineries all around; this is serious grape country.

168 Miles Turn left, staying on Foxen Canyon Road, while Zaca Station Road continues straight.

172 Miles STOP sign—turn left onto CA 154.

173 Miles The town of **Los Olivos** will be off to your left, along with **Mattei's Tavern,** a good place to eat. If you take the Grand Avenue turn to your right, you will be in Los Olivos. In the middle of that little village is a recently defunct gas station that has been operating as a garage since 1901, and pumping gas since 1912. Its owner, Bob Cole, claims that it was the first gas station in California, and he is currently looking for a buyer who will keep it a gas station. The EPA forced him to shut down, due to old tanks.

178 Miles CA 276 goes off to the right.

185 Miles The entrance to **Lake Cachuma Recreation Area** will be on your left, with camping available. No swimming here, just boats polluting the water with gas.

191 Miles On your left you will see Stagecoach Road, the old way over the pass. The much newer CA 154 is far less interesting, except for the **Cold Springs Bridge,** which was recently reinforced for protection against earthquakes—good luck when an 8.1 hits.

Alternate Route

Take the turn to the left and follow Stagecoach crossing over Paradise Road, to arch under the Cold Springs Bridge—way up above you. Deep in the shadows of the trees lies **Cold Springs Tavern,** a motorcycling mecca on the weekends, but quiet the rest of the time. This is where the stagecoaches of yore would stop to rest the horses and liquor up the passengers so they wouldn't notice the bumps so much. After your sarsaparilla, continue on up the road, take your first left, and you will be back on CA 154. ✹

---

195 Miles You will be on **San Marcos Pass** (2,224 feet), only seven linear miles from the sea. Off to the left goes East Camino Cielo (East Sky Road— see Trip 6). In front of you there will be a superb view of the ocean, with the **Channel Islands** off in the distance, about 25 miles offshore. And the few oil-rigs set up in the channel will remind you of where the stuff in your gas tank comes from. On a clear day, you can see the 70 miles to the Palos Verdes Hills in Los Angeles.

It's a hazy day, but from the East Camino Cielo road, Kurt Grife can look out over Santa Barbara Channel, almost 4,000 feet below.

Down at the Santa Barbara marina, I am getting ready to winch the Beemer aboard my 45-foot yacht.

Two passers-by on Santa Barbara's Stearns Wharf admire the sleek lines of my motorcycle . . . or are they debating the mechanical wisdom of the opposed twin?

195+ Miles To the right is the start of West Camino Cielo, 20 miles of bliss, about half of which is unmaintained dirt; a d-p bike would be recommended.

197 Miles At a discreet intersection, Painted Cave Road heads off to the right, and the Old San Marcos Pass Road goes down to the left; the latter is a twisty delight, and you will have to wonder how the stagecoaches made it up—or down. Slowly, I suppose.

From here, CA 154 winds down the south face of the **Santa Ynez Mountains.**

201 Miles Cross over CA 192, a/k/a Foothill Road, which goes along the backside of Santa Barbara.

202 Miles Traffic light—turn left after crossing over US 101, merging into 101 going south (east, really).

206 Miles Exit at Garden Street—turn right, toward the beach.

206+ Miles STOP sign—turn right onto Cabrillo Boulevard.

207 Miles Arrive back at ground zero, at **Stearns Wharf.**

Trip 6 Mountain & Beach

Distance *41 miles*

Highlights *This is a very short, but very, very tasty little circle, cruising along the crest of the Santa Ynez Mountains behind Santa Barbara. It is a pretty rough section of asphalt climbing to 3,500 feet before plummeting down to town and returning along the waterfront, past the beaches to Stearns Wharf.*

0 Miles Head west along Cabrillo Boulevard.

0+ Miles STOP sign—go straight along Shoreline Drive, as CA 225 turns off to the right. This will take you past the harbor, where you could turn in and admire how yachtsmen spend their money.

From here, the road wends along the bluffs for a bit, and I'd bet those houses on the sea-side of the 1600 block are really, really expensive.

3 Miles Traffic light—turn left onto Cliff Dr./CA 225.

4 Miles STOP sign—stay straight on Cliff Drive as CA 225 turns right on Las Positas. Past the **Brown Pelican** restaurant, Cliff turns into Roble de Marina Drive, and winds past **Hope Ranch** (where the working rich live) on Las Palmas Drive, past the **La Cumbre Golf & Country Club,** and finally over the top of US 101.

8 Miles Traffic light—turn left onto State Street. Right there on the left corner you'll see the **Five Points Plaza** shopping center, where the aforementioned **Fresco!** could tame your appetite.

8+ Miles Traffic light—turn right onto CA 154.

Hang-gliding off the Camino Cielo behind Santa Barbara is popular—though the glidist sometimes wonders where he will end up.

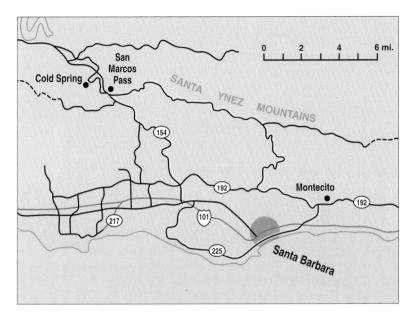

9 Miles Turn right at the traffic light onto CA 154, a broad, smooth road which soon starts climbing.

17 Miles Turn right at the top of **San Marcos Pass,** onto the road marked EAST CAMINO CIELO, going by the California Dept. of Forestry fire station and the **Cielo Store.**

19 Miles To the right, you'll see Painted Cave Road; straight ahead a sign will probably read CAUTION STORM DAMAGE. East Sky Road has a lot of potholes, but virtually no traffic, and unbeatable views. For the next nine miles, go slowly and stop a lot, as you will be running right along the ridge of the **Santa Ynez Mountains.** To the left you will see the great, long valley of the **Santa Ynez River,** as well as part of the **Los Padres National Forest** and the **Dick Smith Wilderness.** To the right you will spy the rooftops of Santa Barbara, the Pacific Ocean, and a bunch of oil-rig platforms out in the channel. You will be close to 4,000 feet above the sea, which is just six miles away.

28 Miles Stay right at the fork in the road, heading for Santa Barbara. If you went left you would end up in **Big Caliente Hot Springs** down in the Santa Ynez River Valley.

As you drop quickly into **Rattlesnake Canyon** and pass a hang-gliding take-off, the road changes names, becoming Gibralter Road.

34 Miles STOP sign—turn left onto El Cielito Road, and at another STOP, go straight across Mountain Drive.

34+ Miles STOP sign—turn left onto CA 192.

The aquarium out on Stearns Wharf is a focal point for Santa Barbara tourists.

Accelerate, brake, turn—again and again and again—on the winding East Camino Cielo road in the Santa Ynez Mountains.

36 Miles Stay straight on CA 192 as CA 144 goes off to the right. CA 144, to my thinking, may be the shortest state highway in all of California, running for just two miles down to US 101; how short city streets become state highways like that baffles me—unless, of course, it is because the CA designation makes the state, rather than the city, responsible for maintenance costs.

38 Miles Turn right onto Hot Springs Road, keeping right again on Hot Springs after half a mile, to pass the **Montecito Country Club.**

39 Miles Go under US 101 as Hot Springs turns into Cabrillo Boulevard, passes the **Santa Barbara Cemetery** (prime real estate!), and puts you right along the shore by the **Santa Barbara Zoological Gardens.**

41 Miles Arrive back at Ground Zero, **Stearns Wharf.**

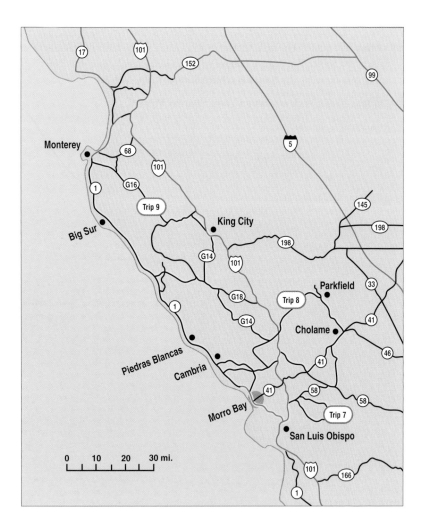

Big Sur & the Central Coast **5**

Headquarters *Cambria*

Chamber of Commerce *805-927-3624 This organization will provide you with long lists of motels and B&Bs in the area, and I promise that there are many of them since this is the southern gateway to Big Sur and, more importantly for the tourist business, the home of the Hearst Castle.*

Best Time to Visit *All year*

Getting There *CA 1 is the way, either coming north from San Luis Obispo, or south from Monterey. Or, you could take CA 46 West from Paso Robles to meet CA 1 just south of Cambria. Coming from the south, you will climb a longish hill which is crowned by a traffic light and a sign reading CAMBRIA pointing to the right. This will take you along the old Coast Highway, dropping down into East Village and the center of activity. At the north end of town there is another traffic light on CA 1.*

Ground Zero *Start at the traffic light on CA 1 at the north end of town, where Main Street goes off inland, and Moonstone Drive heads toward the ocean.*

This is my backyard. And I dwell in this part of the Golden State because the local roads, in my humble estimation, make for the **best year-round motorcycling in the world.** You can talk enthusiastically about the Alps, and wax eloquent about the Rocky Mountains, but I will gladly exchange high passes

In Monterey, the tourist action is always heavy on Cannery Row, but motorcyclists come in droves during the races at Laguna Seca.

A troop of motorcyclists come south along the Big Sur Highway, a road that every motorcyclist should ride at least twice in his or her lifetime—once in each direction.

for a 12-month riding season. Especially since I also have high passes in the **Sierra Nevada mountain range** a mere half a day away.

A motorcyclist cannot go wrong in this part of California. Unless, of course, he arrives right after a big storm and CA 1, the **Big Sur Highway,** is shut down due to landslides. Fortunately, there are the other places, like Pozo and Parkfield, and Carmel Valley Road, which also offer fine destinations.

I was rather undecided as to where to locate the Headquarters for this chapter. I could have chosen the county seat of **San Luis Obispo** (SLO), a college town with lots of activities and much to recommend it, but I decided to take a very different approach and have instead put you up in the small coastal town of Cambria, which is 30 miles north of SLO-City and 100 miles south of the **Monterey peninsula.**

Cambria was named by a homesick Welshman who lived in this little valley along the **Santa Rosa Creek**—or at least that is the romantic side of the story. The old part of town, called **East Village,** is more than a mile from the ocean. Along Main Street and its few offshoots you will find a worthy bar, **Camozzi's,** a selection of eateries from the bakery to **The Brambles,** and half a dozen motels. Farther along, the new part of town (West Village), offers a row of quaint-looking tripper-traps selling everything from olive oil, to toy soldiers and used books. The **West Village** is prone to flooding, however, something which kept the old-timers from building there in the first place.

I recommend you lay your head in the old part of town, at the **Blue Bird Motel,** which is nothing special, but rather a wooden, two-story affair with 37 rooms (no phones) that is just plainly and simply nice ($50+; 805-927-4634; 1880 Main St.). In addition, it is walking distance to **Linn's** for breakfast, and to **Robin's** or **The Brambles** for dinner. And to **Camozzi's** for your evening's entertainment, as they host live music on most weekends, everything from blues to rock to folk.

Down on the seashore is Moonstone Drive, with another dozen or more motels packed in cheek by jowl, each earnestly portraying their romantic possibilities and trying to capture the tourist trade with names like **Best Western Fireside Inn By The Sea** ($75+; 800-528-1234; 805-927-8661; 6700 Moonstone Beach Drive). You will note, however, that there is a road between these motels and the sea, and that the motels are usually built on narrow lots at right angles to the coast, so the views will be limited. But you could always go out for a walk.

Trip 7 Pozo Loop

Distance *191 miles*

Highlights *From Morro Bay to San Luis Obispo to Pozo, with a bit of seaside, a touch of town, and a good deal of ranching country*

0 Miles Head south on CA 1.

5 Miles Stay straight as CA 46 goes off to the left.

7 Miles The village of **Harmony** will be off to your left (pop. 18, elev. 175 feet), where a couple of dozen craftsman try to earn a living selling to the tourists. The whole place, such that it is, is owned by one man who threatens to turn it into some sort of theme park. We hope he fails.

As you come over a rise on CA 1, the whole of **Estero Bay** will be before you, with the houses of Cayucos about five miles in front of you and **Morro Rock** another seven miles beyond that. On a clear day, this is a damned fine view . . . except for the three great smokestacks of the Morro Bay power plant, a fossil-fuel generator. We all need and use electric power, but making it is never a pretty sight.

16 Miles Turn right into **Cayucos,** down Business CA 1, which parallels CA 1 proper and will actually return you to it in about two miles. The cheerfully retrograde **Old Cayucos Tavern** on Ocean Avenue, the main street, will

---

Morro Bay

When Spanish explorer Juan Cabrillo first spied the big rock which protects the harbor, it reminded him of a moor's turban, hence the name. Since then, major quarrying in the early part of this century has substantially altered the rock's moorish look. The town used to have a reasonably-sized fishing fleet, but while several dozen boats do still fish out of Morrow Bay, their main business is now tourism.

Down on the waterfront, the **Embarcadero,** there is a long strip of restaurants and tripper-traps (a/k/a souvenir shops). You can get reasonably good fish at the **Great American Fish Company,** right down on the wharves, but I prefer **Dorn's Original Breakers Cafe,** on Market Avenue, up on the low bluffs above the Embarcadero. And kitty-corner across Market, on the corner with Morro Bay Blvd., will be the **Breakers Motel** ($80+; 24 units; 805-772-7317).

You will find the local action in MB at the intersection of Harbor and Main streets, where two bars compete for the beer-buck, **Legends** and **Happy Jacks,** and a third, **Bay City Grill,** promotes its food as well. ✸

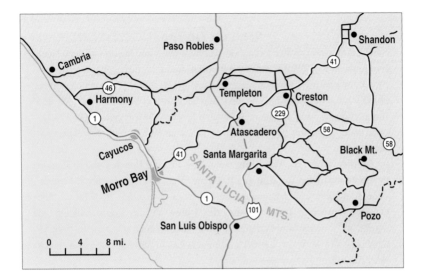

gladly pour you a Virgin Mary. If you are there on January 1st you can partake in the annual **Polar Bear Dip.**

32 Miles   Pass the turn for CA 41, which you will be using as a return route later.

32+ Miles   If you want to visit Morro Bay, exit at the MORRO BAY, MAIN ST sign (see Morro Bay sidebar).

45 Miles   Traffic light—turn right, immediately after crossing over US 101, following US 101 NORTH signs. This follows your coming through the **Chorro Creek Valley** on the Cabrillo Highway, alongside a row of smaller versions of Morro Rock stretching off to the east. Once on US 101 North, you will pass **Cuesta College** on your right, and the **California Men's Colony** (a white-collar prison) on your left. As you approach San Luis Obispo, Cabrillo will turn into Santa Rosa Street, and you will pass **California Polytechnic University** on your right, and intersect with US 101 (see San Luis Obispo sidebar).

54 Miles   Exit right off US 101 onto CA 58/Santa Margarita. As the road crests the Santa Lucia Range, you will have just climbed the highest spot on US 101 between Los Angeles and San Francisco, the **Cuesta Grade** (a redundant name, as "cuesta" is Spanish for "grade"). At 1,522 feet, the Cuesta Grade does not sound like much of a climb, but after miles and miles of flat terrain, it is an impressive and picturesque ascent. The road into **Santa Margarita** is called **El Camino Real** ("The Royal Road") which was the Spanish name for the road that ran from San Diego to San Francisco.

San Luis Obispo

San Luis Obispo is a nice town, both a college town and the county seat. Head into town on Santa Rosa, and at the fourth traffic light, turn right onto Higuera Street, the one-way, main drag through town. The center of the action will be about three blocks down, between Chorro and Broad Streets. You'll need to find a place to park, and there are even a few motorcycle parking slots scattered about—but you'll pay as much as does a car for a big space, which is not fair at all.

Mother's Tavern, The Library, and the **Frog & Peach Pub** are right in the middle, with the **Russian Tea Room** nearby, as well as the **Novel Experience Bookstore** (which happens to sell my book on Baja). A block away is the old **Mission San Luis Obispo de Toloso** (Saint Louis, Bishop of Toulouse . . . which is in France, for those weak on such trivia). Construction began in 1772, and they are still holding services in the restored chapel; it is a beautiful place just to wander about.

For breakfast, I like **McClintock's Dining House** at 686 Higuera; for ribs, try **Mo's Smokehouse BBQ** at 970 Higuera. If you are in town on Thursday evening, you will find five blocks of downtown Higuera closed off for a large farmers' market featuring lots of fresh food.

If you are looking for a place to stay, SLO-City has lots to offer. I cannot help but recommend the **Madonna Inn,** at 100 Madonna Road off US 101 on the south side of town. You cannot miss it, as bright pink is **Alex Madonna**'s favorite color, and it advertises itself as having "109 unique rooms and suites." Unique is right, as each has a different decor, from Caveman to Hawaiian, and Old West to Fifties Funk. It is an experience; whether you wish to miss it or not is up to you ($90+; 800-543-9666; 805-543-3000; Madonna Rd. Exit off of US 101).

At the other end of town, the more conventional, **Apple Farm Inn,** at the Monterey Street exit off of US 101, has 68 rooms ($75+; 800-255-2040; 805-544-2040); the Apple Farm is full of old-fashioned goodness, from chicken and dumplings to brownies and apple pie. The Apple Farm also owns the neighboring **Motel Inn,** which claims to have been the first motel in the world—or the country, or the state, or something. It opened in 1925 as the **Milestone Mo-tel,** an obvious contraction of Mo(tor) and (Ho)tel. Unfortunately, the restoration of this Motor Hotel seems to have been caught up in some bureaucratic mess, and it has been closed for the past ten years. ✱

Morro Bay is the only safe mooring at the south end of Big Sur; that is Morro Rock in the background.

55 Miles Turn right, following CA 58 across the railroad tracks. You will have just passed through Santa Margarita, a small town which was originally built to service the railroad that came through here in the 1880s. Although the **Union Pacific** still sends a dozen trains a day through here, the need for personnel has been greatly reduced over the years. On your left in town, you'll find **Hoover's Roundup Cafe,** which serves good breakfasts and burgers seven days a week, shutting down after lunch.

57 Miles Go straight to stay on Pozo Road, though CA 58 goes off to the left.

Good road, Pozo, recently surfaced. Pass La Pilitas Road to your left, pass the left turn at Rinconada to **Lake Margarita,** pass River Road to your left—all the time hurtling along straightaways, around bends, and over hills. This is 16 miles of very good riding.

73 Miles Arrive in **Pozo,** a great Saturday or Sunday destination, albeit a very quiet one the rest of the week. There is a forest service fire station, a few houses, the old **Pozo Saloon** (open Thursday through Sunday, 438-4225) . . . and that would be about it for the town of Pozo. A hundred years ago, this place was a stage-stop on the San Luis Obispo to Bakersfield run, but them days is long gone. On the weekends there might be a couple dozen bikes outside, everything from cruisers to dirt bikes.

A rough dirt road, Hi-Mountain Road, runs south out of Pozo, past the forest service fire station, back over the Santa Lucias to **Arroyo Grande** and

San Luis Obispo. East of Pozo in the Los Padres National Forest, you will find **Turkey Flats** and a big ORV area.

74 Miles Stay straight, on Park Hill Road, as Pozo Road goes off to the right. You could follow Pozo Road out to CA 58 if you wished, but there are about ten miles of unpaved going; I took a ZX11 through there, but I can't say I would recommend it to the sporty brigade.

77 Miles Stay straight, on Park Hill Road, as a sign points to the right indicating TURKEY FLATS and BLACK MOUNTAIN. The road to the top of **Black Mountain,** the highest spot in the county (3,625 feet), is paved, albeit a bit roughly, since the FAA has all sorts of instruments up there. It makes a nice, if gnarly, side trip.

Continue along Park Hill Road, which, depending on recent weather, could be clean or a bit dirty, especially the section along the **Yaro Creek.** Take it easy, as there are a couple of deceptive turns.

79 Miles This is one of those deceptive turns, as River Road runs off to the left, and Park Hill goes to the right, if you went straight you would find a big ditch.

84 Miles There will be a big curve in the road, and Las Pilitas Road will go off to the left; a hundred yards farther on, Huerhuero Road will go to the right, but you will stay on Park Hill.

92 Miles STOP sign—turn right onto CA 58, going up a hill in an absolutely wonderful series of tight curves (second gear, stay on the throttle).

94 Miles Curve right, staying on CA 58, as CA 229 goes off to the left.

Detour

If you want to add a few extra miles and a lot of extra fun, take CA 229, which twists very tightly over a low range of hills, down to the **Huerhuero Valley.** After eight miles you will come into **Creston** (pop. 270) and pass the **Loading Chute Saloon** and then the **Long Branch Saloon,** both on your left. Opposite the Long Branch, take a right-hand turn onto O'Donovan Road. You will tear flatly along the **East Branch Huerhuero Creek** for a little more than five miles before rejoining CA 58. Good little excursion.   ✱

---

99 Miles O'Donovan Road will come in from the left, as CA 58 whistles along some rolling countryside, around some curves, and past La Panza Road going off to the left.

108 Miles Turn left onto Shell Creek Road. It is easy to miss this, as there is a paucity of signage, but a watertank and windmill on your left should alert

Dirt riders will gather at the Pozo Saloon, in San Luis Obispo County, for a hit of sarsaparilla after a grueling day in the forest.

you. If you cross the bridge over **Shell Creek** you will have gone a hundred feet too far.

Shell Creek Road, for my limited money, is one of the most fun roads in the state: no traffic worth mentioning, lightly-curved, and as fast as you want it to be. Of course, there is a bit of open range along the way, so you will need to watch out for beef. And also for antelope, who disregard all fences but will generally stay away from the road.

At the north end of the valley, the road hugs the east wall and the going will be a bit slower.

118 Miles Turn left onto Truesdale Road. If you inadvertently went straight you would find yourself fording **San Juan Creek,** which is usually dry, but it can be flooded.

121 Miles Truesdale Road will make a right-angle turn to the right and enter a large grape-growing area, all part of the wine-drinking mania that has infected the United States in the last 15 years. Of which I approve.

122 Miles Turn left onto Clark Road, in the middle of the vineyard, at an intersection with nary a STOP sign anywhere.

123 Miles STOP sign—turn left onto CA 41. The next 10 miles will be very nice indeed, as the road winds through the hills, climbs to 1,500 feet, and drops back down to **Huerhuero Valley.**

CHAPTER
5

134 Miles Stay straight on CA 41, as CA 229 goes off to the left, to Creston. Follow CA 41 down the **Atascadero Grade,** with all of the **Salinas Valley** and the town of Atascadero spread out before you.

145 Miles Traffic light—go straight at the intersection with El Camino Real in downtown **Atascadero;** go under US 101, following CA 41 west along Morro Road toward **Morro Bay.** After two miles, you will leave the **Salinas River Valley** and climb up the **Santa Lucia Range** to the 1,438-foot saddle, before descending through **Devil's Gap,** past the **Half-Way Station** (open Thursday through Sunday with food and music), and into the **Los Padres National Forest.** You will pass the forest service fire station, and the **Cerro Alto Campground** before beginning the winding descent into **Morro Creek Valley.**

161 Miles STOP sign, blinking red light—turn right onto CA 1 going north.

165 Miles Traffic light—turn right, the signs reading OLD CREEK ROAD (right) and STUDIO DRIVE (left). Old Creek is a back way of getting back to Cambria, and it's a very worthwhile route. There might still be a sign saying LAND-SLIDE, LOCAL TRAFFIC ONLY, but it has become a fixture, and the road is likely fine; if the road is actually unusable, a barrier will stop you.

Follow Old Creek up the hill, around the top of the **Whale Rock Reservoir,** and down the hill.

169 Miles Stay straight as Santa Rita Creek Road (dirt) goes to the right, eventually getting back to US 101. Then a bridge will cross over Old Creek, and Cottontail Creek Road will go off to the left, a dead-end. If you have an interest in looking at guns, go up Cottontail to **Storni's Gun Ranch.** You can just walk out his back door and try out the ten-gauge howitzer.

Old Creek Road wiggles along under a magnificent bower of oak trees—followed immediately by a very steep, very sharp, right-hand turn, and up and over the Santa Lucias, cresting a 1,415-foot summit.

Atascadero Colony

In 1913, a businessman by the name of **Edward G. Lewis** decided to build a planned community on the west bank of the **Salinas River.** It was to be a self-sufficient town, serving the nearby agricultural and ranching business with retail merchants, light industry such as wagon and barrel making, and social services. He began by building about 60 "colony" houses, and many are still lived in. He also built a lovely city hall in the Palladian style, and over the entrance is a quote by Abraham Lincoln: "The most valuable of all arts will be the art of deriving a comfortable subsistence from the smallest area of soil"—a Greenie before his time. Lewis went broke and left, but the community continued to grow and now has 24,000 inhabitants. ✱

174 Miles STOP sign—turn left onto CA 46, which will lead to CA 1 and the coast. Back in the Sixties, if you wanted to go down to the coast from Paso Robles, a small city on US 101 to the east, you would come to this intersection, with Santa Rosa Creek Road going to Cambria, and Old Creek to Cayucos. Although neither of these were easy roads, the tourists were nevertheless determined to visit **Hearst Castle.** In the early Seventies, the project was approved to build a highway from this intersection to meet up with CA 1, and it opened in 1974. Now it carries a lot of traffic. About two miles on, you will reach the summit, at some 1,500 feet, and from there you'll have a scenically inspiring ten-mile drop down to CA 1.

186 Miles STOP sign—turn right onto CA 1.

191 Miles Arrive back at Ground Zero.

The Motel Inn in San Luis Obispo opened up as the Milestone Mo-Tel (motor-hotel) in 1925, and it is credited as the first establishment to use the word "motel."

Trip 8 Parkfield Loop

Distance *214 miles*

Highlights *Via Santa Rosa Creek Road, Shandon, Parkfield, San Miguel, Hunter Liggett, the Nacimiento Road to the coast, and south on CA 1*

0 Miles Head back through Cambria along Main Street, past the Blue Bird and Camozzi's, right out of town.

2 Miles Turn left onto Santa Rosa Creek Road; remember that this rustic paradise used to be a main road into town back in the Sixties. Once you are past the high school, it is just good fun. The first five miles will be quite easy.

7 Miles Stay right, as Curti Road goes off to the left. From here, the road will get a good deal twistier, until it finally enters a very shaded stretch and emerges in a valley. At the end of the valley, the road makes a 180-degree turn

---

Wineries

San Luis Obispo County is working very hard to compete with Napa Valley, with more than 40 commercial wineries in the area and a large number of private little vineyards whose owners have not gone to the hassle of legitimizing their product with the authorities so that their wine can be sold to the public.

Part of the grape growing happens just south of San Luis Obispo in the **Edna Valley,** but the major portion takes place around **Paso Robles** and **Templeton.** California has more than 400,000 acres of land dedicated to wine grapes (as opposed to grapes for eating or raisins), and the dream of every vintner is to cultivate a following that will pay $50 a bottle or better. San Luis Obispo County has more than 15,000 acres under vines.

Historically, the padres brought the first grapes to the region in the late 18th century to make sacramental wine. In 1882, a gent from Indiana, **Andrew York,** set up the first commercial winery. But it was the wine-crazed Seventies that had everybody turning rough ranchland into expensive vineyards, doubling and tripling the price of land.

Many wineries have tasting rooms. In the good old days, if you showed up at a winery you would be rewarded with a sample of their best, and then you would buy a few bottles and be off. Nowadays, wineries have become major tourist attractions, and many now charge you for the privilege of tasting. They realize that most of their current visitors have no real knowledge of wine, and no intention of purchasing an '87 cabernet, but a small profit can be made off these samplers, especially if they can sell them a T-shirt or corkscrew.

For local wines, a **Wild Horse Merlot** is usually a good bet. ✻

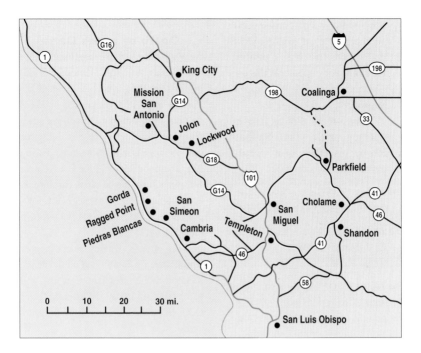

and then climbs up to make a second 180-degree turn. If you stop to look, you will realize that you have seen this road many times before—it is a favorite place for motorcycle magazines to photograph bikes.

Climb up, as Cypress Mountain Road (dirt) goes to the left, to the summit at 1,860 feet. You will have crossed the **Santa Lucia Range** and will now be heading down the east side, along **Rocky Creek.** It is a superlative stretch of road, but not necessarily a fast one.

18 Miles STOP sign—turn left onto CA 46. This is wide and fast and very well patrolled by the CHP.

20 Miles York Mountain Road will be off to your left. If you would like to see a New Era motorcycle (circa 1912), take this little road and stop at the **York Mountain Winery** tasting room; the motorcycle is part of the decor. Afterward, you could just continue on York Mountain Road to get back to CA 46 (see Wineries sidebar).

24 Miles Turn right onto Vineyard Drive, past the **Mastantuono Winery** and tasting room.

27 Miles Cross over US 101, having gone past the **Pesenti** and **Creston Vineyards** tasting rooms—or maybe you stopped?

27+ Miles Traffic light—go straight, onto El Pomar Drive. If you took a left at the light you would be on Main Street in **Templeton,** an un-incorporated, one-street town that has several good places to eat. For breakfast and lunch, try the **Country Kitchen;** for dinner, **McPhee's Grill;** and for steak, **A.J. Spurs Saloon.**

Stay on El Pomar Drive, crossing over the **Salinas River,** as the road winds through the countryside.

34 Miles STOP sign—go straight, continuing on El Pomar.

37 Miles STOP sign—turn left as El Pomar T-bones into Cripple Creek Road.

38 Miles STOP sign—turn right onto Creston Road, curving around to your right and going alongside an exquisitely expensive horse-breeding place called **Creston Farms.**

Death of James Dean

A mile to the east of the memorial, where CA 41 and CA 46 split, James Dean met his end in 1955 when he crashed his Porsche into a Ford coupe. The intersection has been substantially altered since then, but you can see the possibility for disaster, with Dean driving into a setting sun. The poor fellow in the Ford, a man with the uninspired name of Turnipseed, had probably not even seen his low-profile Porsche as he made his left turn onto CA 41.

Who knows where Dean's career would have taken him had he lived. We do know that he was a motorcyclist, and had a Triumph T100C. A Japanese fan of Dean put up the memorial some years ago. ✸

40 Miles Turn left at the end of the horse farm railing, onto Camp 8 Road.

43 Miles STOP sign—turn left onto CA 41; you are about to do that gorgeous winding stretch again, as you did in Trip 7, only this time you'll be going the other way.

53 Miles STOP sign—turn right, following CA 41 through **Shandon** along Centre Street.

55 Miles STOP sign—turn right as CA 41 merges with CA 46, becoming a four-laner with double fines if you are caught speeding. Be cool.

61 Miles On top of the rise, to the left, is what remains of the town of **Cholame,** where you'll find the **Jack Ranch Cafe** offering sturdy trucker food, and a memorial to the late **James Dean** (see Death of James Dean sidebar).

62 Miles Turn left (cautiously) onto Cholame Valley Road. A large sign along CA 41/46 reads PARKFIELD and points to the left . . . as well as indicates that the next left goes to Fresno, and straight ahead is Bakersfield. The road heads straight up the valley and has no traffic to speak of, but there is a lot of open range, and, hence, a lot of free-roaming cattle. The road crosses into

There is not much to the town of Cholame these days, just the Jack Ranch Cafe and a memorial to actor James Dean, who was killed near here in 1955.

Monterey County, and every now and then it chooses to change course and move to the other side of the valley via a right-angle turn.

About ten miles along, the road goes past a farm, crosses **Cholame Creek,** and starts winding a bit. An informational sign will tell you that you have arrived at the Pacific Plate side of the **San Andreas Fault.** Turkey Flat Road will go off to the right, dead-ending in a couple of miles. Then you will cross through a girder bridge and see Ranchito Canyon Road (dirt) off to the left.

77 Miles Turn right, over the little bridge, the sign reading PARKFIELD 1/2, COALINGA 29. Not much in Parkfield but a small school, a forest service fire station, and the **Parkfield Inn & Cafe,** a great spot to spend a quiet, uninterrupted night (well, sort of—Parkfield *is* known as The Earthquake Capitol of the World). The inn offers six rooms ($50; 805-463-2421). The cafe is closed on Wednesdays, but they open at 11:30 the rest of the week, and shut the door when everybody goes home.

If you choose to continue on past Parkfield, the road will turn to dirt after about four miles, climbs over the hills, and drops down to CA 198 near Coalinga.

But to continue on our planned route, you will need to go back to that little bridge outside of town and turn right at the STOP sign, which will put you on Vineyard Canyon Road.

CHAPTER

5

81 Miles Turn left, staying with Vineyard Canyon. Were you to go straight ahead, you'd see a sign reading NOT A THROUGH ROAD. Believe it.

In two miles, you will reach the 2,602-foot summit, and then it will be a fast 15 miles down along the valley. As of early 2000, the road had been resurfaced in some of the rougher stretches, and a goodly pace could be maintained. You won't have much to worry about, as the sheriff might come this way but once a month.

98 Miles STOP sign—continue straight to merge with Indian Valley Road. You will see San Miguel in the distance.

99 Miles STOP sign—turn right, and in a hundred feet is another STOP sign where you will turn right again, crossing over the Salinas River on River Road.

100 Miles STOP sign—turn left onto Mission Street, and you will be in downtown **San Miguel.** This used to be a tough-guys town back in the heyday of World War II, when GIs from **Camp Roberts** and **Fort Hunter Liggett** would pour in to spend their money on card games, bad booze, and good women. That has all long since been cleaned up, and San Miguel is now a pretty sleepy place.

Many of the photographs you see in motorcycle magazines are taken on Santa Rosa Creek Road, running from Cambria toward Paso Robles.

Down at the south end of town is a very worthwhile visit, the **Mission San Miguel Arcangel,** begun by Franciscan padres in 1797. The place was secularized (sold to civilians) in 1846, and then bought back by the Catholic church in 1878. In 1928, the Franciscan order returned and the place is now looking spiffy indeed.

Food can be found at **Danny's Cafe** on Mission Street, or at the **Tenth Street Cafe** opposite the (only) gas station at 10th Street and US 101.

101 Miles Merge with US 101 going south.

102 Miles Turn right onto San Marcos Road.

107 Miles STOP sign—turn right onto County Rd. G14/Nacimiento Lake Dr.

109 Miles Turn right, following G14/Nacimiento Lake Drive.

117 Miles Cross the **Nacimiento Dam** at the east end of the lake, and then climb the hill.

119 Miles Turn left, following G14, which has become Interlake Road. Drop down into **Bee Rock Canyon,** then whisk along **Harris Valley,** across the **San Antonio River,** and out through **Tule Canyon** to **Lockwood.** (This is 20 miles of great riding.)

139 Miles STOP sign—turn left, following G14, now known as Jolon Road. There will be a store and a cafe at that little intersection, but it's more often closed than not.

144 Miles Turn left after seeing the sign that reads FORT HUNTER LIGGETT 5, MISSION 6, to the left; if you went straight on G14 you would be in King City in 18 miles. Several years ago you would have been in the middle of downtown Jolon at this point, but now there is nothing there. In 1997 there was a small town, with a large trailer park, big store, gas, restaurant—and one day following the downsizing of Fort Hunter Liggett, it all vanished.

144+ Miles **Fort Hunter Liggett** was named for the general who took over the American forces in Europe in World War I after General Pershing left. Today it is mainly used for training purposes, and it has a very small permanent party. The fort is an open base, so access is not controlled and the entrance gate is usually unmanned—unless some top-secret, hush-hush training exercises are going on, at which point a guard might be on duty to advise you not to dawdle or take pictures.

147 Miles Turn left, following a sign that reads NACIMIENTO-FERGUSSON ROAD, CA 1. This is not a well-marked turn, but it will be the first turn to the left (see Fort Hunter Liggett sidebar).

Stay on the Nacimiento-Fergusson Road.

The Mission San Antonio de Padua, in the middle of Fort Hunter Liggett, began business in 1771, but was completely reconstructed in the 1950s.

Fort Hunter Liggett

If you went straight instead of making that turn onto Nacimiento-Fergusson Road, you would pass the barracks and transportation areas, and then see a large, red-roofed building on the hill to your right, **The Hacienda.** This was the old officer's club, and before that it was one of the many houses in Willie Hearst's far-flung spread. In fact, it was designed by **Julia Morgan,** the same architect who drew up the plans for Hearst Castle. It is now a restaurant serving lunch and dinner most days, and the old **Bachelor Officers Quarters** currently serve as a guest lodge. Rooms run from $28 a night (plumbing down the hall) to $45 and up with a bathroom attached (408-386-2262).

If you continue on past The Hacienda, you will come to the **Mission San Antonio de Padua,** which was begun in 1771. It was a profitable mission (the church was as interested in making money as it was in saving souls) and in 1830, the valley had more than 8,000 cattle and 12,000 sheep. The mission was abandoned in the 1880s, to be knocked down by time and earthquakes. Today, however, the place looks as it did in the early 1800s, having been completely reconstructed. ✹

148 Miles You could cross over the **San Antonio River** on the girder bridge, or you could ford it at the tank crossing just 100 feet downstream; the latter is much more fun, especially when the river is high.

150 Miles A road to the right runs up to Del Venturi Road, which becomes Indians Road, turns into dirt, and eventually, maybe, if the Ventana Wilderness road is open, runs into **Arroyo Seco.** Good d-p riding.

Staying straight, you will come out of the woods into a rather treeless area where you can prance over the open range and have a good time. The **U.S. Army Corps of Engineers** does believe in laying good asphalt, and the road dips and winds around the folds in the land.

156 Miles As you leave the military reservation, you will head up along the Nacimiento River, passing several campgrounds in the **Los Padres National Forest.** After starting a steepish climb, you will pass a ranger station.

165 Miles At the very top, sort of in the woods, you will come to an intersection of sorts, with dirt roads going off to the right (north) and left (south). To the right, Cone Peak Road dead-ends at 4,500 feet—if it is open to vehicles. To the left, South Coast Ridge Road goes to either **Plaskett Creek** or **Willow Creek**—again, good d-p riding, although I have struggled up on a standard on more than one occasion.

Move forward a hundred feet from the intersection, and the **Pacific Ocean** will be visible far away in front of you. Ride carefully down the very twisty seven-mile descent to the Big Sur Hwy./CA 1, as the corners can be dirty. And stop a lot to marvel at the views.

167 Miles Ah, you'll have a grand view of the coast still way below you, and the road as it twists its way down there. There are no guard rails; be cautious, enjoy, stop, and take pictures.

171 Miles Turn left after meeting up with CA 1; the right turn goes to Monterey. Since I will run you all the way up the coast from Cambria to Monterey in the next trip, Trip 9, I'll just touch on just a couple of points of interest right now. If you want more information on this southward journey, just go forward a couple of pages, find the Nacimiento-Fergusson turn-off at Mile 43, and start reading backwards from there. Is that clear?

179 Miles Enter **Gorda,** with gas, food, lodging.

192 Miles Enter **Ragged Point,** with gas, food, lodging.

206 Miles Come upon San Simeon, and the **Hearst San Simeon State Historical Monument.**

214 Miles Arrive in **Cambria,** at Ground Zero.

Trip 9 The Big Sur Highway

Distance *251 miles*

Highlights *Run up the Big Sur coast and down Carmel Valley, then along the west side of the Salinas Valley. This route also serve as a Connector, taking you into the Monterey peninsula. The hundred miles between Hearst Castle and Carmel have some of the very best motorcycling in the world, but you do want to ride it when the traffic is low and the coast is clear (which usually means starting early in the morning in the spring or fall). The road is officially called the Cabrillo Hwy./CA 1, but is popularly known as the Big Sur Highway.*

For those not familiar with pre-American California, the Spaniards used Monterey as their capitol, and to them, that big wilderness to the south, which was virtually impossible to traverse, became known as El Sur Grande.

Or, as the Kingston Trio sang in the Fifties, "The south coast, the wild coast . . . "

0 Miles At the traffic light, head north on CA 1 where the road starts running along the edge of the flatlands that stretch from the Santa Lucia foothills to the sea (good for cattle). Very fast motorcyclists will enjoy the long curves, but you could spot the CHP along this stretch.

4 Miles You will have reached the so-called community of **San Simeon,** which is nothing more than a dozen motels scrunched in on each side of the highway. The only reason for existence is its proximity to Hearst Castle.

7 Miles If you look up on the ridgeline to your right, you will see the towers of **Hearst Castle.** A big sign indicates a right-hand turn, should you wish to get a closer look at this marvel (see Hearst Castle sidebar).

14 Miles You will come up on **Piedras Blancas** ("white rocks," thanks to the guano). The lighthouse (no visitors, please) which you passed after the sea-lion beach had gas and a ramshackle motel.

After the White Rock business center, the road develops a couple of straightaways, then comes around a vicious curve to drop down to . . .

21 Miles . . . **San Carpoforo Creek,** with a house belonging to the national forest on the right just after you cross the bridge. From this point, the **Santa Lucia Mountains** go straight down to the ocean. This is where the serious riding begins, the road twisting up sharply and steeply.

23 Miles **Ragged Point** has a very pleasant 20-room lodge ($90+; 805-927-4502) and a very good restaurant, as well as a coffee shop, hamburger joint, and small store that also sells gas.

From here, the road gets occasionally fast—and occasionally hazardous. If you are a first-timer, take note of the 15-mph signs you will occasionally

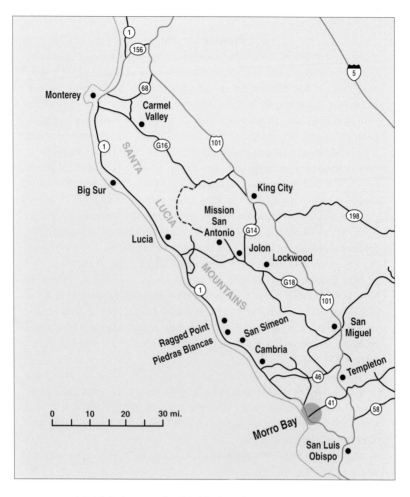

see posted. I think that one should ride the Big Sur slowly in one direction to admire the view and get the feel of the road, go back slowly the way you came—and then you can ride it at any speed you wish.

The real hazard on this road is not the road itself, but the gawking tourists who are constantly wandering over the center line, slowing abruptly to gaze out to sea, and driving in and out of scenic viewpoints.

34 Miles The town of **Gorda** will have gas, food, and half a dozen cabins to lodge in. Beyond Gorda a mile will be the turn onto Los Burros Road (dirt) which scrabbles up to the South Coast Ridge Road (dirt). A couple of miles farther on, Plaskett Ridge Road (dirt) also climbs up to South Coast Ridge Road. Beyond the turn-off, you'll see a campground at Plaskett Creek, and then the road opens up into the **Pacific Valley**. There was a store out there for many years, but it burned down in 1997, and as of January 2000, there had

Hearst Castle

William Randolph Hearst's father, **George,** made a lot of money from mining interests in the late 1800s and bought most of the land around the little seaside community of **San Simeon.** He also purchased a failing newspaper, the **San Francisco Examiner,** for his son, who turned it into a sensationalist paper with lurid headlines and pictures similar to the tabloids you'd find by the supermarket check-out counter today. **Willie** made his money a quarter cent at a time selling his newspapers, but he did sell a lot of them. In fact, he got to be very rich and very powerful, and when he was 50-something he fell madly in love with a showgirl named **Marion Davies,** who just happened to be more than 30 years younger than he was (how predictable). He built his castle on the coast so his mistress could throw great parties, and the construction went on from 1919 to World War II. He called the place **La Cuesta Encantada** (The Enchanted Hill), but it is now better known as Hearst Castle; the main section has a mere 40,000 square feet of living space in more than 100 rooms.

Mrs. Hearst, his official wife, was an understanding woman who stayed in New York, spending lots of his money, and having her own version of a good life. Hearst died in 1951, and in 1958, the Hearst heirs realized that they had a great white elephant on their hands and gave the place to the state. It has since become a serious money-maker, as thousands of tourists troop through every week at $14 a head.

The castle is worth a visit, if only to see what excess wealth can do to good taste. After buying a ticket, you can walk around and think about how nice it would be to have all that money. You should allot a half day to this little adventure. There are different tours you can take, including one at night. To get more information, call 800-438-4445.

Opposite the castle, on the sea side, are the actual remnants of the whaling station of San Simeon, with a small store and sandwich shop. ✸

been no attempt to rebuild. You will drop down to the **Mill Creek Picnic Area,** start back up and . . .

43 Miles   . . . There will be a sign for Nacimiento Road, with a 300-degree turn back to your right, over a cattle guard. **Kirk Creek Campground** will be almost across the road. It is definitely worth going up Nacimiento Road for a couple of miles, as there are stupendous views of the coast in both directions. Remember, you are in no hurry.

45 Miles   Cross over the bridge at **Lime Kiln Creek State Park.**

47 Miles   You have come upon the not-so-bustling community of **Lucia,** with nought but a small store and restaurant, usually open for early lunch and breakfast on the weekends. The ten motel rooms of Lucia Lodge sit in a row,

When William Randolph Hearst wanted to impress his mistress and friends, he did it in a big way, building a veritable castle at the south end of the Big Sur.

one out on the edge of the cliff over the sea, the rest coming inland. You'll want to stay in #10, right at the end; it's expensive, but the view is worth it ($100+; 408-667-2391).

Beyond Lucia, you'll find more fast road, often improved by CalTrans in an effort to defeat the landslides of the winter.

55 Miles Pass the **Esalen Institute,** with a sign reading BY RESERVATION ONLY. This place is a very pleasant hangover from the Sixties, one of those holistic feel-good resorts where you can check in for a couple of nights, eat vegetarian food, attend soul-searching seminars, and, best of all, hang out in the natural hot springs that are on the cliff high above the water (408-667-3023).

59 Miles Coming up, the **Julia Pfieffer Burns State Park** has good hiking and a wonderful waterfall falling into the ocean. Just north of here, in 1983, a landslide came down from **Partington Ridge** and closed the highway for more than a year.

From here, the road repeatedly sweeps around the outside curves of the hillside, then cuts inland for even tighter curves around the watercourse. Soon, however, you afwill see signs of civilization, such as art galleries, inns, and even the **Henry Miller Museum.** You will be approaching the community of Big Sur.

Looking north from Hurricane Point to Bixby Bridge—this is the Big Sur at its best.

67 Miles **Nepenthe**—loosely translated as "the place to lose oneself in"—is probably the nicest lunching spot on the coast. Go up on the high terrace and order an ambrosiaburger—the view will be worth the ten bucks.

Crest the rise to the two fanciest places on the Big Sur coast; the **Ventana Big Sur Inn** is inland ($260+; 408-667-2331; 800-628-6500), and the **Post Ranch Inn** is on the edge of the sea. Choose the latter if you have a spare $365+ to spend (408-667-2200).

Down in the stretched-out community of **Big Sur,** there will be other options, including the **Big Sur Lodge** at the **Pfeiffer Big Sur State Park** ($100+; 800-424-4787; 408-667-3100), as well as a half a dozen commercial places to stay along CA 1.

Just south of the entrance to the state park, you'll find the turn down Sycamore Canyon Road to **Pfeiffer Beach;** it used to have free access, but in 1998 the state began charging five dollars.

71 Miles When I'm not staying at the Post Ranch, my favorite spot is the **Ripplewood Resort,** with a dozen cabins down by **Big Sur River** that were built to house workers back in the Thirties ($75+; 408-667-2242). Ask for #8 or 9, right on the river's edge.

76 Miles **Andrew Molera State Park** will be on the left, giving pedestrians access to four miles of unblemished beach; it's worth the hike. Opposite the park, off CA 1, a dirt road goes up to the right, the Old Coast Road, where a sign reads IMPASSABLE IN WET WEATHER. True, but it's a great ride on a dry day.

Pass the **Point Sur Light Station** (begun in 1887), now a state historic landmark with guided tours on weekends (408-625-4419), and head down to **Little Sur Creek,** to a curving bridge that would beg speed—were it not for those concrete rails.

83 Miles At **Hurricane Point,** it can get righteously windy.

84 Miles Ride over **Bixby Bridge,** made mildly famous in the opening credits of the Sixties TV show, **"Then Came Bronson."** On the north side of the bridge, the Old Coast Road will reconnect with CA 1. This bridge, finished in 1932, was built with the help of prisoners who wanted to take time off their sentences. I'd say their labor was put to good use, and we should do something similar today.

The road will straighten out a bit as it tears over **Rocky Creek Bridge,** past Palo Colorado Road, over **Garrapata Creek,** and past **Garrapata State Park,** to cross **Malpaso Creek** and enter **Carmel Highlands.** The show is almost over.

95 Miles Off to the left will be **Point Lobos State Reserve,** a very nice, but very crowded park where the hordes from Monterey come to see a bit of wild-

Bixby Bridge, the keystone to the success of the Big Sur Highway, was completed in 1932 and made briefly famous in the opening shots of the TV series, "Then Came Bronson."

Monterey Peninsula

The Monterey Peninsula is a Tourist Destination, so ordinarily I wouldn't be too keen on it. Although there is lots to do and see, it is not really motorcycling—with one exception: the national and international motorcycle races that are held every year out at the **Laguna Seca Raceway,** a few miles east of town on CA 68.

The big show pieces on the peninsula are **Cannery Row,** with the **Monterey Bay Aquarium** at the west end and a dozen restaurants serving overpriced food. The glorious tourist trap of **Fisherman's Wharf** is very picturesque. And let's not forget the gated community of **Pebble Beach** and its overrated **17-Mile Drive.** Motorcyclists cannot pay at the gate and cruise the 17 miles unless they have dinner or room reservations somewhere inside the fence. Or a friend who can buzz them in.

Food is everywhere. Down on Cannery Row, **Trattoria Paradiso** (654 Cannery) serves everything from California cuisine to Calabrese-style Italian food. On Fisherman's Wharf, I gravitate to **Abalonetti's Seafood,** which has the most scrumptious fried calamari. You'll find more good seafood at the **Monterey Fish House,** 2114 Del Monte Avenue. If someone else is picking up the tab, try **Club XIX** at **The Lodge** in Pebble Beach.

For fine accommodation, check in at the **Monterey Plaza Hotel** on Cannery Row, with 290 rooms and suites, and prices starting at $200 (800-334-3999; 408-646-1700). On the more economical end, you can go to North Fremont Street, where a long line of motels await your business, such as the **Best Western De Anza Inn** ($65+; 43 rooms; 2141 North Fremont; 800-858-8775; 408-646-8300). ✴

life. From there, you will pass the **Carmel River State Beach** and a Carmelite nunnery.

99 Miles   After crossing the **Carmel River** you will come to a traffic light. You are now on the southwest edge of the **Monterey (King's Mount) Peninsula.** A left would take you into Carmel; straight up the hill heads into Monterey. For lots of info, go directly to the Visitors Center (831-649-1770) at 380 Alvarado Street in downtown Monterey (see Monterey Peninsula sidebar).

99+ Miles   Traffic light—turn right onto Carmel Valley Rd./G16, where the sign points toward Carmel Valley.

109 Miles   Stay straight as Los Laureles Grade/G20 goes off to the left, which is, by the way, a good way to get to Laguna Seca Raceway.

111 Miles **Carmel Valley Village** will provide your last chance to gas up for a while. There will be great riding for the next 40 miles, down Carmel Valley, over a rise, and down toward the **Salinas Valley.**

140 Miles STOP sign—turn left following G16; the right turn goes to **Arroyo Seco.**

147 Miles Turn left, heading down to the girder bridge, the sign reading GREENFIELD; cross the bridge over the **Arroyo Seco River** and keep going, now on Elm Avenue, running through flat farmland.

151 Miles Turn right onto Central Avenue—a turn that is hard to anticipate right out there in the middle of those flat, flat fields; you will be headed south, paralleling US 101.

158 Miles Turn right onto US 101 as Central Avenue ends.

161 Miles Exit right onto G14/Jolon Rd., where there will be gas and a convenience store.

177 Miles Pass the turn to Fort Hunter Liggett and the **San Antonio Mission** (see Trip 8), to stay on G14.

182 Miles Turn right opposite the **Lockwood Store,** following G14 down Interlake Road.

202 Miles STOP sign—turn right, following G14 and dropping down to the **Nacimiento Dam.**

212 Miles STOP sign—turn right, leaving G14 and going onto Chimney Rock Road, a very nice piece of under-utilized asphalt.

218 Miles Turn left at the **Adelaida Cemetery** onto Adelaida Road.

219 Miles Stay left on Adelaida Road as Klau Mine Road goes off to the right.

220 Miles Turn right onto Vineyard Drive.

229 Miles STOP sign—turn right onto CA 41.

246 Miles STOP sign—turn right onto CA 1.

251 Miles Arrive back at Ground Zero.

Connector

If you are in Monterey and want to keep going north toward San Francisco, just stick to CA 1. ✱

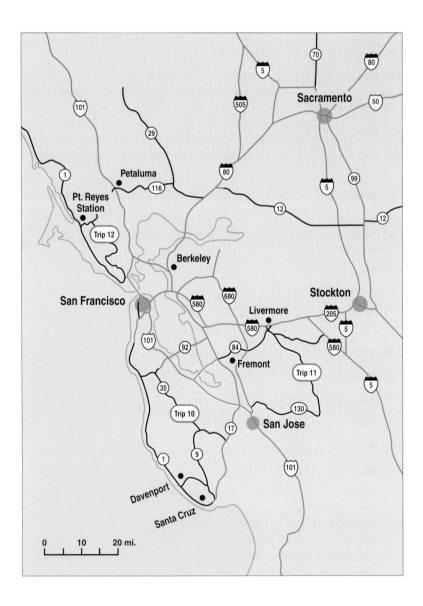

The San Francisco Bay Area

6

Headquarters *San Francisco, The City by the Bay*

San Francisco Visitors Bureau *415-391-2001*

Getting There *The main north-south route is US 101, but you could come up I-280 from San Jose in the south, which connects with I-80 coming from the east across the Bay Bridge, making an arc from south to east. Or vice-versa.*

Best Time to Visit *All year, though it can be wet in winter*

Ground Zero *There isn't one. Again, like Los Angeles, you will have to do a little work for yourself and figure out where the Interstates and freeways are. For the two southern loops, I will have to rely on you, the faithful, competent, geographically-aware reader, to make your way through the city to pick up either I-280 or US 101 (It's not very difficult, I promise—Van Ness Avenue south from Fort Mason comes to mind, or 19th Avenue from Golden Gate Park to Daly City).*

This is a broad sweep of land and water, the *terra firma* cluttered with millions of people—but there is great riding in the area. How many times have I used the expression, "great riding?" But I do mean it. The Bay has a lot of hills around it which provide the under-populated riding venues we seek. And San Francisco is the finest big city that California has to offer.

Alcatraz Island, out in the bay, is now a tourist destination; many people think the government should return it to its original use, rather than building new prisons.

The City of Saint Francis constitutes the **smallest county** in California, about 46 square miles, a lot of it hilly. And the better part of a million people live in this nice city. **San Francisco,** as the locals like to refer to it—only the good ol' boys from Modesto are apt to talk about "going to Frisco"—offers a great deal in the way of entertainment, from tawdry thrills in North Beach strip joints to excellent museums with lots of good culture.

San Franciscans have managed to prevent an Interstate from carving a great swath through their fair city. The standard way through the city is via US 101; the freeway ends downtown, putting you on Van Ness Avenue going north, where you could hang a right on Lombard Street and, Bob's your uncle, you would be at the **Golden Gate Bridge.** Your second choice would be to come up CA 1, which merges with I-280 in **Daly City** for

Down in San Francisco's Marina district, if you follow these 49 MILE SCENIC DRIVE signs, you will see a good bit of The City by the Bay.

a few miles, then leaves and cuts north through San Francisco on 19th Avenue and Park Presidio Boulevard, to meet with US 101 at the bridge. Or, you could opt to take I-280, which connects CA 1 and US 101, and eventually just ends in the downtown area.

I've chosen three noteworthy rides out of SF, one to the Santa Cruz Mountains and Alice's Restaurant, another to Mt. Hamilton east of San Jose, and a third to Marin County, on the north side of the Golden Gate Bridge.

Exploring San Francisco itself is not really within the intended scope of this book. The official **49-Mile Scenic Tour** found on most city maps will take you about a day. If I tried to direct you in this brief guide, it would take about 30 pages, so instead I will leave you more or less on your own, to procure a good map for your tankbag.

With limited enthusiasm, I do recommend **Coit Tower** on Telegraph Hill, the wiggly bit of **Lombard Street** between Hyde and Leavenworth (one-way from Hyde), **Chinatown, Ghiradelli Square, the Palace of the Legion of Honor** in Lincoln Park, **Twin Peaks,** and for those of us who remember the '67 Summer of Love, the **Hashbury** (those 20 blocks around the intersection of Haight and Ashbury streets) though it is much, much changed. And, by all means, take a trip to **Alcatraz Island** (why the California authorities don't reopen that place instead of building new prisons is beyond me).

And no list would be complete without mentioning **Fisherman's Wharf** and **Pier 39** (which has an official Welcome Center with lots of maps), near the **Best Western Tuscan Inn** ($160–$230; 425 Northpoint St.; 800-648-4626; 415-561-1100), with 221 rooms. The Tuscan Inn is as good a location as you can find, within walking distance of just about everywhere. If you are looking for less expensive digs, there are a whole bunch of motels along the west end of Lombard Street heading for the Golden Gate bridge.

I'd suggest places to eat, but the choices are too numerous—though I always go to **Chinatown.** If you want to soak up the local motorcycling scene, head to **Farley's Coffee House** at 18th and Missouri, or **Zeitgeist,** a bar at Valencia and Duboce.

Although it is not the most romantic of hotels, the Best Western Tuscan Inn has safe parking and is within walking distance of many of San Francisco's better sights.

Trip 10 A Day In The Life Of Alice's Restaurant

Distance   *Roughly 144 miles from and to I-280*

Highlights   *A ridge of big hills comes up the San Francisco Peninsula, the Santa Cruz Mountains, which run from Salinas all the way to South San Francisco, right behind the seaside city of Santa Cruz. And along the northern portion of the crest is Skyline Boulevard, a glorious stretch of wooded, two-lane road running some 26 miles. CA 35/Skyline Blvd. technically begins in the southwest corner of San Francisco, right by the zoo, but that initial stretch is pretty urban and boring, so I shall speed you to the good parts.*

Go south on I-280, past the CA 1 SOUTH exit. CA 35 flows in going south, as you continue down I-280/CA 35, past Crystal Springs Reservoir on your right, to the big green exit sign reading CA 35, CA 92 HALF MOON BAY.

0 Miles   Exit right to the STOP light, and turn right onto CA 92/35, crossing between the upper and lower reservoirs, to head up the east side of the **Santa Cruz Mountains.**

2 Miles   Turn left at the top of the hill, onto a major road marked CA 35. A sign will read JUNCTION 84 13, JUNCTION 9 23; the latter is some three miles short of the mark, but who is to argue with the CalTrans mileage counter? You will

There's not much happening at Alice's Restaurant at ten o'clock on a weekday morning—but just wait until the weekend.

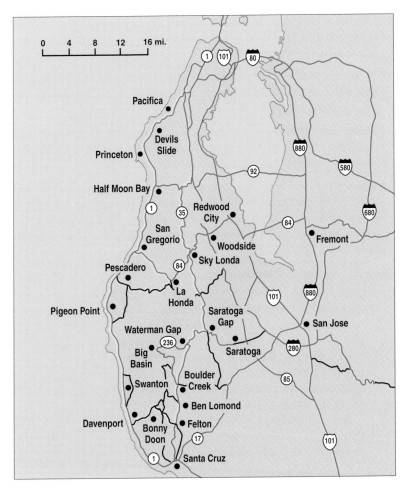

have reached the good part of **Skyline Boulevard,** where leather-clad *Ducatisti* (with one-piece Dainese) and Harley riders (Brando jacket by First Gear, chaps by MotorClothes) collide . . . sometimes literally.

A short uphill run will take you into the woods. In the summer, your visibility may be limited by the fog that typically hangs out here, so watch out. And remember also that a lot of weekend riders will be hustling along at speed, because they know all the turns.

A smooth two-laner will cross over **Kings Mountain,** a pricey rural community with the **Kings Mountain Country Store** on your right, the **Bella Vista** restaurant (dinner) on your left, and the **Mountain House** restaurant (dinner) on your right, at the corner of Henrik Ibsen Road (how some cultured type came up with that literary resource, I know not).

9 Miles Stay straight at the small crossroads. Kings Mountain Road will go down to the east, and Tunitas Creek Road will go to the west (which is a good ride in itself).

15 Miles The road will descend into a wide open area, and CA 84 going east-west will cross CA 35 North-South at an intersection called **Sky Londa** (see Alice's sidebar).

22 Miles At another intersection, Alpine Road drops off to the right, and Page Mill Road down to the left. Alpine will run you back down to **La Honda,** should you wish to explore.

28 Miles STOP sign—turn right onto CA 9 at the **Saratoga Gap,** 2,634 feet above the Pacific Ocean. Skyline Boulevard continues straight, turning very narrow and twisty, while to the left, Congress Springs Road goes down to the town of Saratoga; you want to go right on CA 9, down toward Boulder and Santa Cruz.

34 Miles Stay left at **Waterman Gap,** although the road off to your right, CA 236 ends up in the same place as CA 9—Boulder Creek.

Detour

CA 236 is a beautiful, if slowish, road consisting of 17 winding miles through the **Big Basin Redwoods State Park,** California's first state park; take it if you want to loiter a bit—and loitering is good, despite what the forces of law and order are apt to say when you do it on Main Street.

But we'll stick to CA 9 and head south along the **San Lorenzo River.** ✸

---

42 Miles Enter **Boulder Creek** (see Hemp History sidebar).

44 Miles The **Brookdale Lodge** will be on your right, and I recommend a stay there ($60+; 831-338-6433). Not only is it old, it's nice, and recently refurbished. There is a real live brook running through the dining room—and you can't beat that with a redwood tree. Although this area was timbered in the 1870s and 1880s, the railroad was already accommodating tourists by the turn of the century. Originally built in the 1920s, the lodge has since undergone a lot of adjustments, but it is still reputed to have ghosts.

46 Miles Entering **Ben Lomond** you will see Henfling's on your left; if you reach the traffic light you will have gone 100 feet too far. **Henfling's,** a rowdy bar and grill, will usually have motorcycles out front on the weekends; it opens at 11:00 o'clock six days a week, and 9:30 on Sunday mornings, for those who like to pray over a pint of **Boulder Creek Brewing Company's** best and a plate of ham and eggs.

Alice's

Other than the post office, no one refers to this intersection as **Sky Londa;** it is always Alice's. On any Sunday there will be motorcycles all over the place. A short stretch of low buildings sits on the east side, and on the right side is an angled parking lot in front of **Alice's Restaurant,** a name which originated from a lady named Alice, and not a singer named Arlo (his Alice had a restaurant in western Massachusetts). Occasionally you will see a row of motorcycles fall over, as parking is dodgy on the slope. It's best to leave your bike in gear and use your sidestand.

Alice's is a **classic hangout,** with a small deck and a few tables out front, and a dozen tables inside; they open for breakfast at 7:30 on weekdays, 8:30 on the weekends. Next door, **Alice's Station** pumps gas for those with tiny, tiny tanks, or those who forgot to fill up before coming.

Across the road, at the **Boulevard Bar & Grill,** the parking is flat, but all the spaces have faded signs reading CAR PARKING ONLY. Although there are no tables out front from which to admire the motorcycle scene, there is a big deck overlooking a grassy stretch with a volleyball court. According to the fire marshall, the place can seat 350 people, with probably another 200 standing around.

Taking a left down CA 84 would put you in **Woodside** after seven miles, a very upscale community best known for **Buck's Restaurant** and **Robert's Market.** Buck's is where you would go to have breakfast and eavesdrop on all the venture capitalists talking about where to put money, and Robert's is where you would go to buy the makings of a picnic lunch. If every town had a market as nice as Robert's, the world would be a far better place; it is a glorious establishment, with a lovely produce department, and a meat counter to die for.

Back at Sky Londa, a right (heading west) on CA 84 would take you down to the little intersection at **La Honda** after seven miles. More on that later.

Right now, go straight along the ridge of the mountains, as it rises pleasantly amidst lots of open space preserved by San Mateo County. ✳

Although she is not Alice, this very fine wait-person posed next to Outlaw Biker Steve "The Beast" Bergren.

Go through the traffic light, heading down CA 9.

50 Miles Traffic light—turn right, going up Felton Empire Road.

At this light, you will be in the middle of **Felton,** home of the **Roaring Camp Railway;** if you were to take a left at the light, you would find the entrance to the railroad yards a half-mile up the road. Once there, for a reasonable sum of money, you could chuff along behind a steam engine all the way down to the **Santa Cruz boardwalk,** which is probably the best way to get to that benighted spot.

Instead, Felton Empire Road will take you uphill along narrowingasphalt.

Hemp History

Many inhabitants of the **Santa Cruz Mountains** are in the forefront of environmentally-correct thinking and farming. And one of the more profitable crops is hemp, a crop whose strong fibers can be made into durable material, rope, and thousands of other products. Did you ever see an old movie about life at sea on a sailing ship, where some sailor cuts off the end of a bit of rope and stuffs it in his pipe? That's hemp.

Back in 1937, the passage of the **Marijuana Tax Act** made criminals of anyone growing hemp. In 1998, however, an outfit called **Californians for Industrial Renewal** tried to put an initiative on the state ballot, saying that hemp plants with less than one percent THC (the stuff that gets you stoned) could be legally cultivated. Didn't happen.   ✳

54 Miles At the STOP sign, go straight, as Felton Empire meets **Empire Grade;** continue straight, as Felton Empire turns into **Ice Cream Grade.** (No one I spoke with claimed to know how that name got attached.)

56 Miles STOP sign—turn left onto Pine Flat Road.

58 Miles Keeping straight, Pine Flat becomes Bonny Doon Road.

62 Miles STOP sign—turn right at the intersection with CA 1; you will be going north up the coast, past the remains of Davenport on **San Vicente Creek.**

63 Miles **Davenport** is a small community complete with a store, eateries, and a St. Vincent de Paul church set back from the road. The town was founded in 1867 by **John Davenport,** a shore-whaler who set up a business harpooning grey whales as they migrated from Alaska to Baja. The whaling is long done, but a big cement plant now employs the town and a live railroad still occasionally services the plant.

67 Miles CA 1 will go straight; Swanton Road angles off to the right.

71 Miles   Arrive at the northern end of Swanton Road.

76 Miles   Just after passing into **San Mateo County,** the 400-acre **Coastways Ranch** will be on your right; it's a nice place to live—and to sell produce. Between the road and the sea, you'll find the **Año Nuevo State Reserve,** your best opportunity to see what the coastline looked like before the road and the automobile arrived.

79 Miles   CA 1 will continue straight; Gazos Creek Road angles off to the right, opposite the coastal access.

82 Miles   Pass the **Pigeon Point Lighthouse & Youth Hostel;** it's worth getting a hostel membership just to stay there, but don't forget to make a reservation (650-879-0633).

88 Miles   Turn right at the hand-painted PESCADERO sign, onto Pescadero Road.

90 Miles   A flashing overhead light will tell you that you are at the intersection where Stagecoach Road meets downtown Pescadero. I recommend stopping at **Duarte's** ("do-arts," with a silent "e") noted for excellent food since 1894, be it fried calamari, menudo, or steak; they have everything from crab cioppino to PB&J sandwiches. It's definitely worth your while, and you can eat in the bar as well. Just a hundred yards up from Duarte's, on the other side of the road, you can buy artichoke bread at the **Country Bakery & Grocery.**
Stay on Pescadero Road heading east into the Santa Cruz Mountains.

101 Miles   Keep left at the intersection where Alpine Road goes off to the right.

102 Miles   STOP sign—turn left onto La Honda Road and head downhill.

If you turned right at the STOP sign onto La Honda Road and went up a few hundred yards into the center of the village of La Honda, **Applejack's** (circa 1879), a weekend hangout for the biker crowd, will be on your right. Good sarsaparilla. Another hundred yards down the road, in a little shopping center on the left, you will find the **Merry Prankster,** where the Dainese crowd tends to loiter on weekends, comparing carbon-fiber license-plate holders.

109 Miles La Honda Road will have descended 400 feet in the last few miles, into **San Gregorio.** In 1880, the town had two churches, a school, a hotel, and a saloon. All it has now is the **San Gregorio General Store,** on your right, with a pleasantly eclectic collection of "stuff" for sale.

110 Miles STOP sign—turn right onto CA 1.

In case you don't recognize it, that is the Golden Gate bridge.

117 Miles Tunitas Creek Road goes off to the right, if you are looking for a twisting, tree-shaded nine miles back to Skyline Boulevard. But we will continue along CA 1, just to explore a couple of other choices.

After a few miles you will begin to enter **Half Moon Bay,** a fishing village gone tourist, and going residential.

125 Miles You'll reach the middle of **Half Moon Bay.**

Alternate Route

A right onto CA 92 would take you back over the ridge to connect with the crowded bay side of the peninsula and I-280. However, the road tends to be heavily trafficked, with commuters on the weekdays and tourists on the weekends. After five miles you may recognize the intersection you were at 117 miles ago, where Skyline Boulevard meets CA 35. Two miles farther along you will be back at I-280.

Stay straight, going north, on CA 1.

130 Miles Two miles past **Princeton** and the Half Moon Bay airport, you will see the **Point Montara Lighthouse & Youth Hostel,** which is booked out every weekend (650-728-7177).

135 Miles Past the **Devil's Slide,** the road is often blocked during the winter rains, as it is cut into the ocean side of **Mt. Montara** and runs 1,900 feet above sea level. CalTrans continues to do battle with Mother Nature on this steep section, but the lady always wins. Keep this in mind if you are coming through here on a stormy day, hundreds of feet above the crashing waves.

137 Miles Drop down sharply to **Pedro Valley, Rockaway Beach,** and a bit of congestion. A couple of miles farther on, CA 1 will become a freeway as it enters **Pacifica,** a suburb of San Francisco with some 50,000 residents.

144 Miles Merge with I-280, heading north into **San Francisco.** From here, you will be on your own.

Trip 11 Mt. Hamilton

Distance *94 miles from getting off of I-880 to getting on US 101*

Highlights *You'll be riding through some unexpected wilderness at the southeast end of the Bay.*
If you found I-280 for the Alice's Restaurant loop, you can find it again for this one. Go south of your CA 92/35 exit about nine miles and take CA 84 going east toward Redwood City and US 101. Follow 84 South/US 101 for two miles, then exit onto CA 84, always east, heading for the Dumbarton Bridge and Fremont.
Cross the south end of the Bay on Dumbarton (no toll in this direction), and stay on CA 84 as it slides into I-880 going south.

0 Miles Exit I-880, following signs for CA 84 to Fremont and Livermore.

1 Mile Turn right onto Fremont Boulevard, following CA 84.

1+ Miles Turn left onto Peralta Boulevard, following CA 84.

4 Miles Turn left onto Mission Boulevard, following CA 84.

4+ Miles Turn right at traffic light, following CA 84 onto Niles Canyon Road. If you want a sugar and fat rush, **Niles Doughnuts** on the corner can provide it.

Finally, you will be breaking loose of the megalopolis that is the Bay Area and getting into a bit of the unbuilt-up. CA 84 will wind up along **Alameda Creek,** along with an old railroad whose various bridges you will see crossing this two-lane road time and again as you go east (see Overpopulation sidebar).

9 Miles The community of **Sunol** will be off to your left, a short loop off of CA 84; not much there but the **Sunol Lounge** on Main Street, a motorcyclists'

Overpopulation

If you happen to be on the road at rush hour, you will appreciate just how many people now live well beyond the 80 towns and cities that make up the **Association of Bay Area Governments,** which include 5.5 million inhabitants themselves. Around 1990 the Bay communities more or less put a moratorium on building new housing—but people were still flocking to the area for high-paid, high-tech jobs. So developers went to communities outside the Bay area, such as **Livermore,** and began putting up houses as quick as they could drive nails. Unfortunately, the highway arteries did not follow suit, and many semi-rural roads that used to be lightly-trafficked are now packed with cars. The establishment of a commuter train running through **Niles Canyon** from Livermore to San Jose is but a band-aid on a gaping chest wound. ❋

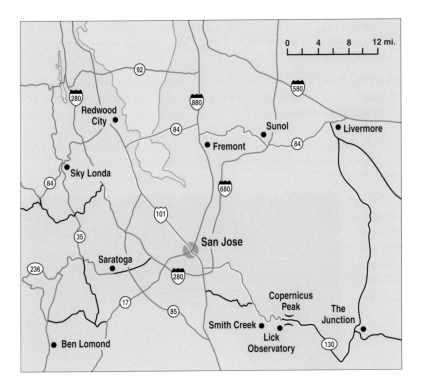

hang-out on weekends, and the **Old Town House Cafe** by the railroad tracks.

9+ Miles STOP sign—turn right at **Sunol Corners;** you'll see a Greek-looking temple off to your right, some sort of self-congratulatory symbol built by the water department to celebrate their bringing water from the **Hetch Hetchy Reservoir** in the Sierra Nevadas to this bit of the world.

10 Miles Go under I-680 and immediately curve 270 degrees to the right to get on the Interstate going north, which you will stay on less than a quarter of a mile.

10+ Miles Get off I-680 at the first exit, marked CA 84, LIVERMORE. You will be on Vallecitos Road, going along the **Vallecito Valley** past the **Vallecitos Nuclear Center** (scientists have been doing lots of atomic research in Livermore these past 50 years). It is a nice road rolling through the hills, but it was a lot less crowded ten years ago.

20 Miles Once you are in downtown **Livermore,** going east on 1st Street, you will see a tall flagpole ahead of you, almost as though it is in the center of the street.

20+ Miles Turn right at the flagpole. First Street curves off to the left, but you want to go right on South Livermore Avenue, also known as County Road J2, although there is no sign to indicate either name. It's best to gas up along here, as there will be nothing for the next 70 miles. You will be clearing town in just a mile or two.

23 Miles Turn right onto Mines Road, just as you pass the **Concannon Vineyards;** the sign indicating MINES also reads DEL VALLE REGIONAL PARK. Old **Jimmy Concannon** established his vineyard here back in 1883, proving that good grapes could be grown in California.

From this point, you will be getting into the back of beyond. And you are only some 20 crow-flying miles from the Bay area.

The Lick Observatory on Mt. Hamilton was completed back in 1875, before the encroachment of light pollution.

CA 130 is one steep road as it comes down off Mt. Hamilton.

27 Miles Turn left, staying on Mines Road, marked MT. HAMILTON, while Del Valle Road goes to the park. Mines Road will be following the **Arroyo Mocho** for the next 20 miles or so.

35 Miles A cautious county bureaucrat has mandated a sign saying ONE LANE ROAD, which means that rather than have a yellow line down the middle, the road has a white line down each edge. It is a reasonably good road, not a real one-laner at all, and since you will be seeing only one vehicle every five minutes or so, the width of the road shouldn't worry you. Along the way, you'll cross from Alameda into **Santa Clara County.**

52 Miles Your arrival in the **San Antonio Valley** will be marked by several scattered houses, a sign outside a small trailer reading RUTHIE'S MALL (makes you want to go see what Ruthie's Mall is all about, doesn't it?), the Sweetwater forest service fire station on your right, and **The Junction** cafe

Down on the east side of Mt. Hamilton, in the San Joaquin Valley, The Junction, a sometimes-open cafe, sits at the spot where three roads converge from Livermore, San Jose, and Patterson.

on your left—which might or might not be open. Mines Road will end, turning into San Antonio Valley Road, and Del Puerto Road will go off to the east, the sign reading PATTERSON 31.

Go straight, noting that San Antonio Valley Road is now officially called County Road West 130.

Great wilderness out here, with just a few ranches hidden off in the valleys. Cross **San Antonio Creek,** make a sharp turn to the right and go up the **Arroyo Bayo.** You'll start a serious climb up the **Diablo Range** to 4,200 feet, with great views looking down into the valleys below.

71 Miles A complex of observatory buildings will appear, with **Copernicus Peak** (4,373 feet) on the north side of the road, and Lick Observatory south of the road on top of **Mt. Hamilton** (4,209 feet).

Lick Observatory was built in the 1880s, as part of the **University of California,** long before the Bay area grew up and created intrusive light pol-

CHAPTER

6

112

lution. It is still an active place, however, with lots of astronomy students making use of all the telescopes, including the 120-incher installed in 1959.

CA 130 (as opposed to County Road 130) will start here and head downhill in a precipitous fashion.

78·Miles Cross over **Smith Creek,** with a fire station on your left, and enter **Joseph Grant County Park.**

82 Miles Quimby Road goes off to the left, a short-cut down to south San Jose.

90 Miles STOP sign—turn left onto Alum Rock Avenue.

93 Miles Access US 101 going north; San Francisco will be just 50 miles away.

That is the Golden Gate Bridge behind me.

Trip 12 Up the Coast and Over Mt. Tamalpais

Distance *83 miles—which does not have to be done on Sunday morning. As a matter of fact, if you want to enjoy the scenery, best do it on a weekday.*

Highlights *All this will be covered in the beginning of the next chapter, the North Coast, which deals with CA 1 from the Golden Gate Bridge to the Lost Coast.*

First off, you have to get to the **Golden Gate Bridge.** US 101 or CA 1 going north through the city will take you right there. Or just look for the bridge towers, if the day is reasonably clear.

The south end of the bridge has a **Vista Point** on the east side, which means the access is off 101 going north.

From the Vista Point, a road goes down to the marina section of San Francisco. There is also a subway passage at the Vista Point if you need to turn around and get on US 101 South. You'll get a good view of foggy towers on most days, but if the weather is clear, the place will certainly offer a Kodak Moment (see Golden Gate Bridge sidebar).

0 Miles Begin at the south side of the bridge, at the non-functioning toll booths, and cross over the bridge to North Vista Point, on the east side of the road. If it is a clear day, you will have a great view of San Francisco—but there are not many of those kind of days.

2 Miles Just up from the Vista Point, the Alexander Avenue exit from 101 will run you down to **Sausalito** (see Marin Headlands sidebar).

Back on US 101, now officially called the **Redwood Highway,** you will go through the **Rainbow Tunnel** and then start down the hill.

6 Miles Take the freeway exit that reads CA 1, STINSON BEACH to go back under 101 toward Mount Tamalpais Junction.

Marin Headlands

For a little excursion, take the Alexander Avenue exit, then go left through the underpass marked SAN FRANCISCO US 101 SOUTH, and emerge on the west side, where you will hang a right at the brown-and-white sign reading MARIN HEADLANDS, which is part of the **Golden Gate National Recreation Area** (415-550-0560, for information). The trip out to the headlands on Conzelman Road runs about five miles, and you won't get lost; you can loop back to Alexander Avenue on Bunker Road, which has a long tunnel. If the day is clear, it will be a delight. The whole area was part of the defense complex protecting the entry to **San Francisco Bay** from the Spanish-American War to World War II. There are great views, and you can clamber over all the old gun positions. ✸

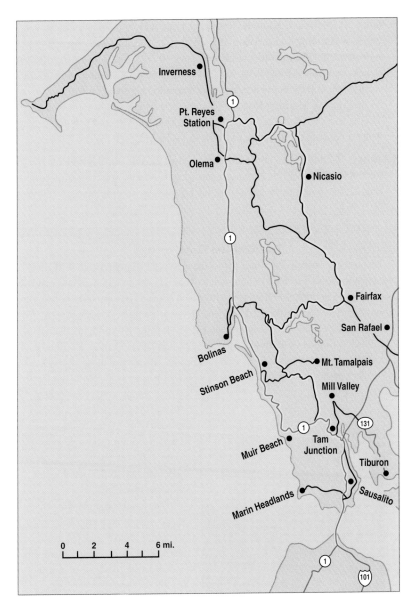

6+ Miles STOP light—turn left onto the road marked STINSON BEACH. This is **Tam Junction,** and Mill Valley will be to the right. The ARCO gas station on the corner, run by genial, turbaned Sikhs, has been a well-known Sunday meeting spot for Bay Area motorcyclists for nearly 50 years (see The Sunday Morning Run sidebar).

9 Miles Stay left on CA 1 at the fork in the road, which will occur after several miles of climbing and arriving at a slight rise. The road goes up and to the right, and the **Panoramic Highway** goes to Mt. Tam and on to Stinson Beach; you want the one to the left that starts a steepish, twisting, winding descent down to the shore—not for the agoraphobic nor those suffering vertigo; on the Sunday Morning Run, this is considered the most hazardous stretch. This byway originated as a stage road back around 1870, and I could imagine many a passenger preferring to walk.

13 Miles On the corner, at the left turn to **Muir Beach,** sits the **Pelican Inn,** a romantic retreat for those taking a short trip from the city. It does the whole English bit, with grassy lawn, rose bushes, beams and mullioned windows,

The Golden Gate Bridge

The idea of a suspension bridge across the entrance to San Francisco Bay first came around in the 1870s, when such technology was still in its infancy, and getting to San Francisco from the north meant a rough ferry ride. Bad weather could ground the whole operation, and if you were prone to seasickness, it could be especially unpleasant. Around 1918, the notion of bridging that gap called the Golden Gate (think of the setting sun) began to be taken seriously, and 15 years later construction began. The bridge was opened in April, 1937.

The resulting towers stretch 760 feet above the water—with 420 feet between them, and the cables, moored in solid rock and concrete at each end of the bridge, are 7,650 feet long. The roadway is some 260 feet above the water, high enough to let the biggest ships pass beneath.

Today, more than 30,000 vehicles use the bridge on a daily basis and tolls pay for its maintenance. To simplify matters and expedite the flow of traffic, the toll is charged only when you are going south ($3 for both motorcycles and cars, which is grossly unfair, although during rush hours motorcycles are waved through). That adds up to $45,000 a day. Not bad. ✱

The towers of the Golden Gate Bridge are often shrouded in fog.

The Sunday Morning Run

If you happen to be at Tam Junction at 7:45 on a Sunday morning, you may see anywhere from ten (rainy day) to 100 (sunny day) or more motorcycles gathered at the ARCO; this is the start of an infamous weekly run, one of America's longer-lived and more firmly established unofficial motorcycle events since the 1950s. At eight o'clock, the bikes head north along CA 1 to Point Reyes Station.

If you wish to partake, feel free, but I very much recommend your hanging back toward the rear of the pack. The guys up front go really, really fast, and they know the road as well as they know the number of their bail bondsman. The more sensible riders at the rear of the pack will be out to enjoy the ride and the camaraderie, rather than risk life, limb, and losing the old driver's license.

Over the years, there have been a small number of bad accidents, but that has not diminished the pleasure of the run. Occasionally the forces of law and order will descend with helicopters and patrol cars to arrest a bunch of people for speeding, at which point all the lawyers along on the ride will volunteer their services, and the state gets to spend a lot of money for little result.

Should you be in the area on a Sunday morning, I do recommend this little fraternal adventure.   ✵

and Guinness and Watney's on tap—all pleasantly camp. With only eight rooms at $158+ a night, plus 10% tax, it is a bit selective (415-383-6000). The management does include a decanter of sherry and a big breakfast with the price of a room, however.

14 Miles You will pass the **Muir Beach Overlook** off to the left, as CA 1 continues along a spectacular cliffside route. Screw up on a corner along here . . . you do not want to think about it. Next you will see **Bolinas Lagoon** and the long spit of land that runs out from Stinson Beach, which is where you would want to have a house if you lived in that part of the world.

18 Miles Pass the north end of Panoramic Highway and enter **Stinson Beach,** founded by one **Nathan Stinson** in 1880 as a resort where the city folk could refresh themselves. In "downtown" Stinson, the **Sand Dollar Restaurant** and **Stinson Beach Grill** sit on opposite sides of CA 1; the latter offers a dozen tasty "Cajun" pan-fried oysters for $17.25. Early on a Sunday morning, there is often a group of motorcyclists who come in from Tam Junction to meet at the **Parkside Cafe,** which is on the left a hundred yards from the only STOP sign in town.

Leaving Stinson Beach, the road weaves along the edge of the **Bolinas Lagoon,** flat and fast, occasionally luring an overly exuberant rider into the drink.

22+ Miles At the north end of the lagoon will be a small crossroads that is hardly marked at all; the road to the left goes to Bolinas, while the road to the right goes to Fairfax on the old, little-used Fairfax-Bolinas Road (you will be getting on the east end of that road in another 26 miles). The privacy-loving inhabitants of Bolinas are noted for destroying any sign on CA 1 that indicates their town's whereabouts, but this has actually had precisely the opposite effect, as San Franciscans think it is a lark to go out and visit this place that the inhabitants do not want visited.

Detour

Do go out to **Bolinas,** a little throwback to the Sixties. Go up the road a mile, take a left at the STOP sign, and soon you will be in the town. The Bolinians love where they live, and seem to hate that strangers come to enjoy their little town, even though places like **The Shop Cafe** and **Smiley's Schooner Saloon & Hotel** (est. 1851) do make their living off of visitors. If you are interested in deceased literary types, this is the town where author **Richard Brautigan** did himself in in his own house, and his body was not found for a week.

When leaving Bolinas, retrace some of your steps, but there is no need to make a right and retrace your entire route, as you can go straight along Horseshoe Hill Road to reconnect with CA 1. Take care as you speed along under the imported eucalyptus trees; these quick-growing rascals from Australia tend to leave slippery bark on the road in shedding season. Note that you will be running right along the **San Andreas Fault Line** as it runs between Bolinas Lagoon and Tomales Bay. ✸

32 Miles Enter **Olema,** with several Hippie-Era merchants surviving quite well. The **General Store,** on the right, has excellent spinach and feta stuffed bread. At the flashing red light (which means STOP), Sir Francis Drake Boulevard will go off to the right, heading southeast to Fairfax, San Anselmo, and US 101. This is a major access road to **Point Reyes National Seashore,** and it can get downright crowded on Sunday afternoon. At the intersection, the **Olema Farmhouse Restaurant** will be open for lunch and dinner, breakfast on the weekends, and next door, the **Point Reyes Seashore Lodge** (415-663-9000) has room rates starting at $85 + 10% (off-season, weekday, creek view), going up to over $200 (see Point Reyes Station sidebar).

34 Miles Continuing from Olema on CA 1, you will see the sign indicating Sir Francis Drake Boulevard going left to **Point Reyes National Seashore,** while you go straight, crossing **Lagunita Creek.**

Point Reyes National Seashore

Point Reyes National Seashore consists of 70,000 acres of pretty nice real estate, and developers would dearly, dearly love to get their greedy hands on just a little bit of it. If the San Andreas were to creak just a little, this could be one fine island. Turn left off CA 1 (now Sir Francis Drake Blvd.) just after the blinking light in Olema, onto Bear Valley Road, which runs by the **Bear Valley Visitor Center** and onto the road (Drake Boulevard again) to Inverness, a small town on Tomales Bay.

There are several places to stay and a couple of restaurants, but the main glory of Point Reyes National Seashore is its beaches. Sixteen miles beyond **Inverness,** the road ends at **Point Reyes Lighthouse,** and it is a beaut ride. On the way you will pass the turn to **Drake's Beach.** Supposedly, Sir Frank careened his ship in the vicinity in 1579, which means he ran it on the beach at high tide so the sailors could clean the bottom. Whether or not this was the place remains open to debate—but it makes for a good story.   ✳

34+ Miles   When you are in downtown **Point Reyes Station,** you will see **The Station House Cafe** on your right. Yes, a railroad, the **North Pacific RR,** did run between here and Sausalito from 1874 to about 1935. On a Sunday morning the cafe will be crowded with leathered motorcyclists who have just raced these last 29 miles from Tam Junction at speeds most motorists would consider unconscionable. Sensible riders who want to avoid the crowd will go up to the **Pine Cone Diner** at the end of Main Street, where CA 1 turns right on Fourth Street.

Point Reyes Station will be the apex of this loop, and from here you will have a variety of ways to get back to San Francisco, including retracing the previous 34 miles, which is not a bad idea. However, given my druthers, I would go north out of town half a mile, and then head back toward SF on a different route, one which will go over Mt. Tamalpais.

35 Miles   Turn right onto Petaluma-Point Reyes Road.

41 Miles   Turn right onto Nicasio Valley Road.

48 Miles   STOP sign—turn left onto Sir Francis Drake Boulevard.

53 Miles   Traffic light in downtown **Fairfax**—turn right onto a commercial frontage road which leads to the Fairfax-

To The Top of Mt. Tamalpais

If the day is clear (Ha ha!) you should definitely go to the top of Mt. Tam, which has unparalleled views of the San Francisco Bay. At the **Rock Spring Junction** (Mile 67), take a left onto East Ridgecrest Blvd., and in three miles you will be at the top of Mt. Tamalpais.   ✳

Bolinas Road; this road will become nicely twisty as it disappears into the Marin Water District watershed.

61 Miles Cross **Alpine Dam,** and the road will start to climb steeply.

63 Miles At the crest, turn left onto West Ridgecrest Boulevard, which leads to Mt. Tam. If you were to continue straight on the Bolinas-Fairfax Road you would end up at the Bolinas/CA 1 junction that you passed at Mile 22+.

67 Miles Go right at Rock Spring Junction, which is a huge parking area (see To the Top of Mt. Tamalpais sidebar).

69 Miles STOP sign—turn left onto the **Panoramic Highway.**

74 Miles STOP sign—turn left onto CA 1.

77 Miles Traffic light—turn right at **Mt. Tam Junction.**

83 Miles Arrive back at the **Golden Gate Bridge.**

This is the viewing area at the south end of the Golden Gate Bridge.

The North Coast

From the Golden Gate to the Lost Coast, CA 1 is a straight stretch of winding road running for 200 miles up the California coast through Marin, Sonoma, and Mendocino Counties. At the end of CA 1 in Leggett, you can either continue north to Humboldt County and Eureka (see Chapter 8), or you could loop south on US 101, to be back in San Francisco in less than four hours.

This is one of the great rides in California, if not the world. I have thrown in a number of detours, alternatives, and little loops, and I truly hope that most of you will not stick just to CA 1. The ocean is backed by the Coastal Range of low mountains, and dashing in and out of the many valleys is downright good fun.

The first part of the chapter is a repetition of the first 34 miles of Trip 12, so I will only reiterate the main points. For details and a far better description of those 35 miles, flip back a few pages.

You could do the whole stretch from the Golden Gate Bridge to Leggett in one long day, but would be about as bright as buying a $150 bottle of Johnny Walker Blue Label and mixing it with Coke. Savor this ride.

Craig Stein looks down on the beach at Usal Bay.

Trip 13 A Linear Route Up the Coast

0 Miles Begin at the south side of the **Golden Gate Bridge,** at the non-functioning toll booths, and head north on CA 1/US 101.

6 Miles Take the freeway exit that reads CA 1, STINSON BEACH, which will go back under 101 and wind around to Mt. Tamalpais Junction.

6+ Miles At **Tam Junction** is a STOP light, where you will turn left onto the road marked STINSON BEACH.

9 Miles Stay left on CA 1 at the fork in the road.

32 Miles Enter **Olema,** where the flashing red light indicates you should stop, and then continue straight.

34+ Miles Arrive in downtown **Point Reyes Station.**

35 Miles The Petaluma-Point Reyes Road will go off to the east; CA 1, the road you want to stay on, goes straight. The next dozen miles will provide splendid riding, rolling along beside **Tomales Bay,** curving and bending past magnificent views and idyllic farms—idyllic to a city boy who doesn't understand the work involved.

44 Miles The town of **Marshall** has but a few decaying buildings and boarded-up businesses on the narrow bit of land between the road and the bay. However, if you are there on a weekend, there will be lots of cars parked in front of **Tony's Seafood,** open noon to nine Friday through Sunday—oysters a specialty.

In fact, commercial oyster raising has become big business along Tomales Bay. It all began more than 100 years ago using oysters shipped in from Chesapeake Bay, and it now makes a number of oyster farmers quite wealthy.

This beached boat is in Inverness, in the Point Reyes National Seashore.

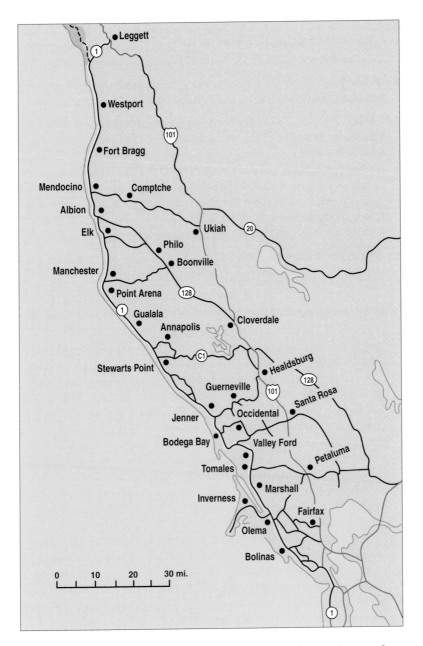

After another three or four miles, the road will begin to angle away from the bay, going along **Keyes Creek** and past the remnants of the old bridge, before crossing over the creek.

51 Miles Stay left on CA 1 as the Tomales-Petaluma Road goes off to the right. In the village of **Tomales,** the **William Tell House** offers Italian food, and the **Tomales Bakery,** baked goods. North of Tomales is ranching country.

56 Miles Stay left on CA 1 after crossing the **Americano Creek,** entering **Sonoma County,** with the Petaluma-Valley Ford Road going to the right.

57+ Miles The village of **Valley Ford** was momentarily famous in 1976 when **Christo,** an artist who thinks big, created a white cloth fence that ran for 22 miles across the Sonoma countryside, through Valley Ford, and on to the sea. He then took it down, all 22 miles of it. Transient art. In town, **Dinucci's** restaurant serves up pasta and all the Italian trimmings (must be a lot of Italian influence on the coast). If you like historical sleeping, stay at the **Valley Ford Hotel,** which dates from the Civil War era and has seven rooms ($75+; 707-876-3600; 800-696-6679) and a Mexican-flavored restaurant.

61 Miles The **Bodega Highway** will go off to the right, where the sign reads BODEGA 1.

Bodega Bay

Tourism now tops the economic ladder in Bodega Bay, with commercial fishing a distant second. The newer, more expensive lodgings are on the south side of town. The first place you will pass is the **Bodega Bay Lodge** ($170–$375; 707-875-3525; 800-368-2468 x5), its 80 rooms showing upper middle-class aspirations; it does have a good restaurant, **The Duck Club.** A mile up CA 1, a Chamber of Commerce tourist bureau on your right, open weekends, will have piles of folders on additional places to stay (800-905-9050). Down on the water at the Lucas Wharf is the **Lucas Restaurant** and a fish market, and just up the road is the **Tides Wharf & Restaurant,** with oysters and eggs for breakfast. Cheaper digs can be found in town, notably at the **Bodega Harbor Inn,** which has 14 conventional motel rooms ($53+; 707-875-3594), plus a number of house rentals available.

Take the well-marked East Shore Road down to the waterfront at the north part of town; as you get to the bottom, you will see the **Sandpiper Restaurant,** the place for breakfast. There is still a good deal of commercial fishing out of **Bodega Harbor,** thanks to the constant efforts of the **U.S. Army Corps of Engineers** to keep the harbor dredged. The West Shore Road out to **Bodega Head** skirts the shore and several marinas. As you walk out on the head, realize that a nuclear power-plant was almost built there back in the Sixties; construction had actually started when more rational people decided it was not such a good idea after all, sitting as it does right on the **San Andreas Fault.** You can look across the narrow channel to the slender **Doran Spit,** which protects the southern approach to the harbor. ✹

This detour takes in the inland **Bodega,** not to be confused with Bodega Bay, and it is worth detouring through this pleasantly small collection of Victorian buildings and places to eat, sleep, and spend your money.

Continue for four miles beyond Bodega on the Bodega Highway, crossing over **Salmon Creek.** Go left onto the **Bohemian Highway** toward Occidental. Three miles up the Salmon Valley, you will come to **Occidental,** a modestly-guised old-world resort.

The town has basically four blocks, with a STOP sign in the middle. The **Union Hotel & Cafe** (est. 1879) sits to the east, with the associated **Union Motel** ($40+; 707-874-3635) just a block away. **Howard's** cafe, the place for breakfast, is on the next block. On the opposite side of the road is **Negri's Occidental Lodge** ($45+; 707-874-3623).

To get back to the coast, you must take Coleman Valley Road, which starts when you head west at that aforementioned STOP sign in Bodega. After a mile and a half, the road turns left, and then in a hundred feet goes right; if you went straight instead, Joy Road would run you back down to the Bodega Highway. Aim for the right, where the sign reads NARROW WINDING ROAD NEXT 8 MILES. It is a beaut, through ranching country—when the sea will suddenly appear in the distance, a stunning sight. From there, you'll have a steep descent to a STOP sign that meets CA 1 about four miles north of Bodega Bay. Coleman Valley Road is one of the more scenic stretches of asphalt on this planet. ✹

62 Miles Back on CA 1, if the road is packed with Winnebagos and you wish to avoid the hurly-burly of Bodega Bay, turn right on Bay Hill Road, to bypass BB entirely. It will put you back on CA 1 just north of town. If you have not seen Bodega Bay, however, stick to CA 1.

66 Miles Arrive in **Bodega Bay,** in all its charm (see Bodega Bay sidebar).

Heading north from Bodega Bay, the last outpost will be the **Bodega Bay Grill**, before you reach the northern end of Bay Hill Road, where the road goes along the bluffs. It is a beautiful ride, which accounts for the numerous vacation houses on the inland side of the highway, all of which seem rather low and designed to hunker down when the winter storms come in. Practically the whole of this stretch of coast is part of the California State Park system, so it remains well-protected from development.

70 Miles Pass Coleman Valley Road to your right. If you did not do the **Occidental** detour, it would be worth your while to ride the two miles up the road,

CHAPTER

7

Fort Ross, north of Jenner, was founded in 1812 by Russian fur-traders, and it served as the last outpost of the Czarist empire in California. It is now a state historical park.

turn around, and come back down, because the view is outstanding as you descend to the sea. Or ride up for the view, continue on Coleman all the way into Occidental, and take a left onto the **Bohemian Highway.** Seven downhill miles later you will come upon Monte Rio and the bridge over the **Russian River.** From there, a left on CA 116 would swing you back to the coast in eight miles.

In fact, there are lots of options available along the North Coast, and the idea is *not to rush.*

75 Miles   After passing the entrance to **Goat Rock Beach,** the road will curve right and drop down to **Bridge Haven** on the **Russian River** (with the **Sizzling Tandoori Restaurant** and **Bridge Haven Campground**), then cross over the river on the 1931 bridge to meet up with CA 116.

75+ Miles   STOP sign—turn left on CA 1, going toward Jenner.

Detour

This detour through Guerneville, Healdsburg, and Lake Sonoma will bring you back to the coast about 20 miles from here. From CA 1, take a right onto CA 116 and head up along the north side of the Russian River for 12 miles, past **Duncan Mills** and **Monte Rio,** and into **Guerneville,** which is hectic in the summer, sleepy in the spring and fall, and often flooded in the winter.

12 Miles   Stay straight at the second traffic light, staying on River Road, as CA 116 goes right over the river.

17 Miles   Turn left after you enter **Hacienda,** angling onto the **Westside Highway** headed for Healdsburg, while River Road crosses the river.

26 Miles   Turn left onto Kinley Road, just as you are approaching US 101.

28 Miles STOP sign—turn left onto Dry Creek Road.

39 Miles Below the dam, you will come to the **Lake Sonoma Visitor Center;** the man-made **Lake Sonoma** has become a big recreation center. Leaving the Visitor Center you will be on Skaggs Creek Road.

41 Miles Turn left as you ascend a grade, following a sign that reads HWY 1 45 M., STEWARTS POINT SKAGGS SP RD (the distance is more like 36 miles, however). If you accelerate madly up the hill and miss the turn, going straight, a sign reading NOT A THROUGH ROAD will remind you of your error. The next dozen miles along Skaggs Springs Road will be blissful. The **U.S. Army Corps of Engineers** has certainly proved to the world that when given an almost infinite amount of money, they can indeed build a marvelous road that doesn't have to handle much traffic.

54 Miles Stay straight, as the old Skaggs Springs Road disappears down to the right. From here, the Corps of Engineers give way to the **Sonoma Dept. of Highways,** who don't have nearly as much money to spend, and the asphalt will be pretty beat up the rest of the way to the coast. Although the going may be slower, the road is lovely, running through thick woods.

72 Miles Stay straight as a girder bridge spanning the **Gualala River** goes off to the right, headed for Annapolis. From here you will start climbing.

75 Miles Bear right, staying on Stewarts Pt./Skaggs Springs Rd. as you enter the small rag-tag community of **Point Stewart Indian Rancheria.** Tin Barn Road will drop off to the left.

80 Miles At the STOP sign, you will be in **Stewarts Point** on CA 1.   ✱

---

76 Miles The nice village of **Jenner** has a tiny post office in a trailer, and a gas station with some rudimentary foodstuffs. A quarter mile up the road you will find **River's End,** a very nice place to spend the night ($95; 707-865-2484), as well as a lot of money on a tastily prepared dinner (it is a gourmet's retreat). You will be looking over the mouth of the **Russian River** as it curves around a great sand spit to meet the Pacific Ocean, a view that is spectacular.

From Jenner, CA 1 will wind along the coast, drop down into **Russian Gulch,** climb up past a bluff and viewing area, and then . . .

81 Miles . . . The road will go straight, as Meyers Grade Road angles off to the right, threatening grades of 18 percent. In several places along the coast where it was difficult to construct a road, and where a road, even if constructed, might easily have been washed out in a winter storm, the old-timers built a road in the hills of the coastal range. Though the route might have been more stressful for horses and passengers in the stagecoach, with steep ups and downs, at least the mail would get through. If you are tired of seeing the sea and surf, you could zip down this wooded run and return to CA 1 at Fort Ross or Timber Cove.

Running as it does along the **Jenner Cliffs,** some 700 feet above the ocean, CA 1 has often slipped into the sea, which is why the Meyers Grade Road is so well paved, as it has gotten frequent use as a detour. From here, you will be riding over **Jewel** and **Timber** and **Mill Gulches.**

87 Miles Oh Lord! Time warp! A stockaded fort will appear on your left, and you will half-expect a sentry to hail you (see Fort Ross State Historical Park sidebar).

Past the Fort Ross Road going up into the hills, CA 1 will rush through the woods.

90 Miles Once over **Timber Cove Creek,** Timber Cove Road goes off to your right. On the left, the **Timber Cove Inn** has a very tall totem pole bringing peace to the world. Although it is a pleasant enough place to escape the hustle of San Francisco, once you are there, you are there, and there is nothing much else nearby. The inexpensive rooms ($80 on a weekday) don't have an ocean view, while the best rooms can run up to $350 on a Saturday night (707-847-3231; 800-987-8319). The place does have a good lobby and bar, but if I'm paying three and a half for a room, I am not likely to be hanging around the public places.

The road will go back into the woods, with occasional glimpses of the ocean, curving and cresting as it goes over creeks, past the **Ocean Cover Store,** the **Salt Point Bar & Grill & Lodge,** and on toward . . .

96 Miles . . . **Stewarts Point Store** (est. 1868) with general merchandise and gas, on the left. Stewarts Point Skaggs Springs Road, the end point for the previous detour, is to the right. The next ten miles along CA 1 will be all **Sea Ranch,** a tastefully planned development begun in the 1960s, so the wealthy could have second homes on the Sonoma coast and deny the hoi polloi access to the beaches. Money does have its privileges.

99+ Miles A sign for the **Annapolis Winery** will point off to the right, along Annapolis Road, to the community of **Annapolis.** Eventually, the road will loop back south to meet Stewarts Point Road. CA 1 will continue along through grazing land, a mile or so in from the coast.

107 Miles Drop down to the **Gualala River,** cross into **Mendocino County,** and enter the town of **Gualala,** with a useful collection of stores, restaurants and motels.

At the very, very south end of town, just before you come to the first buildings, old state highway. 501A goes up the hills to the right, becoming the Old Stage Road and returning to the coast some 16 miles later at **Point Arena,** changing names a few times along the way.

On the sea side of the highway is the **Gualala Country Inn** ($80+; 707-884-4343), and the more upscale **Breakers Inn** ($100+; 707-884-3200; 800-273-2537). On the inland side of the highway, the **Gualala Hotel** has been renting rooms since 1903 (707-884-3441; $55+ with bath, $44 with bath down the hall); you might have to lug your bags upstairs, but it is a nice piece of history, with a good restaurant and bar. At the north end of town is the **Sandpiper Restaurant,** open working-man's hours, 6 a.m. to 3 p.m., with good, honest, solid food.

Leaving Gualala along CA 1, the road runs straight and woodsy. On the right, a remarkable structure, called the **St. Orres Inn,** looks a bit like a Russian fairytale by way of Disneyland; it has 20 rooms and cottages on 50 acres ($60+; 707-884-3303). As you continue past **Anchor Bay,** several small paved roads to the east climb up to the Old Stage Road. Remember, all those bridges over the gulches and creeks were not around a hundred years ago.

Fort Ross is a friendly place, with few DO NOT ENTER signs to spoil your day.

Fort Ross State Historical Park

Welcome to one of the farthest outposts of the Czarist empire. Russians involved in the fur trade came here in 1812, and theirs was an uneasy relationship with the Spanish and then the Mexican governments. Over the next 30 years, however, the sea otter became an increasingly endangered species, and the Russians finally pulled out, leaving behind the name of the river and a crumbling fort. The state took over the site some 30 years ago, and it has been fixed up and properly maintained. Great place! History the way I like it. ✹

121 Miles Point Arena was a major coastal town a hundred years ago. Although farming was the main business, the roads were pretty rudimentary and wagons did not move very fast, so most of the local wheat, beef, and whatnot

The original Point Arena Lighthouse was destroyed in the 1906 earthquake; this is its replacement.

went out of **Arena Cove** on ships. And now it is out of the mainstream of the tourist industry. But there is a movie theater, and next to it, the **Point Arena Cafe;** down the road, the rooms at the **Sea Shell Motel** (707-882-2000) start at a modest $50. Several good restaurants, like **Giannini's** and **Sign of the Whale** could provide dinner.

At the south end of town, Port Road goes down to the wharf, and it's worth the visit. (Remember to enjoy yourself, not rush along.) Up at the north end of town, just before CA 1 cuts left 90 degrees, Riverside Drive goes off to the right, the northern terminus of the Old Stage Road that began in Gualala.

123 Miles Off to the left goes Lighthouse Road, at **Rollerville Junction,** and the two-mile stretch of bumpy asphalt that leads to the **Point Arena Light Station;** it is $3 to get close to the 156-foot lighthouse, which was built after the 1906 earthquake destroyed the previous lighthouse. The old lighthouse keepers' cottages are for rent, if you are of a mind to stay (707-882-2777).

CA 1 will drop down to the wetlands of the **Garcia River.** Try to imagine getting a wagon laden with produce across this stretch during a rainy winter a hundred years ago.

125 Miles A tall windbreak of eucalyptus trees will be ahead; CA 1 keeps to the left, Mountain View Road to the right. To get to the town of **Elk,** go 15 miles up CA 1, or 51 miles via the **Anderson Valley.**

CHAPTER
7

Detour

You will see a lot interesting scenery if you head due east on Mountain View Road. The windbreak ends after a short stretch, and the newly-paved road winds into the coastal range—and "winds" is the operative word. This is a twisty one: up and down, up and down, over the **Mendocino Ridges,** before dropping down to cross **Rancheria Creek,** the road narrowing as you start up. Then you will ride through some redwoods to emerge in **Anderson Valley,** near the town of Boonville on CA 128. The tripmeter should read 25 miles.

25 Miles   At the STOP sign, you will be in **Boonville.** To your right, you will see a couple of stores, two gas stations, several cafes (the **Horn of Zeese** has excellent blueberry pancakes), and the **Boonville Hotel,** a pleasantly old place. However, the best rooms in this hotel, airy and spacious, are in front, and they are subjected to the noise of the passing traffic on the highway . . . though trucks and RVs tend not to travel at night (707-895-2210; $75+—ask for a quiet room at the back). Breakfast will be included, and the restaurant also serves lunch and dinner.

Heading west on CA 128, you will find wineries to your right and vineyards to your left. **Anderson Valley** is working hard to develop a reputation among oenophiles, and at least ten vineyards and tasting rooms will be in evidence. Pass through **Philo.**

33 Miles   Turn left onto the Philo-Greenwood Road, where you will see a sign for Elk. Then you'll get back to a little ridge-hopping and valley-following.

51 Miles   STOP sign, and you will have returned to the sea at **Elk.**   ✦

126 Miles   CA 1 will bring you to the small village of **Manchester,** with some unexpected topiary work (shaped trees) on your right. You could go down to **Manchester State Park,** where a five-mile stretch of shoreline is famous for its beachcombing, as is the north side of **Point Arena;** the wind and currents have brought lots of flotsam and jetsam to rest here.

CA 1 continues along through ranchland just waiting to be gobbled up by 21st-century city-folk looking for country homes, to . . .

140 Miles   . . . The little town of **Elk.** It was a mill town, until the mill closed 40 years ago, and now it has a relatively unspoiled air, with several cafes, B&Bs, and the **Elk Cove Inn** with 14 rooms ($120+; 707-877-3321), and the **Greenwood Pier Inn** with a dozen rooms and cottages ($110+; 707-877-

Mendocino

Stories about the founding of Mendocino differ as to who the principals were, but whatever the truth is, the town began lumbering in the early 1850s, cutting, milling, and shipping trees down to San Francisco. While going off to the Sierra Nevadas with a pick and shovel to seek your fortune might or might not pan out, selling lumber to the construction industry was a guaranteed way to get rich.

Mendocino had 50 good, booming years before **Fort Bragg,** up the coast a few miles, got a railroad in 1911, and sent the community into decline. After World War II, Mendocino became an artists' colony (quaint expression), and inevitably, the tourists followed. Rather than schlep their wares down to The Big City, artists opened little galleries in town to sell their work. And the word spread, and the art lovers came and wanted to spend the night—and so it went.

Today there are probably 50 places to stay within five miles of the old **Presbyterian Church** (dedicated in 1868). Right on Main is the **Mendocino Hotel,** dating from 1878, where you can get a room with a bath down the hall for $85, with an ocean-view suite going for $275 (707-937-0511; 800-548-0513). For a B&B I recommend the **John Dougherty House** (circa 1870) on Ukiah Street, just two blocks from the hotel ($95+; 707-937-5266); not only

The Menodcino Hotel, established in 1878, still serves up good food and clean beds.

does it have a beautiful garden and superb views of the bay, the owners, **Dave and Marion Wells,** are motorcyclists.

For large breakfasts, the upstairs **Bay View Cafe** on Main serves large portions. For more formal food, I gravitate toward the **MacCallum House** on Albion Street, built about 1882; the raspberry cheesecake souffle with fudge sauce is to die for . . . and it just might kill you. And the best place in town to loosen up is **Dick's Bar,** just two doors from the hotel, where the drinking is taken quite seriously.

The only trouble I have with Mendocino is that I sort of would like to move there myself. Except I know how long and wet the winters are. ✹

Ah yes, artistry abounds in Mendocino.

9997). The place could be compared to Mendocino 30 years ago, but on a much smaller scale. On weekends, the beds will usually be booked far in advance, as the San Francisco contingent which has come to love this place keeps on coming back.

From here, the road hangs on to the edge of the land, and it sometimes gets washed away in the winter, keeping CalTrans very active along this stretch.

146 Miles Swooping around a long curve, you'll find yourself looking down on the **Navarro River.** The original bridge was put across in 1917, as the automotive age came to the Mendocino coastline.

STOP sign—turn left on CA 1 on the north side of the river where CA 128 ends; if you took a right onto 128, you'd be in Boonville in 28 miles, and back on US 101 in 47 miles. At this point, you are less than three (boring) hours from San Francisco, which explains why the Mendocino coast is so populated in the summer. But since you don't want to head back to the Golden Gate, go left, toward Fort Bragg, along the B&B Highway.

This is all tourism, but a tasteful tourism; if you want tasteless, go to Orange County in Southern California and visit Disneyland and Laguna Beach. On a sunny summer day, this stretch of coast is unbeatable, which is why a lot of people from the south try to figure out how to make a living up here.

The road will swoop around **Navarro Point,** up past the village of **Albion,** over the high bridge above the **Albion River,** through **Dark Gulch** and the **little Van Damme State Park,** to the village of **Little River.** Beyond that, you will see Little River Airport Road off to your right, as well as the **big Van Damme State Park.** Cross over the river and slip around the inside of the bluff and down toward **Big River.**

CHAPTER
7

156 Miles The Comptche-Ukiah Road will go off to the right, with the **Big River Lodge** on the corner; if you want a rural, untrafficked, motorcycle-friendly way back to US 101, this would be it. It is 14 miles to the hill community of **Comptche** and another nine miles to a small intersection where Orr Springs Road goes straight, and Low Gap Road goes off to the right; stay straight on Orr. Another three miles, and the road will run through **Montgomery Woods State Preserve** before passing **Orr's Hot Springs** on its way to Ukiah.

CA 1 will cross the **Big River,** with the beautiful sight of **Mendocino Bay** off to your left, the road widening as you climb to the bluff that is the site of Mendocino. Big River, the site of the old mill, was where the ships would load the lumber.

157 Miles Once in **Mendocino,** take the first turn to the left, Main Street. Although the town is hopelessly hyped in the tourist and travel industry, it will be almost as good as promised (see Mendocino sidebar).

161 Miles Cross **Caspar Creek** and take a left into **Caspar.** The funky old **Caspar Inn** on the first corner features blues music on the weekends.

163 Miles On the seaside of CA 1, the **Mendocino Coast Botanical Gardens** offer 47 acres of floral and arboreal splendor. Six bucks will get an adult in, and those who appreciate flowers and ferns and foliage can spend a good few hours walking about. A cafe offers sustenance after all that physical exertion.

164 Miles CA 1 meets up with CA 20; a right onto CA 20 would bring you to CA 101, and you would be in Willits in 34 miles. It's a nice road, even if it is a major truck route for getting in and out of Fort Bragg.

164+ Miles Cross over the bridge high above the **Noyo River** and look down to your right into **Noyo Harbor** (see Fort Bragg sidebar).

This fishing boat was leaving Noyo Harbor, just south of Fort Bragg; CA 1 crosses high above the water on the bridge in the background. I took this picture from my room in the Wharf Lodge.

Fort Bragg

In the 1850s, a small detachment of American troops set up camp on a heavily-wooded bluff to oversee a nearby Indian reservation, and the post was named for a company commander, one **Captain Bragg.** When the Indians were pacified, however, the lumbering interests moved in, and Fort Bragg was incorporated in 1889. **Charles Johnson** founded the **Union Lumber Company,** and the original mill was a few miles north of town, moving into Fort Bragg in 1885. In 1911, the railroad arrived from Willits, and business began to boom. And soon there was not a tree to be seen.

Union Lumber was merged into **Boise Cascade** in 1969, and then acquired by **Georgia Pacific** in 1973. Now the company is closing down the mill, which takes up more than a mile of seashore on the south end of town.

So Fort Bragg is going into the tourist business. A call to the CoC (707-961-6300) at 332 North Main St./CA 1, will get you a passel of information. For entertainment, the famous **California-Western RR's Skunk Train** (800-777-5865), will take passengers on a 40-mile trip up along **Pudding Creek** and **Noyo River** before dropping down to **Willits;** they typically have both steam and diesel locomotives. Note that the train is usually packed with children who will likely be enjoying themselves noisily as you are trying to soak up the grandeur of the redwoods.

The town has several museums, the best of all being the **Guest House Museum** by the railroad station, which both informs and entertains. And the **Paul Bunyan Days,** usually the first week in September, promises to become a Big Time affair, showing the logging industry the way it never was.

For sleeping, I gravitate to the south end of town, at **Noyo Harbor.** At the first right turn after crossing the bridge, the **Harbor Lite Lodge** offers "view" rooms starting at $70 (707-964-0221). For a more unconventional setting, follow the road down to Noyo Harbor, and check in at the **Wharf-Anchor Lodge,** where five rooms below **The Wharf** restaurant (18 to 22) are right on the water, with the fishing boats chuffing by a few feet away; these waterfront units start at $65 (707-964-4283). The **Anchor Lodge,** with another 17 rooms, is behind the restaurant, and quieter—but not nearly as much fun. In the middle of town, one block off Main at the corner of North Franklin and Oak is the **Old Coast Hotel,** which began life in 1892 as a working man's hotel, so a view was not important; it has since become a fancy-ish sort of place, still without views, but their chef does serve up some very tasty dishes . . . try the cioppino, a shellfish stew ($155+; 707-961-4488; 888-568-3550).

For other food, the **Tradewinds Restaurant** on Main feeds a lot of lumbering types, while the **Cliff House,** south of town, has "dramatic" ocean views. And **North Coast Brewing,** at 444 North Main, has a good grill and some excellent brew (sample the Old Rasputin stout). ✸

Riding through the Chandelier Tree in Leggett should be on every motorcyclist's list of "Must-Do" events.

180 Miles The village of **Westport,** a thriving lumber-town a hundred years ago, is now a somnolent place with a general store and gas pump. A mile beyond Westport, a paved road, the Branscomb Road will head off to the east, going to Laytonville and US 101, 20 miles away; however, there is about a five-mile stretch in the middle which is not paved. Just so you know.

CA 1 will be running close to the coast, along **Westport-Union Landing State Beach,** crossing **Juan Creek** before wiggling inland. You may now kiss the coast goodbye. Climb over a low ridge and head down to the nonexistent town of **Rockport** and several small grassy valleys.

193 Miles You will have just come through an open grassy area of a dozen acres or so, with several abandoned buildings. As the road curves to the right, you will see a dirt road going to the left, County Road 431, the Usal Road.

Detour

This dual-purpose stretch of Pacific seashore gets a lot of comment, but very few visitors—which is a good thing.

The Usal Road, whose dirt surface does get minimal maintenance, climbs steeply to a ridge overlooking the ocean, and then disappears into the woods. After six miles, the road reaches **Usal**

Bay. It is a splendid ride for a dual-purpose bike—but a bit arduous on a street machine.

After crossing **Usal Creek,** the road tends not to be maintained at all as it runs through the **Sinkyone Wilderness State Park.** It can be a tough road, especially after a tough winter, but this is where you would expect to see a stagecoach and four horses tearing around the corner in front of you.

This hundred-mile stretch from **Usal Creek** to the **Eel River** in the north is known as **The Lost Coast.** It is one of the most dramatic stretches of California coastal land left, and is definitely worth taking several days to explore it. A paved road connects the 35 miles from **Garberville** on US 101 to **Shelter Cove,** the only community on this stretch of coast. After some 35 miles, the Usal Road meets Shelter Cove Road, but you could continue north on Kings Peak Road, in the **Kings Range National Conservation Area,** which goes on to **Honeydew** (see Trip 14). ✹

From here, you will likely be sharing CA 1 with logging trucks, as the road zigs and zags upward through the forest.

207 Miles When CA 1 ends, take a right into **Leggett,** where food and gas will await you. The **Chandelier Drive-Thru Tree** is the town's main attraction. For a $2 entrance fee, you can get a picture of yourself driving through the hole cut in this large redwood.

Connector

From Leggett, a turn south onto US 101 would put you in San Francisco in less than four hours, while north would have you in **Eureka** (Chapter 8) in less than two hours. Anyone going north should definitely get off US 101 right after **Garberville,** and follow the well-marked 31-mile **Avenue of the Giants** (CA 254) through the **Humboldt Redwoods State Park.** And if you want to do a Eureka loop, look for the HONEYDEW sign just past **Weott** and head over to the Lost Coast. I describe this stretch, albeit in reverse, in Trip 13. ✹

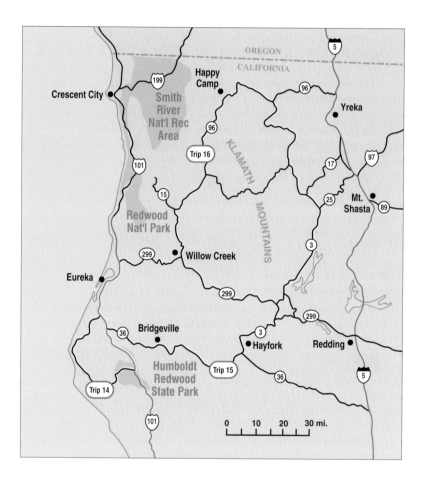

The Far Northwest

8

Headquarters *Eureka*

Chamber of Commerce/Visitors Center *707-442-3738, 800-356-6381*

Best Time to Visit *May through September*

Getting There *Either take US 101 from north or south, or CA 299 going west from Redding. Or, sail into Humboldt Bay on your 45-foot ketch with your bike lashed to the mast.*

Ground Zero *Starting point will be at the intersection of CA 255 and US 101 in Eureka—which is not to be confused with 255 and 101 in Arcata, seven miles to the north, as 255 does a long 180-degree curve around Arcata Bay to rejoin CA 101. (Don't worry, it's not all that difficult to figure out.)*

Although this area has some of California's bestest riding, it is the least visited. You might not want to be up here in the winter, which is the rainy season, but for most of the year the place will be motorcycling nirvana. This chapter will have three Trips—but the last one will offer several options.

This mansion in Eureka was built by lumber baron William Carson in the mid-1880s, not as an ostentatious display of wealth, but rather as a way to keep his workers employed during a slump in the business; would that all employers were so gracious.

This section has I-5 to the east, the Pacific Ocean to the west, the Oregon border to the north, and CA 36 to the south, and covers roughly 10,000 square miles, including the **Six Rivers, Shasta-Trinity, and Klamath National Forests.** The riding will take you through mountains and along rivers, where good roads are never straight for very long. The place will be sparsely populated, but each little community has at least one cafe, and since their business likely depends on locals, rather than tourists, the food will usually be good. Lots of families depend on CalTrans (California Department of Transportation) wages to keep the larder stocked, so the roads also tend to be in good condition.

You will be bedding down in **Eureka,** way up on the California coast, farther north than most tourists go. A seaside city, albeit a mite chilly for bathing suits, Eureka made its money from fishing and lumbering. However, these days, small-scale fishing is pretty iffy, and the wood business has its ups and downs, depending on how many trees are left to cut, so tourism is becoming a more important source of revenue.

A **Captain Winship,** working for the **Russian-American Fur Company,** sailed through the well-concealed entrance to **Humboldt Bay** in 1806 and recorded it as the best place to put in a ship between Puget Sound and San Francisco Bay. After the gold rush began, searching miners poured into the mountains east of the bay, starting a town in 1850 which was incorporated 25 years later. Apparently all these highly-educated miners spoke ancient Greek and liked to holler "Eureka!" ("I found it!") when they hit a vein, hence the origin of the name, as well as the California state motto. The supply of gold eventually petered out, but there were a lot of trees to be cut down, and Eureka began supplying timber to build buildings and shore up mines in other parts of the state.

I like to visit the old part of town; the buildings are Victoriana at its best. At the north end of 2nd Street, you'll find a large, tall house, with enough gingerbread trimming to keep a housepainter or two busy the year around. It was built by an early lumber baron, **William Carson,** in 1885, when the lumber industry was in a slump and he wanted to keep his boys employed. It has now become a private club, called the **Ingomar;** obviously no one person, except perhaps Bill Gates, could afford to keep the place up.

US 101 goes right through the heart of Eureka, and nearly everything can be found within a couple blocks of the highway. The place to stay is the **Eureka Inn,** a gorgeously large pseudo-Tudor hotel that takes up the entire block between 7th and F Streets. It was completed in 1922, during the city's financial heyday, and the lobby is a suitably grand place, with a real fire burning in the huge fireplace even in summer, as the fog tends to keep the place cool. The main structure has just over 100 rooms, with another 70 rooms in the newer annex. Prices start at $110, while the Grand Suite, with its own fireplace, is a mere $250 (518 7th St.; 800-862-4906; 707-442-6441; fax 707-442-0637). There is safe parking for bikes. The hotel is locally owned, and the community is justifiably proud of the place.

Down at the other end of the pricing structure, rooms at the string of motels along US 101 start at $26, or so read the marquees late in 1998. These places tend to be on the noisy side, as traffic motors through town constantly, but that is the price of saving a buck. The **Matador Motel,** at the corner of 4th and C Streets, is AAA approved (approval is easy to get); prices start at $37, more if you want a jacuzzi in your room (800-404-9751; 707-443-9751).

For food, you could cheerfully stay at the Eureka Inn and visit the **Rib Room** for a rare sirloin and an '83 cab from the Wild Horse Vineyard. Or you could walk a few blocks to the **Sea Grill** (316 E Street) for some splendid bass with garlic and shallots. For breakfast or lunch, there is **Betty Moes's** superb kitchen at 207 2nd Street and D; the chicken-fried steak

The best place to overeat is the Samoa Cookhouse, just across Humboldt Bay from Eureka, the last of the real lumbermen's cookhouses.

will be worth the trip. If you just want coffee and a croissant, you could sit on the sidewalk at **Humboldt Bay Coffee Company,** at 2nd and F. And, for a modern brew-pub in a hundred-year-old building, try the **Lost Coast Brewery** at 4th and G Streets.

On the other hand, you should not leave Eureka without checking out the famous **Samoa Cookhouse,** which began as a cookhouse for the lumbermen 100 years ago. Take CA 255 (a/k/a R Street) over the **Samoa Bridge** to the peninsula at the far side of the bay, turn left at the T-bone at Samoa Road, and immediately left again. The side dishes are served family-style at long tables, and the waitresses will bring you the meats of the day: steak, fried chicken, baked ham, grilled salmon—everything your doctor advised you against. It's all-you-can-eat for $6 at breakfast, $7 at lunch, and $11.50 at dinner.

If you want to stay at a slightly unusual place, continue south on Samoa Road for three miles beyond the Cookhouse, and you will come to the old **U.S. Navy blimp base,** now a general-aviation airport. The World War II officers' quarters have been turned into the **Samoa Airport B&B** ($70; 707-445-0765); it's very nice, and if you fly in, the management will provide you with a car at no extra charge.

The city of Eureka will offer museums, shopping (especially antiques, of which you can't carry many on your bike), and general hanging out.

Trip 14 The Lost Coast

Distance *130 miles*

Highlights *If you do not like tight and twisty roads, stay away from this little stint—but it is otherwise a righteous ride, one on which you should dine often. This run along the north section of the Lost Coast is a beaut—and then you will get into the redwoods. Too much fun.*

0 Miles Take US 101 South.

15 Miles Exit right at Ferndale/Fernbridge/CA 211, going straight.

15+ Miles Turn right as the sign for Ferndale comes up, and cross the bridge over the **Eel River.** On the far side you will cross several miles of flat, estuarial land.

Ferndale, which prospered as a farming community, has many examples of its Victorian heritage along Main Street.

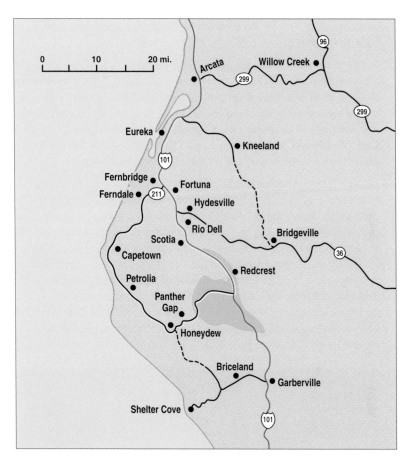

20 Miles Enter the charming town of **Ferndale,** the Main Street decorated in turn-of-the-century Victoriana. The town was founded in 1852, on the flat fertile land between the Eel River and **Bear River Ridge,** and it came to be noted for its dairy herds.

20+ Miles Turn right at the intersection of Main and Ocean, and the **Victorian Inn** (12 individualistic rooms, $85 to $100; 707-786-4949, 888-589-1808) will be to your upper left, and a NO THROUGH ROAD sign will be in front of you) and go past the rather ordinary **Fern Motel** (8 units, $60+, 707-786-9611). On the upper side of the scale, the **Gingerbread Mansion,** a B&B just off Main at 400 Berding Street, has 11 very nice rooms going from $120 to $350 (707-786-4000). And a great breakfast that includes eggs benedict.

21 Miles Turn left as you arrive at the Mattole Road junction; a tall sign will stand to your left, two poles with the words CAPETOWN PETROLIA at the top. Unfortunately, the arrow fell down long ago, but it would have pointed left to

CHAPTER
8

direct you onto Mattole Road, which begins a steep climb up to the top of **Bear River Ridge.**

27 Miles   Once on Bear River Ridge, Upper Bear River Ridge Road will go off to the left (east), back to Rio Dell on US 101. You will stay straight, however, dropping down into **Bear River Valley,** past a lone ranch sitting by the river; this area was once known as **Capetown,** hence the sign back in Ferndale. You will climb out of the valley onto **Cape Ridge,** the western end of which is **Cape Mendocino,** and you will be atop **The Wall.** It will be a helluva steep descent down to the beach, with pitches of better than 20 degrees.

39 Miles   As the road comes off The Wall and flattens out by the sea, a regular sort of house will be sitting off to your left; this would be the place to live if you liked the lonely life and didn't mind occasionally hearing a vehicle come crashing down after losing its brakes. From here, the next six miles will run through uninhabited, pristine beachfront—quite a sight on the California coast. To get a proper appreciation for **The Wall,** stop after a mile or so to look back on it. You will also pass one ranch tucked back a-ways into the **Branstatter Ridge.** This area was originally developed to raise cattle to feed the lumberjacks, and you can still spy a few head. Nowadays, however, I'd imagine that transporting the hamburgers on the hoof out of this area would eat up whatever profit might be made.

This plaque in the community of Petrolia, on the Lost Coast, makes note of the first oil-drilling in California, which was done here in 1865.

45 Miles Start climbing inland, away from the sea.

51 Miles Enter the community of **Petrolia,** with an historical marker at the first left turn; the plaque commemorates the site of California's first drilled oil (as opposed to natural seepage). In 1865, a ship at the pier near **Mattole Point** was loaded with barrels of crude that were taken down to San Francisco for refining (that little tidbit could win you a barroom bet). Not much in Petrolia, except a general store, post office, and the **Yellow Rose** restaurant and bar, serving lunch and dinner six days a week, brunch and lunch on Sundays. **St. Anthony's Church,** a lone bastion of Catholicism, has services on the first Saturday of every month; the only other church in town, insofar as I could see, was Seventh Day Adventist.

52+ Miles As you are approaching the bridge over the **Mattole River**

The Emerald Triangle

Around these parts, farming is a mainstay of the local economy—but the farmers are not raising rutabagas or squash, they are concentrating on a far more profitable crop: marijuana. Since transportation is always expensive, and an ounce of *Cannabis sattiva* can fetch more than a ton of potatoes, one can understand why so many people are cultivating Mary Jane.

The Emerald Triangle consists of three adjoining counties, Humboldt, Mendocino, and Trinity, where the land is good for growing this illegal product, and there is much wilderness—which is useful for hiding the small plots that the farmers use. If you happen to be motoring along happily in this pristine part of the world, and suddenly a helicopter swoops in low over your head, fear not—it is merely the local authorities out to destroy the evil weed before it is shipped down to San Francisco to eventually destroy our entire civilization. ✷

(Mattole, by the way, was the name of a local Indian tribe), down on the left will be **The Hideaway,** with food and drink available seven days a week. It opens at 11 a.m. Tuesday through Sunday, mid-afternoon on Monday, and the burgers (sorry, imported, not Lost Coast, beef) are tasty; the bar stays open until the last client leaves. By the way, credit cards will be useless in Petrolia's eating and drinking establishments.

63 Miles If you really want to get away from the hustle and bustle of regular life, spend the night at the **Mattole River Resort,** a collection of six cottages under shady trees, kitchens included ($40–$120, depending on size; 707-629-3445). If you don't want to cook your own grub, you could go back to The Hideaway.

65 Miles Keep left at the fork as you enter the booming(?) hub of downtown **Honeydew,** which has one store that is combined with the post office and two free-standing phone booths. The store is open seven days a week and does have gas, should you be on a Sportster with a peanut tank. Usually a collec-

The tops of those giants are a long way up.

Avenue of the Giants

If you have come from the south on US 101, you might well have already ridden along the Avenue of the Giants, a/k/a CA 254. The southern end of the avenue begins at the well-marked exit off US 101, about six miles north of **Garberville.** From that point, you will soon enter a delightfully gloomy tunnel of trees running along the east side of the **Eel River.** After 12 miles, both you and the river will go under US 101 and start ambling down the west side of the big road. In another four miles, you will come to **Humboldt Redwoods State Park** headquarters and information center, and four miles beyond that, having once again moved to the east side of US 101, you will be at the Honeydew turn-off.

If you haven't ridden this stretch already, zip back south on US 101 and do it.

If you are doing the Lost Coast loop, head north on the Avenue of the Giants, where stunning, lovely, tall, tall trees line the road. The **Eel River** will be just off to your right, and you'll see many places to pull off. However, as soon as you've killed your motor, the noise of nearby 101 does tend to intrude. Note that logging trucks will be sharing the narrow two-lane avenue with you, with hardly a dotted line in sight. ✸

tion of congenial folk will be sitting on the porch, sipping sodas, and discussing the important news of the day.

In front of the store, the road will fork. Wilder Ridge Road goes to the right (south), past the phone booths toward Garberville via the Briceland Road, or Shelter Cove (that one is gravel, but it is usually in good shape).

However, you want the left fork (straight, really). Mattole Road will cross the **Mattole River** (for the fifth and final time) on a long, single-lane girder bridge. From here, you will head uphill, and up, and up, to gain half a mile in altitude. You will be going around **Catheys Peak** and into the **Humboldt Redwoods State Park** (see The Emerald Triangle sidebar).

The wife and I are taking a break along one of the many small roads in one of the many national forests.

80 Miles Continue through unmarked **Panther Gap,** at 2,744 feet. From there, the road comes down off the mountain and into a small open valley along **Bull Creek.**

83 Miles The road will go into redwood-shaded dappled darkness which reminds me of the "Star Wars" episode in which little rocket ships were darting amongst the trees. Do not forget, a big redwood tree is not forgiving if a mere motorcycle happens to crash into it. This main portion of the state park will go on delightfully for miles.

88 Miles Turn left onto the **Avenue of the Giants.** All of a sudden you will be out of the redwoods and beneath US 101. Instead of going up the ramp, go straight a hundred feet and you will run into the middle of the Avenue of the Giants, 30 glorious miles of huge, tall redwood trees running along the **Eel River.** It's not to be missed (see Avenue of the Giants sidebar).

93 Miles Redcrest is a bit of private property in the midst of the state park. On one side of the road, the **Redcrest Resort** offers hospitality; the post office and the **Eternal Tree House Cafe** will be on the other side of the road.

94 Miles Pass the **Immortal Tree,** which seems to be more of a marketing gambit than anything else.

99 Miles Avenue of the Giants will meld with US 101, to go north to Eureka, past the lumber mills at **Scotia** and **Rio Dell,** and the sign for CA 36 at Alton (see Lumbering Problems sidebar).

115 Miles Pass the Fernbridge exit.

130 Miles You're back at Ground Zero.

Lumbering Problems

The mills you see beside the highway are big and the lumber will be stacked high, waiting to be turned into houses. However, the war between the loggers and the Greenies continues to be a tough one, with extremists on both sides. Back in the days of smaller logging operations, a company might have had several thousand acres, but the lumberjacks would only cut a small percentage of the trees every year, thus allowing for grow-back and re-cutting; this approach provided both wood for the market and jobs for the locals. Everybody knew that you could make more short-term money by doing a simple clear-cut, taking all the trees in a couple of years and then closing the mill, but local pride and civic responsibility kept things moving smoothly.

Times have changed, and the biggest piles of sawn wood that you will see beside US 101 near **Scotia** belong to the **Pacific Lumber Company.** This outfit was seized by a Texas mega-corp, **Maxxam Corporation,** in a hostile takeover in 1986. And Maxxam CEO **Charles Hurwitz** needed to start paying back all the people who had loaned him the $900,000,000 for the takeover, so clear-cutting became the norm on the company's 211,000 acres. And the tree-huggers came out in force, including the briefly-famous **Julia "Butterfly" Hill,** who climbed up a Pacific Lumber tree in 1997 and stayed there for just over two years to make sure it would not be cut down.

In 1999, Hurwitz worked a couple of very good deals. First, he sold 7,500 acres, including much virgin redwood growth, to the U.S. government for $380,000,000, cutting his debt load by 45 percent, while reducing his property by less than five percent, in order to create the **Headwaters National Preserve.** The taxpayers may have winced, but Maxxam shareholders loved the idea. Then he had Pacific Lumber produce a 2,000-page blueprint to describe in detail the logging operations on the remaining 200,000+ acres over the next 120 years, which met with the approval of most environmentalists.

Not all, of course, as there are many Greens who refuse to accept the fact that Mother Nature did not intend any species to last forever, and consequently rail against fate for not allowing them to save the pterodactyl and woolly mammoth. Butterfly did come down from her tree in December 1999, after Pacific Lumber signed a document stating that the tree would never be cut.

In a reasonable world, where we do need lumber, we can draw up sensible compromises to allow for the preservation of remaining old-growth trees, while allowing sustainable-growth cutting and preserving the lumbermen's jobs. ●

Trip 15 The Trinity Return

Distance *244 miles*

Highlights *Ah, wilderness! This is a joyful ride along rivers, through valleys, and over mountain ridges, with lots of trees and very little traffic, mostly along CA routes 36 and 3 and 299.*

0 Miles Head south from Eureka on CA 101, past the Ferndale exit, and past **Fortuna,** to the point where the highway is no longer a freeway and you see a sign for the village of Alton.

20 Miles Turn left where a small green-and-white sign indicates CA 36 going off to the east. This is a little-trafficked road which connects 101 and I-5 begins by cutting across the flatlands.

23+ Miles Turn right as the two-laner enters Hydesville, going toward Bridgeville. A sign will read NO TRAILERS ADVISED PAST BRIDGEVILLE; motorcycles are just fine, however. The pavement which runs along the **Van Duzen River** is not really in great shape, but it will be perfectly sound.

45 Miles **Bridgeville** celebrates its name with a defunct concrete bridge built in 1925. The new highway bypasses the tiny town, but if you were to turn left

Eureka is located on Humboldt Bay, one of the few safe anchorages along the northern stretch of the California coast.

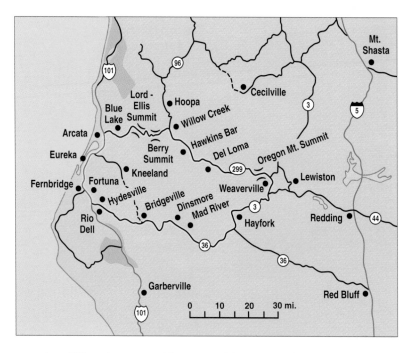

and go 200 yards, you would see several houses, a defunct store, and a sign for Kneeland, to the north. Since you want to go east, backtrack to CA 36, and start climbing up the south side of **McClellan Mountain;** the river will go around to the north. Drop down toward **Dinsmore,** with a gas station and a small airstrip, rejoining the Van Duzen in a narrow valley. In a couple of miles, you will enter **Trinity County,** and the road will get better as you leave the Van Duzen behind to cross over a low ridge and come down to Mad River.

68 Miles The community of **Mad River** has a small general store and two pumps out front, one selling diesel, the other low octane. The sign over the store door reads DON'T BLINK OR YOU'LL MISS US; the post office will be next door, and the only other business in town, the **Burger Bar,** appears to be open whenever the burgermeister chooses. Just a 100 yards from the store, a sign down the road will warn NEXT SERVICES 39 MILES

The road will start to climb, and a beautiful climb it is. The Trinity County engineer had to have had some appreciation for motorcycling, as the curves are banked precisely right. The road will crest **South Fork Mountain Summit,** at 4,077 feet, on the "longest continuous ridge in the North American Continent" before plummeting beckoningly down the east side. The riding along this 20-mile stretch will be so perfect you will be tempted to go back and do it again.

Mt. Shasta, at 14,162 feet, is by far the most impressive mountain in California, rising more than 10,000 feet from the plain it sits on.

98 Miles Turn left at an unmistakable intersection in the middle of the woods, following CA 3 to the north, while CA 36 goes straight, toward Red Bluff.

Connector

Red Bluff is on Interstate 5, a mere 56 miles to the east along CA 36, and a nice ride it is. But there is some grand riding north of here, so you really don't want to take this road unless you are in a goldanged hurry. Also, remember that Red Bluff lies at a 300-foot altitude in the upper **Sacramento Valley,** which means it gets powerful hot in the summer, and real cold in the winter. ✹

---

110 Miles **Hayfork** and its roughly 2,000 inhabitants are located in a lovely valley watered by the **Hayfork Creek.** For nearly 100 years, gold was mined and dredged in the area, but after World War II the economy turned to farming and timbering. Recently they've fallen on hard times, though, ever since the "environmentalists" closed down the lumber mill.

Weaverville

Weaverville, a town of about 3,000, has its own rustic charm, even as it struggles to stay solvent as a tourist destination. Three miners found gold up here in 1850 and, as the story goes, they drew straws to see who would get immortalized. Mr. Weaver won.

The downtown is rather attractive, with a number of two-story buildings lining the tree-shaded thoroughfare. Several have outside curved staircases going to a second floor porch, which was often the access to the shop-owners home. It's a very nice architectural touch.

In the 1870s, after most miners had left because the original easy-to-get wealth was gone, a large number of Chinese miners showed up willing to work harder for less money. The 1874 Joss House is a historical relic of that time.

Food in Weaverville will be plentiful, with some two dozen places catering mainly to the tourists—but in the eight non-tourist months they have to please the locals, so the chow will be okay. My personal favorite is the **Brewery Restaurant** on Main Street, which serves everything from scrambled eggs at 6 a.m. to roast duck at 8 p.m.; **Gerard Kaz,** who has been running it since 1976, also has a splendid collection of microbrews on hand.

Should you imbibe too much, the **49er Motel** is just a couple of hundred yards down the street ($45+; 530-623-4937). ✹

The artistry of the Weaverville architecture is a delight; this spiral staircase leads to the shop-owner's living quarters on the second floor.

Leaving Hayfork, the road will be flat for several miles before climbing to **Hayfork Summit** (3,654 feet). From the top you can see Mt. Shasta in the distance, some 75 miles to the north-northeast; at 14,162 feet, the top of **Mt. Shasta** will be two miles higher than you are.

133 Miles Turn left where CA 3 meets up with CA 299 at a bridge over the **Trinity River.** Hanging that left onto CA 3/299 will take you toward Weaverville. The right goes to Redding.

140 Miles Enter downtown **Weaverville** (see Weaverville sidebar).

As you leave town, stay on CA 299, heading over **Oregon Mountain Summit** (2,897 feet), to re-find the Trinity River at **Junction City** (1,460 feet). CA 299, blessed by our government with the name of **Trinity National Scenic Byway,** is another east-west crossover, but it has 15 cars for every one that was on 36. Which still is not a lot, as there are typically very few cars on 36. It will be a great river ride.

169 Miles Enter **Del Loma,** with cheap cabins for rent.

184 Miles **Hawkins Bar** has a permanent population of 20 or so, and a cheerful general store where the village action takes place.

195 Miles Enter **Willow Creek,** a major metropolis with several motels and two gas stations (see Willow Creek sidebar).

Heading back toward Eureka, the road will continue alongside Willow Creek for a few miles, climb up and cross over **Berry Summit** (2,859 feet), drop down to cross **Redwood Creek,** climb back up over **Lord-Ellis Summit** (2,262 feet), and make a long, long descent to **Blue Lake** and the coastal plain. As you climb over the last ridge you can see the clear-cutting down on

Willow Creek

The community of Willow Creek supports about 1,500 souls and has two motels, a hamburger joint, a pizza place, and **Cinnebar Sam's.** "Cinnebar" is the old-fashioned name for mercuric sulfide, which I can only presume was mined nearby. Considering the nature of the town, Sam's place is a tad on the pretentious side, but it does have a verandah, which unfortunately overlooks a down-at-the-heels parking area and some trailers. I tried the Toad-In-The-Hole, and it was, in a word . . . interesting; should I eat there again, I would probably order something more identifiable, like steak or fried chicken. A number of local microbrews are available in bottles.

If you wish to stay here, in anticipation of your heading north and east of CA 96 to Yreka (see Trip 16), your motel of choice would be the eponymous **Willow Creek Motel,** which took over the old stage stop and hotel that was built in 1890. The motel is not on The Strip, but a half mile north of town on CA 96, just after you cross over **Willow Creek** on the bridge. It's very quiet, very pleasant, and very old-fashioned, with coffee makers in the rooms. ($35; 800-724-1762; 530-629-2115). ✸

the far side of the valley—seriously ugly, but so isn't a lot of life. We hope it grows back.

229 Miles Enter **Blue Lake,** where CA 299 will turn into a divided highway.

235 Miles Merge left, taking the southerly side of US 101, heading toward Eureka.

244 Miles You will be back in **Eureka.**

Trip 16 The Klamath River Run

Distance *399 miles*

Highlights *I have done this as a long loop, but I imagine that most readers will use this trip as a Connector to either Oregon or Mt. Shasta, the latter being the most scenic way to Lassen Volcanic National Park.*

If you want to stay in California, you will head for Mt. Shasta, which I cover in Chapter 9. I will also describe a Connector via Redding, just to give another option. If you do the full 399-mile loop, you will repeat the Weaverville-to-Eureka section that is described in Trip 15, but that means you just get to enjoy it a second time.

0 Miles At the intersection of CA 255 and US 101 in Eureka, head north on US 101.

9 Miles Exit right, take the well-marked exit for CA 299, Blue Lake, and Redding; the first six miles of 299 are divided freeway. Leaving the flat lands and climbing into the mountains CA 299 will become the **Trinity Highway,** going up over **Lord Ellis** (2,262 feet) and **Berry** (2,859 feet) **Summits.**

49 Miles Turn left after entering **Willow Creek** . . . for more on that little community, see Trip 15. In the center of town, take the well-marked left turn onto CA 96; 150 miles of unwedded bliss will be ahead of you. Leaving Willow Creek CA 96 runs alongside the **Trinity River.**

Going down slippery dirt tracks does have its moments.

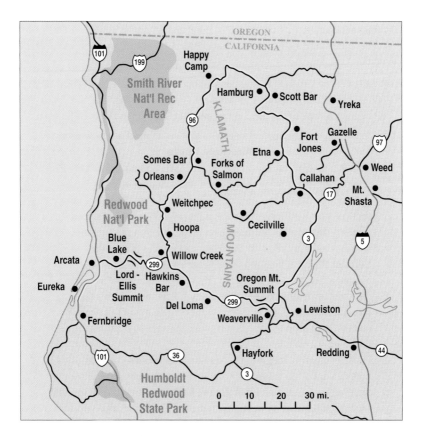

57 Miles An official **Vista Point** on your right overlooks the Trinity River and the **Tish Tang A Tong Creek** (don't ask, I do not know). You are about to enter the **Hoopa Indian Reservation,** where the football team is called the Warriors, and nobody has yet raised a fuss about it.

61 Miles The village of **Hoopa** has a motel and a casino, though the latter is very small-time, with nickel, dime, and dollar poker. It even had the audacity to be closed when I went through there at about 8:30 in the morning.

71 Miles Turn right after you cross the bridge at **Weitchpec,** where the **Trinity** and **Klamath Rivers** converge. You will be going upstream along the Klamath; going left would follow the Klamath downstream and run you into the reservation panhandle.

83 Miles You will see Cedar Camp Road to your left, and the **Klamath River Lodge** down to your right, a rustic fisherman's paradise with few amenities; you have to bring your own food and drink, and do it up in your cabin.

87 Miles Enter **Orleans,** population 630 at last count; on the left will be the **Orleans Mining Co. Cafe,** with lots of skillets on the walls and a skilled

157

cook in the kitchen. The road will be good and fast, and should be treated with respect; it would be a hassle getting a Med-Evac helicopter in along these parts.

103 Miles Stay left on CA 96, after crossing another bridge, going into another county (Siskiyou), another confluence of rivers (the Salmon joins the Klamath). A road off to the right would take you to the Forks of Salmon.

Alternate Route

This is a highly recommended route to **Mt. Shasta** . . . as long as you do not suffer from vertigo (seriously) and do want to experience one of the most scenic roads in the state. At the little intersection after the bridge, take the right turn to Forks of Salmon. Superb! The narrow Salmon River Road will run through the woods, emerging right on the edge, and 40 feet above, the **Salmon River.** A hundred or so years ago some enterprising folk blasted a narrow path along the cliff that went straight up from the river for a hundred feet; some say it was for a narrow-gauge railway, and narrow it is. There will be no guard-rail between you and the long drop to the river. If two cars were to meet, one would have to back up a long way.

After clearing the cliff, the road will reach **Forks of Salmon** (17 miles), which has a store, a sometime gas station (generally open after noon), and the **Grab & Growl Cafe,** serving sandwiches and such from noon to dark. Right after the village, the road will fork, and I recommend you go right, which will take you along Cecilville Road beside the **South Fork Salmon River.** In **Cecilville** (35 miles) you'll find **Doyle's Camp,** which aims to please fishermen, hunters, and motorcyclists, with a restaurant open from 10 a.m. to 8 p.m., a few beds for the weary (5 cabins, $21+; 530-462-4685), and low-test gas pumped out of a fuel truck.

The road from Cecilville to Callahan is one of those mysteries: a perfectly-surfaced road that must average 30 cars and trucks a day, at most. Somebody went to a lot of time and effort to construct this road, and for that I am grateful. From this point, the road will go up over the **Pacific Crest Trail,** with a couple of major switchbacks, before descending into the valley of the **South Fork Scott River.** You will enter **Callahan** at 65 miles, turning right at the STOP sign onto CA 3. ✸

Back on CA 96, follow CA 96 through **Soames Bar,** a huddle of houses just beyond the Forks of Salmon turn. The next 30 miles of CA 96 will run deliriously fast along the **Klamath River.**

137 Miles Slow down as you enter **Happy Camp** (pop. 1,110). One sees the sheriff and his crew a lot, and I think ticket revenues fund the annual X-mas party. Where Second Street runs into 96, the **Frontier Cafe,** on your left, offers good eats, six days a week 6 to 8, Sundays 7 to 2. If you want to spend the night, the **Forest Lodge Motel** will be up the road a half-mile, at 63712 Hwy 96 to be exact ($45+; 530-493-5424). Right opposite the motel is the turn for Indian Creek Road, which runs up into Oregon, meeting US 199 at O'Brien. It you are Oregon-bound, this is a good route to take.

CA 96 is labeled, according to my AAA map, **State of Jefferson National Scenic Byway;** it's another little mystery, as I can find nothing pertaining to Jefferson anywhere. You will pass through **Seiad Valley,** then **Hamburg** (where the **Rainbow General Store** sells cold juice).

167 Miles Turn right at the intersection of CA 96 and Scott River Road, just after you cross over **Scott River.** To your right, a loose private campground sits in mild desolation, a sign indicating some connection with the **Lost Dutchman Mining Association.**

Connector

If you want to head off east and pick up I-5, go straight on CA 96—no worries, you won't get lost. However, after 32 miles you will be at the intersection with CA 263. If you are going north and up to Oregon, stay to the left and you will meet up with the Interstate in two miles; if south, take the turn to the right onto CA 263 headed for Yreka, and in nine twisty miles you will be at an I-5 interchange in **Yreka.** ✹

Our original plan, however, was to follow Scott River Road. The pavement will be a bit narrow to **Scott Bar,** a very small community, and it will rise up higher on the hillside as it follows **Scott River** upstream.

186 Miles **Jones Beach,** a spit of sand out in the cold, cold river, bears no resemblance to the one on Long Island. The Scott, an official **Wild & Scenic River,** continues to slither between the **Marble Mountains** and the **Scott Bar Mountains.**

192 Miles Stay straight as Quartz Valley Road goes off to the right.

193 Miles This is the beginning of **Scott Valley,** and the **Scott Valley Winery** will be off to the left; soon there won't be a town in all of California without its own wine label.

198 Miles Turn right at the T-bone junction with CA 3 at Fort Jones. CA 3 South through **Scott Valley** will be a pretty mundane two-laner with a reasonable amount of traffic.

In July of 1998, Forest Road 17, a/k/a the Trinity Heritage Scenic Parkway, which runs between Weed and CA 3 via Stewart Springs, was still not open.

210 Miles Although **Etna** has a main street and late 19th-century brick buildings, it has a long, long way to go before it could consider itself gentrified. To your right, Sawyer's Bar Road offers yet another alternate route through some great back country.

Detour

It will be 13 dullish miles down to Callahan on CA 3, but would be a 89 brilliant miles if you went via Sawyers Bar Road to **Forks of Salmon,** and then cut back on Cecilville Road. This could be a two-hour (really fast) or four-hour (leisurely) detour. Go down Etna's main street, which becomes Sawyers Bar Road, and in ten miles you will be at **Salmon Mountain Summit** (5,958 feet), between the **Marble Mountain Wilderness** to the north and the **Russian Wilderness** to the south. A steep downhill will bring you along the north side of the **North Fork Salmon River,** past Snowden and Sawyers Bar, to **Forks of Salmon** (41 miles).

From there, hang a very sharp left over the bridge onto Cecilville Road and have a splendid 48-mile ride back to CA 3 at **Callahan.** ✹

If you don't take the detour, go south from Etna.

223 Miles **Callahan,** a town which isn't even really trying to succeed, consists of just a couple of ramshackle old buildings on each side of the road selling groceries and whatnot.

224 Miles A big sign just before the bridge over the **East Fork Scott River** will indicate that CA 3 goes off to the right; to the left or, more accurately, straight ahead, will be the Gazelle Callahan Road.

Connector

To connect over to **Mt. Shasta** and **Lassen National Park,** head out on the Gazelle Callahan Road going up a valley, past the turn to **Kangaroo Lake** (kangaroo and gazelle in California?), over **Gazelle Mountain Summit** at 4,921 feet, and down into the broad valley of the **Shasta River.** The road goes through lush grazing land, and as you go by the entrance to the **Double RR Ranch,** you will suddenly see a giant, snow-capped mountain, Mt. Shasta.

For many years, **Mt. Shasta** was thought to be the highest mountain in the Lower 48, at 14,162 feet. It wasn't until the 1860s that the little needle-nosed peak in the middle of the southern Sierra Nevada, **Mt. Whitney,** was measured and found to be 332 feet higher. Shasta is much more impressive, however, a huge, great cone sitting out in the middle of nowhere. A sight to behold.

After 25 miles, Gazelle Callahan Road will end at Old Hwy. 99; take a right, going south toward the town of **Weed,** named not after wayward vegetation, but rather in honor of timber magnate **Abner Weed,** who prospered in the area around 1900; the **Weed Lumber Mill** is now part of the **International Paper Company.** Once you reach the town of **Mt. Shasta,** hook onto CA 89, which will get you to the national park in two hours. Or you might just want to have a closer look at Mt. Shasta itself. The closest you can get to the top on a motorcycle is **Panther Meadow,** at about 7,000 feet, via the **Everett Memorial Highway** which runs out of downtown Mt. Shasta. If you have a d-p bike, you could circle around the east side of Shasta on the old Military Pass Road, which cuts off US 97 about 14 miles northeast of Weed and then connects with Forest Road 31 after another dozen miles, which in turn runs back to Mt. Shasta (town of).

If you want to stay in Mt. Shasta, the nice digs are at the **Strawberry Valley Inn,** an old-fashioned motel (i.e. one-story) which has been turned into an inexpensive B&B, located on the south end of the main drag in town, Mt. Shasta Boulevard. **Susie Ryan,** the innkeeper, gives her clients a glass of wine or bottle of beer in the eve-ning, and a "continental" breakfast in the morning ($55+; 1142 South Mt. Shasta Blvd.; 530-926-2052). Breakfast of a more seri-ous nature, as well as lunch and dinner can be found seven days a week at the **Black Bear Diner** at 401 Lake Street. You'll find more elegant dining at the **Trinity Café,** at 622 North Shasta Blvd.—or ask Susie for her recommendation.

Pick up CA 89 for the run to Lassen, which runs through the high-country pine forest of the **Cascade Range,** along mostly straight shots of two-lane highway—not very exciting, but quite picturesque. Eighty miles along CA 89, you will reach **Old Station,** just north of Lassen (see Chapter 9). ✺

Back at that intersection with the Gazelle Callahan Road, if you'd headed south on CA 3, you would have gone up over . . .

At 5,401 feet, Scott Mountain Summit, between Yreka and Weaverville, is the highest point on CA 3.

229 Miles . . . **Scott Mountain Summit** at 5,401 feet, with big signs indicating that this road is not cleared of snow at night. If you are traveling this road at night in the winter on a motorcycle, you might want to check in with your psychiatrist.

An historical plaque at the summit will tell you that this was the old California-Oregon stage road, which was opened in 1860, and kept running all winter with the help of sleighs. This avenue of commerce and communication fell into decline after the railroad came up the Sacramento River Canyon in 1887, but could you imagine sledding over this mountain 120 years ago? . . . Where *is* my electric vest?

236 Miles As the mountain road comes around a curve and starts to flatten, you will see a big pile of road-work gravel to your left, as well as the start of Forest Road 17, just before the bridge over the **Tangle Blue River.**

Detour

If you want to have a good time and are adept at riding a lot of dirt road, turn left onto Forest Road 17 (a/k/a Parks Creek Road) and head up alongside the **Little Trinity River.** It was paved recently, and even more recently washed out, so there will be a lot of bumpy sections, but since the state is determined to have this stretch as part of the **Trinity Heritage Scenic Parkway,** it might be getting some improvement in 2000.

After ten miles, the road will leave the river behind and begin a serious climb into the **Scott Mountains.** The asphalt is intact along here, and the road will crest after 16 miles. From this point, you will begin the descent to the eastern side, along **Parks Creek.** At 20 miles you will cross a wooden bridge with the medieval-looking gate of the **Stewart Springs** resort to your right, and a straight shot down to Old Hwy. 99 to your left. Twenty-five miles after leaving CA 3 you will be at Old 99, with Weed just four miles to the south.

From here, you could go anywhere you want.   ✹

---

260 Miles Back on CA 3, **Coffee Creek** has a U.S. Forest Service ranger station with information about hiking trails and such, for the athletically inclined. I got so hungry reading about the 19-mile **Grizzly Lake** hike that I went across the road to the **Forest Cafe** and had myself a piece of pie.

263 Miles **Trinity Lake** will be shining in front of you. The third largest lake in California, it covers some 16,000 acres, though logs and other debris floating in many of the coves reduce its aesthetic qualities. The **Trinity Dam,** completed in 1961, has submerged much of the mining history of the area. Since CA 3 stays a distance away from the lake, all you will see are pine trees.

269 Miles Pass the turn-off to **Trinity Center,** where the general store will have gas and food.

288 Miles A left turn will be marked RUSH CREEK ROAD and LEWISTON; if you wish to spend the night in these parts, Weaverville, straight on CA 3, would be a more romantic bet (see Trip 15).

Detour

If you are in a hurry to get to **Redding,** and you wish to be the first person in the world to claim that distinction (sorry, Reddingites, I do apologize), take the Rush Creek Road. After 10 miles you will reach **Lewiston,** an old, ramshackly mining town with a closed girder bridge across the **Trinity River.** Take a left up the hill and you'll find the **Lewiston Valley Motel** ($40+; 530-778-3942), right next to **Mama's Place,** a family restaurant open from 6 to 9 every day. Not a bad place to spend the night.

In the morning, continue toward Redding by taking a right onto Trinity Dam Boulevard. In four miles you will find yourself on CA 299; turn left to go to Redding. ✱

Back on CA 3, follow the Trinity River south.

295 Miles A STOP sign will mean you are in **Weaverville** (see Trip 15). If you want to go back to Eureka, turn right onto CA 299 and follow Trip 15 routing back to the coast.

399 Miles Arrive back at Ground Zero in **Eureka.**

Connector

If you want to go to Redding, which will lead toward **Lassen Volcanic National Park,** turn left onto CA 3/299. After seven miles, keep left after the Trinity River bridge; CA 3 will go right, and CA 299 will go more or less straight toward Redding.

At 19 miles, Trinity Dam Boulevard comes in from the left, and CA 299 goes steeply up to **Buckhorn Summit** (3,215 feet), with lots of RVs in the way. From here, the road will go down steeply for a few miles, flattening out as it passes **Whiskeytown Lake.**

At 44 miles, you will come into the remains of the town of **Shasta** (not to be confused with Mt. Shasta 60 miles to the north). Although it is now a state historical park, Shasta was the county seat from 1851 to 1888, and during the gold-rush days, life was hectic. As many as a hundred wagons would come through in a single day, making merchants very happy (imagine a hundred semis a day stopping in some small town). Now, all that is left are the ruins of brick buildings and the restored courthouse—but it is all very trim and neat.

Fifty miles after leaving Weaverville you will arrive in **Redding,** named for one **Major B. B. Redding,** a land agent for the **Central Pacific Railroad** back in the 1870s. A big place, it is now the Shasta County seat and a major crossroads in the **North Sacramento Valley.** Nevertheless, it has a lousy climate—very hot in summer, and very cold in winter. The last time I was there (July) the temperature was 111 degrees. You'll find motels, restaurants, and all the necessaries. The visitors' bureau number is 800-874-7562.

Cheap digs can be found at the **Redding Lodge** (1135 Market St; 530-243-5141; $30+); as a matter of fact, all of Market Street, which is part of CA 273, the old main drag, is littered with the detritus of motels of eras past. Out at the Interstate's Hilltop Drive exit you'll find the newer chains, from **La Quinta** to **Motel 6.** For more picturesque accommodations, try the **River Inn** down at 835 Park Marina Drive ($60+; 530-241-9500) on the **Sacramento River.** Restaurants will be everywhere.

In Redding, east-west CA 299 will lead you to north-south I-5, at which point CA 299 heads north while CA 44 goes east to **Lassen Volcanic National Park.** ✹

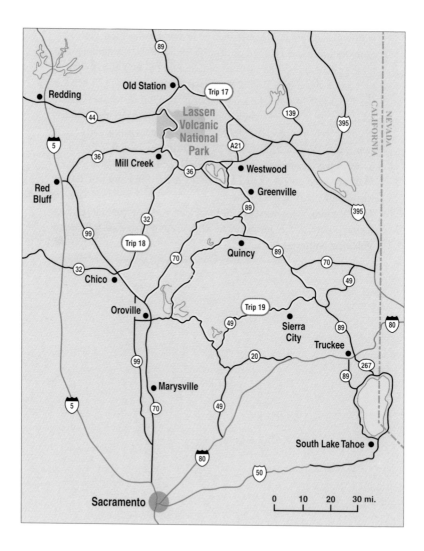

Redding

Old Station ●
Trip 17

89

Lassen
Volcanic
National
Park

44

139

395

5

36

Mill Creek ●

36

A21

● Westwood

Red
Bluff ●

● Greenville

32

89

99

Trip 18

89

Quincy ●

89

395

32

70

70

Chico ●

49

Oroville ●

Trip 19

49

● Sierra
City

89

80

Truckee ●

20

267

99

89

● Marysville

5

70

49

South Lake Tahoe ●

80

50

0   10   20   30 mi.

Sacramento

NEVADA
CALIFORNIA

The Northern Sierras

Headquarters *Quincy*

Plumas County (Quincy) Visitors Bureau *800-326-2247*

Best Time to Visit *May through September, though the road through Lassen Volcanic National Park can stay closed until July*

Getting There *From the north-south, you would arrive in Quincy on CA 89, from the east-west, you'd take CA 70. The two state highways run together for some 30 miles, and the Headquarters is along that stretch.*

Ground Zero *Start right in front of the courthouse, where CA 70/89 takes a right turn*

This is a tootle through **Lassen Volcanic National Park** and the northern third of the Sierra Nevada mountain range. For the most part, you will be in high country, on the ridge of the **Sierra Nevadas** about 4,500 feet above sea level, though two of the loops take you down some 4,000 feet into the **Sacramento River Valley,** where the land is low-lying and distinctly warm in the summertime.

Quincy, the seat of **Plumas County,** gets five feet of snow and four feet of rain every year, mostly during the winter months. Among motorcyclists, Quincy is best known as the site of the annual spring **49er Rally** put on by the BMW 49er Club at the **Plumas-Sierra County Fairgrounds.** The county itself covers some 2,600 square miles, well over half of which is national forest, and it has less than ten bodies per square mile.

Downtown **Quincy** has two parallel one-way streets (Main going east, Lawrence, west), so a brief jaunt and U-turn will show you the whole place. This is a working town, not a resort, but it does have half a dozen places to sleep, like the **Gold Pan Motel** on the north side of town ($40–$65; 200 Crescent St.; 530-283-2265) with 56 rooms, or the older, single-story **Spanish Creek Motel** right across Hwy. 70 ($40; 233 Crescent St.; 530-283-1200) with 25 rooms.

The town has more than a dozen places to eat; the best establishment for breakfast or lunch is the celebrated **Morning Thunder,** at 557 Lawrence Street. For dinner, try **Moon's** (497 Lawrence St.), which has a rather good wine list to accentuate your taste in fish, fowl, or dead cow, or **The Loft** (384 West Main Street) which offers excellent food and the most sociable bar in town.

If you want a nice place to pick up an Associate of Arts degree, try Quincy's own **Feather River College.** For the historians among us, the **Plumas Museum,** right behind the four-story courthouse, has lots on local Indians, mining, and railroads.

Trip 17 Via Lassen Volcanic National Park

Distance *214 miles*

Highlights *This is an easy loop, with easy roads, but the 30 miles you spend inside the park will probably slow you down, as there is much to see and do. Especially if you are a volcanologist.*

0 Miles Head north on CA 70/89, past the airfield. After you climb over a small ridge, the road will wiggle along through the woods.

11 Miles Turn right where CA 70 and 89 split, taking 89 north to **Greenville** and Lassen. The road will take you along the **Indian River** into **Indian Valley,** as well as through the almost defunct mining and lumbering community of **Crescent Mills,** before continuing on through **Greenville** to **Canyon Dam,** a village with several stores and a gas station.

32 Miles Turn right just after Canyon Dam, onto CA 47, which will follow the east side of **Lake Almanor.**

39 Miles Turn left onto A13, angling northwest toward the town of Chester.

With the EPA requirements for expensive new gas holding tanks at service stations, many places, like this one in Greenville, have gone out of business. (Don't worry, there's another station in town.)

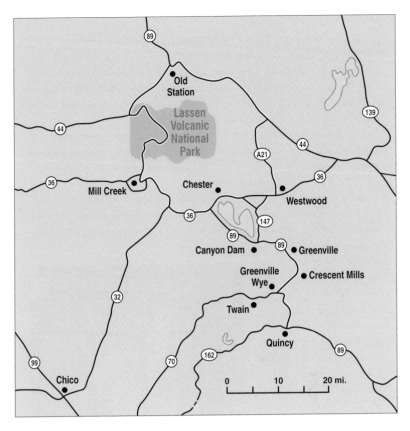

43 Miles STOP sign, and turn left onto CA 36. Cross over the northernmost arm of **Lake Almanor.**

44 Miles At the official **Vista Point,** you can stop and admire Lake Almanor. This big lake was created in 1915 after damming the **North Fork Feather River,** and it has more than 50 miles of shoreline. In the late 19th century, this place, formerly called **Big Meadows,** used to be a good place to raise cattle, and the area became the summer home for wealthy types from the Sacramento Valley.

49 Miles Cross over the **Feather River** and enter **Chester** (see Chester sidebar).

51 Miles Go straight as CA 36 meets CA 89 and the two run west together.

59 Miles The **Black Forest Lodge** will be on your left, an unremarkable building with remarkably good German food, from sauerbrauten to bratwurst, which you can wash down with good beer. And they have nine rooms, should you decide to spend the night ($45+; 530-258-2941).

CHAPTER
9

Chester

Chester is a slightly run-down, but pleasantly touristy town (pop. 2,200, elev. 4,550 feet). It boasts one main street, a half-dozen motels, a dozen places to eat, and a major tourist season about three months long; it's a minor tourist destination the rest of the year—make the bulk of your money in the summer, and play out the profit through the other nine months.

I'm usually not much on B&Bs, for good reason. Show up on a rainy day and you can see the lace curtains fall back into place and just about hear the owners saying, "Oh no, are those the people that have the reservations? They'll muddy everything up!"

But the best B&B in Chester, the **Bidwell House,** is extremely scrumptious, with 14 rooms, and the present owners, **Kim** and **Ian James,** think that motorcyclists are rather nice people (though I could picture some bikers they might not think so highly of). **John Bidwell** built the house in 1901, and it is a lovely sprawling place under large trees. Along with excellent breakfasts, a superb kitchen, orchestrated by Ian, turns out dinner three nights a week. Prices start at $75 (530-258-3338; 1 Main St., at the very east end of town).

If you are into a very rustic setting, 17 miles north of Chester at the end of Warner Valley Road (partially dirt) you'll find the **Drakesbad Guest Ranch** (530-529-1512), stunningly set just within the boundaries of **Lassen National Park.** Reservations are essential, and to get a proper appreciation for the place, I would suggest staying at least two nights. ✱

A father and son are doing a little bonding while riding through the Sierras; they have just spent the night at the Timber House in Chester.

Although these visitors from Germany have great mountain riding in the Alps, riding through Lassen Volcanic National Park is unlike anything in Europe.

62 Miles CA 32 will go off to the left, heading down to Chico. (Keep this in mind for the next loop.)

69 Miles **Childs Meadow Lodge** will be on your right, with 20 motel rooms, several chalets/cabins, and a cafe open from 8 to 6 ($50+; 530-595-3383).

71 Miles CA 172 will go off to the left, while CA 36/89 heads up over **Morgan Summit** (5,155 feet).

Alternate Route

CA 172 is an entertaining, roundabout way of getting to Lassen, taking 14 miles to cover what the direct route would cover in three miles. I suggest you take the detour.

The road will run along **Mill Creek** into a summer community called, curiously enough, Mill Creek, before climbing up to **Mineral Summit** (5,266 feet), and dropping down to intersect with the crossroads community of **Mineral** at the junction with CA 36 (9 miles). **Lassen Mineral Lodge,** at the intersection, has rooms and food ($50+; 530-595-4422). And there will be gas across the road. Take a right onto CA 36, head back up the mountain, and in 14 miles you will intersect with 89 as it goes north into the park. ✹

---

74 Miles Turn right at the fork, staying on CA 89 heading north, while CA 36 goes west toward Mill Creek and Red Bluff.

CHAPTER
9

79 Miles Enter **Lassen Volcanic National Park** and pay $5 (per motorcycle) for the privilege (it's definitely worth it).

79+ Miles To your right will be **Lassen Chalet,** with some souvenirs and basic food. No grand hotel in this park—nothing with gorgeous vistas and a fine restaurant; the Chalet is as good as it gets (the fact that the snow closes the park down from November to June might have something to do with that). It is a great 29-mile trip through the park, with a speed limit of 35 mph (sort of). The road will climb quickly at the beginning, past the stinky **Sulphur Works,** around **Diamond Peak,** and past **Lake Helen.**

85 Miles If you want to take a three-mile hike, park at the **Bumpass Hell** lot and head down into this ten-acre Hades. Apparently, a fellow named **Ken Bumpass** (back when names were names, and nobody laughed) used to take tourists down into this hellish scene of bubbling pits where water is actually boiling from geo-thermal heat. Nowadays, there are boardwalks, but poor old Bumpass had the misfortune of stepping through some fragile crust, and his parboiled leg had to be amputated.

87 Miles South of **Lassen Peak,** the pavement reaches 8,512 feet, the highest point the road gets to in the park. If you wish to leave the bike in the parking area and climb the rest of the way to the 10,457 foot peak, be my guest; it's about a five mile round trip, in which you climb about 2,000 feet (see Lassen Volcanic National Park sidebar).

From here, the road will go down through the **Dwarf Forest** to **Manzanita Lake.**

107 Miles The **Loomis Museum** (**B. F. Loomis** documented the cycle of eruptions back in the late teens, and was instrumental in having the park established) sits at the lake, and will tell you all you wish to know about the park and volcanoes.

108 Miles STOP sign and turn right onto CA 44/89 after exiting the park. CA 44 goes west to Redding.

109 Miles Somebody with a sense of humor named **Eskimo Hill Summit,** at 5,933 feet.

118 Miles Cross over **Hat Creek,** with a store and cafe beside the road.

121 Miles Arrive in **Old Station,** once a stop for the **California Stage Company,** as well as a military post in the late 1850s.

121+ Miles Turn right with CA 44, as CA 89 splits off toward Mt. Shasta; there will be a Forest Service information station at this intersection.

122 Miles This will be your last view of **Mt. Shasta,** as the road ascends to the Pacific Crest via the **Feather Lake Highway.** From this point, you will be travelling through flat, sparsely-grassed high country. Pass the turn to the right for Butte Lake, and the turn to the left for Pittville. A railroad runs just to the north of the road. Long, fency lines will parallel the road, their important, highly-stressed corner sections shored up with rocks.

145 Miles The **Bogard Rest Stop** will be on your right.

Lassen Volcanic National Park

As you enter this park you should not forget that you are standing on a dormant volcano, with bubbly bits perking out all over to remind you that this giant is merely slumbering. The last major eruption was nearly 80 years ago, when it blew its stack more than 300 times between 1914 and 1921. Mess not with Mother Nature. In 1916, in the midst of that eruptive chaos, it was declared a national park, thanks to the efforts of U.S. Representative **John Raker,** for whom **Raker Peak** in the north of the park has been named.

The road runs around **Reading Peak** to **Summit Lake** (7,000 feet), through **Dersch Meadows** and the **Devastated Area** (named after the lava flow of 1915), and over **Emigrant Pass;** if you couldn't imagine taking a wagon train through here 150 years ago, realize that one **Peter Lassen** did just that, and hence claimed his small portion of immortality. The **Lassen Emigrant Trail** was active from 1848 to 1851, and as befits a frontiersman, old Pete died in 1859 while prospecting, attacked by Indians who objected to all the white-man's possessiveness.   ✸

These Beemer riders from Michigan attended a BMW rally in Montana, and then continued on down to Lassen National Park.

Here we see Lassen Peak in the month of July; the snow can stay a long time at these latitudes and heights.

150 Miles Turn right onto County Road A21, at the sign that reads WEST-WOOD 18. If you turned left, a gravel Forest Road would take you to **Feather Lake** in a mile. County Road A21 consists of 18 well-paved, lightly-trafficked miles.

166 Miles Cross railroad tracks just passing through the forest.

168 Miles Turn right as A21 ends at CA 36.

171 Miles Turn left onto CA 147; you will start to retrace your steps in a couple of miles.

182 Miles STOP sign—turn left onto CA 89 at **Canyon Dam.**

203 Miles STOP sign—turn left onto CA 70/89, toward Quincy.

214 Miles End your ride in downtown **Quincy.**

Trip 18   Deer Creek & Feather River Canyon

Distance *185 miles*

Highlights *I could say a lot about this loop, but the Feather River Canyon is simply one of the most delicious rides imaginable—a definite must. I will run you up CA 89, down Deer Creek (CA 32) across CA 99, and back up Feather River CA 70. Easy as eating apple pie.*

0 Miles Leave Quincy going north on CA 70/89 (this is partially a repeat of Trip 17).

11 Miles Turn right at **Greenville Wye,** following CA 89 toward Greenville, Canyon Dam, and the southwest shore of Lake Almanor.

46 Miles STOP sign—turn left to stay on CA 89.

47 Miles Turn left at the well-marked turn to CA 30, where the sign reads CHICO 52—and just follow your front wheel for the next 52 miles. You can't go wrong.

Deer Creek Highway begins through a meadow with a split rail fence, then heads into heavy woods, curving along **Deer Creek;** it is a good road, if not particularly inspiring, but a very pleasant ride with a moderate amount of traffic. About 14 miles along, the road will leave the forest and the creek, and after about 25 miles it will flatten out a tad for a long, long descent alongside **Little Chico Creek** (redundant, as "chico" means "little" in Spanish) into the valley of the **Sacramento River.** Go past **Forest Ranch,** and past the traffic light at Bruce Road, all the way to CA 99 (see Chico sidebar).

99 Miles Turn left after going under the CA 99 freeway. Follow the signs to get on CA 99 South, which goes through flat grassland; there will be no sign of a city anywhere, as it all lies just to the west of the freeway.

112 Miles Exit right at the Butte College/Durham exit, and turn left at the STOP sign, onto Durham-Pentz Road. Go through the fields, crossing over CA 191 and continuing on into the foothills.

Chico

The fabled city of Chico (elev. 200 feet) is home to many events and institutions, including **Chico State College,** which for several years held the dubious honor of being ranked the **#1 party school** in the nation. Chico also has very good BMW and Harley dealerships . . . separate, not combined.

The town began life as the **Chico Ranch,** back in the Spanish land-grant days, and became a cattle-raising center, accessing the markets via the **Sacramento River.** Now it is noted for being very hot in the summertime. ✴

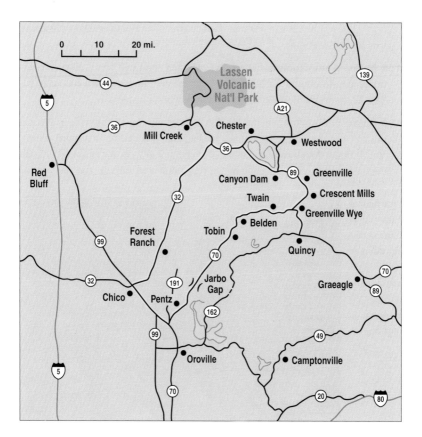

121 Miles Go right when Durham-Pentz ends at Pentz Road, where a sign indicates that CA 70 is to the right.

122 Miles STOP sign—turn left onto CA 70. In a mile or so, CA 70 will become a stretch of freeway for seven miles. You will cross over an arm of **Lake Oroville,** little figuring that this is a product of the **Feather River,** which is running way off to your right, unseen behind the hills.

130 Miles At **Jarbo Gap** (2,250 feet) the road will start to descend, and you will realize that a monstrous river is roiling along below you; do not go over the edge. You can see the **Union Pacific** railroad tracks running well below the level of the road, on the far side of the canyon. It's dramatic.

136 Miles The 1932 bridge, carrying the road, crosses high above the Union Pacific bridge. The road is a sight, with huge sheets of granite curving down on both sides. Watch out for several tunnels along the way, especially if you are wearing darkly shaded glasses on a very bright day. There will be no room for error here. Most of the highway bridges, you will note, date from the 1930s, when FDR had the **Works Project Administration** in full force, and fixing bad roads was a major use of manpower. The **Feather River Highway** was opened in 1935.

150 Miles At the **Tobin** crossing, the rails and road will have changed position, the railroad now higher than the pavement. The old **Tobin Resort** (530-283-2225) seemed closed and boarded up when I last saw it.

159 Miles No problem, as the **Belden Resort** will be in full swing. What a place! Cross the old (1912) girder bridge, and you will be in another world. You'll find a dozen cabins that can sleep from 2 to 7 people (more, if you are very friendly), crowded camping, a restaurant and saloon, and even a gas

Along the narrow Feather River Canyon, the highway and railroad compete for space; here, the road has the high crossing, on a bridge built in 1932.

That 1912 girder bridge crossing the Feather River gives one access to the Belden Resort, a very fine place to spend a night or two.

pump (cabins from $75; 530-283-2906). Every July, the place hosts a motorcycle extravaganza (by invitation only), and 2000 will be the **14th Annual Biker Weekend,** and upward of a thousand people will likely show up. How they will all fit in this relatively small place has yet to be explained.

Back on CA 70, go past the Caribou turn-off, **Rich Bar, Virgilia, Twain** (with its abandoned lumber operation), and **Paxton.**

174 Miles Stay straight as CA 70 meets up with CA 89 at what is locally known as the **Greenville Wye.** For the railroad buffs, the **Keddie "Y,"** which refers to the railroad tracks splitting and going in two directions, will be just a couple of miles farther on.

185 Miles Arrive back in **Quincy.**

Bucks Lake & Yuba Pass

Distance *184 miles*

Highlights *This loop involves two more crossings over the Sierra Nevadas, including the northern end of CA 49, which is a doozy as it goes up along the Yuba River and over Yuba Pass, the northernmost pass of note in the Sierra Nevada Range.*

0 Miles Head west out of town on Forest Road 119, aiming for Bucks Lake.

2 Miles A plaque off on the right side of the road describes the mining operations that existed along **Spanish Creek** from 1851 to 1905. Interestingly, **Gopher Hill,** once the biggest hydraulic mining operation in **Plumas County,** is now site of the county dump (see Hydraulic Mining sidebar).

9 Miles Stay right at the fork in the woods, following the high road, Butte County Road; the RV-ers take the low road, Big Creek Road, to the left. Climb up and over **Bucks Summit** (5,531 feet), then drop down to **Bucks Lake,** at 5,153 feet.

17 Miles **Bucks Lakeshore Resort,** on your right, has 11 cabins starting at $70 a day. The management likes a minimum of a two-day stay, but if you are passing by and they have an empty room, negotiations could be successful. ($50+; 530-283-6900). Down the road, the **Bucks Lake Lodge** also has a dozen rentals ($50+; 530-283-2662).

18 Miles STOP sign—turn right onto Big Creek Road, which is now the **Oroville-Quincy Highway.** This lovely new stretch of road, paved by the U.S. Forest Service, winds along a ridge, generally open to great vistas.

Hydraulic Mining

What's that? Hydraulic mining was an efficient and environmentally disruptive way of separating gold from the rest of the earth. In the early 1850s, miners either hoped to find a nugget lying on top of the earth, or they got a pan and scooped up a bit of gravel from a placer (sort of like a gravel bar, instead of a sand bar), swirled it around with some water, and picked out the gold bits.

After the easy stuff got taken, the big mining companies could either do tunnel (hard-rock) mining or hydraulic mining. The latter ran water by gravity feed into great, huge nozzles which would blast away at the earth and carry everything downstream, where sluice boxes would separate the gold from the dirt. Some of these hydraulic digs moved thousands of tons of earth, and eventually downstream ranchers complained, lawyers got involved, and off to court everybody went. In 1984, the California Supreme Court ruled that hydraulic mining had to stop. Score one for the Greens. ✴

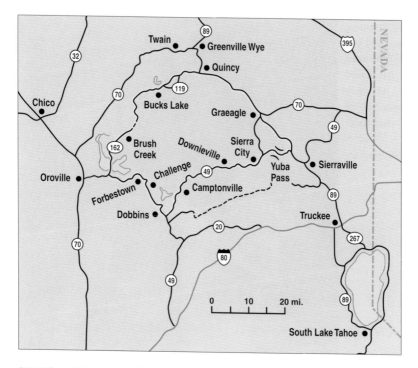

28 Miles The road will enter the woods, and the pavement will be old and patched.

31 Miles The summer community of **Brush Creek** will be scattered through the woods, as the road gets quite steep and twisty. Then the woods open up, and somewhere along that stretch FR 119 will become CA 162.

44 Miles Lake Oroville (elev. 601 feet) can be seen, the result of damming up the **Feather River.**

49 Miles Cross over an arm of **Lake Oroville** on a miniature Golden Gate Bridge.

52 Miles Turn left, where a sign pointing to the left indicates FORBESTOWN ROAD, a/k/a Forest Road 174.

58 Miles Stay right as the road forks; the left goes to **Feather Falls,** while the right (straight, really) will go on to **Forbestown.**

59 Miles Stay right at the fork, continuing on FR 174, a/k/a Challenge Cut-Off Road, after passing through the town named after **Mr. Forbes,** with a general store, open daily, and a museum, open on weekends; the **Yuba Feather Museum** is best known for its thousands of photographs from the last half of the last century which recorded the history of the era.

Sierra City, sitting at 4,200 feet along the Yuba River, has moved from mining to tourism, but the local church still has its congregation.

This couple rode out for a look at New Bullards Bar Reservoir, which dams North Canyon Creek.

68 Miles STOP sign—turn left toward **Challenge** on County Rd. E21/FR 174.

71 Miles Turn right a hundred yards after the **Forest Service Information Station,** which sits on the right, at DOBBINS 16 sign, to stay on FR 174.

82 Miles STOP sign—turn left, onto County Road E20, where the sign says BULLARDS BAR DAM 2.

85 Miles You'll ride along the top of the big damn dam damming **Bullards Bar Reservoir.**

91 Miles STOP sign—turn left onto CA 49 at the junction.

93 Miles A sign proclaiming "historic" **Camptonville** points off to the right, but you will find most of the history has been lost in the detritus of modern civilization, including a lot of abandoned cars. Dual-purpose types could search out the west end of Henness Pass Road if they'd like to have an interesting time crossing the Sierras on a long stretch of dirt.

From here, head up along the rushing **Yuba River** (very nice). Pass **Goodyears Bar.**

111 Miles **Cannon Point** has a real 12-pounder on a pedestal, and from here you can look down on **Downieville** (see Downieville sidebar).

112 Miles As the sign indicates, turn right, go over a bridge along the river for a quarter mile; you'll find the **Sierra Shangri-La** offering both cottages and B&B ($70+; 530-289-3455).

121 Miles In **Sierra City,** the **Herrington's Sierra Pines Resort** ($50; 530-862-1151) serves breakfast and dinner. The **Buckhorn Restaurant** in town also does meals.

Downieville

When it was named for a **Major William Downie** in 1850, the town had more than 5,000 inhabitants in that decade—a good many more than today, where the number 350 is voiced about. It's a nice place to spend the night. Try the **Riverside Inn,** a wonderfully antiquated building right on the river, with ten rooms above the water ($60+; 530-289-1000); the place is often reserved a year in advance on the weekends, but mid-week it will be more accessible. More conventional is the **Downieville Inn,** with 11 rooms ($45+; 530-289-3243; 117 Main St.). You'll find food at the **Downieville Diner** or the **Downieville Bakery & Cafe**—which turns out an excellent Cornish pastie, a traditional miners' meal.

Do go across the river to **Durgan Flat** and the courthouse, if only to admire the refurbished gallows, which were last used to hang someone in 1888. Galloway Road (dirt) will run uphill from the gallows, with a big sign saying that it is very, very steep. You could clamber up and meet the Henness Pass Road at the top, but it is a bear of a ride that is best done on a dual-purpose machine. ✹

Alternate Route

At the 128-mile mark there will be a short-cut, which can lop
about 17 miles off the loop back to Quincy, going north via Gold
Lake Road (a/k/a Forest Road 24), over **Snag Lake Summit**
(6,700 feet) to meet with CA 89 near **Graeagle.**   ✳

137 miles   Crest **Yuba Pass** at 6,701 feet; Forest Road 12, on your right, would
take you south on a dirt road to **Henness Pass,** if you so desired.
From this point, you will begin a steep descent down into **Sierra Valley.**

142 Miles   STOP sign—turn left onto CA 89 to get back to Quincy.

Connector

If you turned right at the STOP and followed CA 49/89, in five
miles you would come to **Sierraville.** CA 49 will go straight, and
you will turn right by the closed general store, keeping on CA 89.

No, that pump by
the STOP sign is
not working, but it
does serve as an
attraction for the
Corner Cafe in
Sierraville, on CA
49/89.

Nine more miles, and you will come over a rise in the woods, and to the right (west) will be Henness Pass Road, which could take you all the way back to **Camptonville** in about 45 miles, the first third of which are paved; the dirt section will drop about 4,000 feet. Easy for a d-p bike.

In 30 miles, you will arrive at Interstate 80. It will be 14 miles to **Lake Tahoe,** 33 to **Reno,** and about 100 miles to **Sacramento;** from here, you'll be on your own. ✹

158 Miles Coming into **Graeagle,** Gold Lake Road goes off to your left. Just ahead will be the bridge crossing over the **Middle Fork Feather River.**

160 Miles STOP sign—turn left at the intersection with CA 70, heading toward Quincy on a long, straightish road through the woods.

184 Miles Enter downtown **Quincy.**

Love these signs: north and south in the same direction.

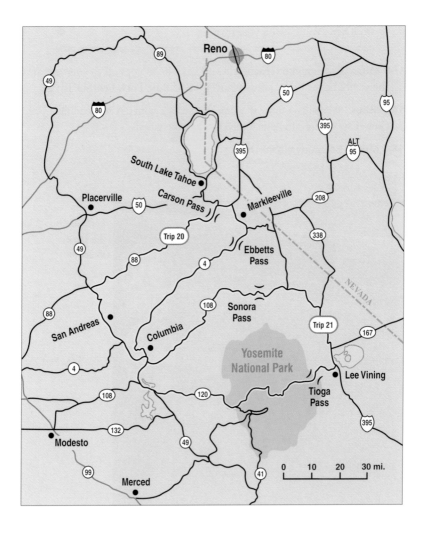

The High Sierra Passes

Headquarters *Sonora*

Tourist Information *209-532-4212, 800-446-1333*

Best Time to Visit *May through November, though check in the spring to make sure the passes are open, and in the fall to make sure that they haven't already been closed*

Getting There *There aren't any big interstates or freeways near Sonora, which is all to the good, but getting there is easy nevertheless. Arrive from the east or west via CA 108, from the north or south via CA 49.*

Ground Zero *Start at the traffic light at Washington and Stockton, right by the Sonora Inn.*

For those of us who love mountain riding, the rides do not get much better than this. Within 70 eagle-flying miles lie four of the great passes across the Sierra Nevada (Snowy Mountain) Range: **Tioga** (9,945 feet), **Sonora** (9,624 feet), **Ebbetts** (8,730 feet), and **Carson** (8,573 feet). Connecting all those passes,

Ebbetts Pass, at 8,730 feet, is, for my motorcycle money, the most entertaining pass in the Sierras to ride.

however, will take about 500 road miles—enough to keep any sporting motorcyclist deliriously happy for a day or two.

Traffic is generally light, except on Tioga in the summer, so a rider can take full advantage of the pleasures of the road. It is best to take these passes two per day, though I have met riders who have gotten up early on a June day and nabbed them all in a day. However, that is a bit more work, and competition, than interests me.

Each pass has an east-west road some 60 to 90 miles long, and then a north-south road connects them at the east or west ends. The landscape will go from the hot **San Joaquin Valley** on the west side, with vineyards and cattle and oak trees, through thick fir forests at the midway point, to break out into rock and lake and isolated evergreen as the road tops 8,000 feet.

The asphalt is usually in good condition, but services are not frequent. Since all these passes are closed in the winter, there is not much call for gas stations and garages at the top.

Sonora, the seat of **Tuolumne County,** is steeped in history, with lovely winding roads to the west going up into the mountains.

The town sits in the **Sierra Nevada** foothills at about 1,800 feet elevation. Although it has a reasonable year-round climate, it can get hot in July and August. Fortunately, the high ridge of the Sierra Nevadas is just behind Sonora, and the temperature will drop as you climb. Of course, when winter comes, it also means that these passes will be closed by snow.

Those with a literary bent will want to stop by the cabin that Mark Twain purportedly lived in during the winter of 1864–65. I'll bet he was cold.

Sonora is a tourist destination, more for the Mother Lode and 49er families than the pass-seeking motorcyclists—but that means that the food and beds will be plentiful.

Smack in the middle of town, at the corner of Washington and Stockton Streets, sits the old **Sonora Inn,** dating from 1896, although it was extensively redone in 1931; in 1998 it was incorporated into the **Day's Inn** chain, which seems to have done it no real harm. The hotel has 30 rooms, while the two-story motel unit (circa 1960) has another 34 ($50+; 160 South Washington St.; 209-532-2400, or 800-329-7466). You must park outdoors in front of the motel units, but Sonora is a pretty safe place. Up Washington Street a quarter mile, you'll find the **Sonora Inn of California,** formerly the **Sonora Townhouse Motel,** a rather bleak, three-storied, asphalted presence with 112 rooms ($60+; 350 South Washington St., 209-532-3633, 800-251-1538). Filling out the old motel category, the **Sonora Gold Lodge,** on Stockton about half a mile west of the Sonora Inn, has 42 ground-level units ($50; 480 Stockton St.; 209-532-3952; 800-363-2154).

Food will be where you find it. I like **Wilma's Flying Pig Cafe** at 275 South Washington; they serve good biscuits and gravy in the morning. **Banny's California Cafe,** a block off the main street at 83 South Steward Street, is also good, as is the **Diamondback Cafe** at 110 South Washington. For more elegant fare, try **Good Heavens** at 49 North Washington.

Trip 20 Ebbetts Pass & Carson Pass

Distance *223 miles*

Highlights *Ebbetts happens to be my favorite pass of the four, because it has some seriously twisty roads that tend to keep other people away. On the downhill sections, you can always tell when there is a vehicle ahead of you by the toasted-brake smell hanging in the air.*

0 Miles Head north on CA 49, right through the center of old Sonora.

2+ Miles Bear right onto Parrotts Ferry Road.

3+ Miles The **Columbia Gem Motel,** a rustic place along the road, rents genuine cabins ($50; 209-532-4508).

4 Miles Enter **Columbia** (see Columbia State Historical Park sidebar).

8 Miles Cross the bridge over **New Melones Lake.**

14+ Miles STOP sign—turn right onto CA 4.

17 Miles The Murphys turn-off will be on your right (see Into Murphys sidebar).

Alternate Route

A very nice alternative to the next 11 miles of CA 4 would be to take Sheep Ranch Road, which goes off Main Street just beyond the **Murphys Hotel;** a big MERCER CAVERNS 1 MILE sign points the way. Follow that, past **Mercer Caverns** (I'm claustrophobic, so spelunking is not high on my agenda), and after six miles the road will fork, **Sheep Ranch** to your left, and Fullen Road to your right, marked CAUTION NARROW ROAD; go right, and there will be a beautiful four-mile stretch over the tops of the hills, with great views. Fullen Road will then merge with Avery Sheep Ranch Road and go on into **Avery,** where you will turn left onto CA 4. ✹

---

24 Miles Enter **Avery,** as the back way to Murphys, Sheep Ranch Road, goes off to your left.

28 Miles As you enter **Arnold, Mountain Mike's Pizza** will be the first place on your right. The town is strung out for more than three miles.

29 Miles **Meadowmont Shopping Center** (what dullard thinks up these names?) will be on your left, and the **Snowshoe Brewing Company** will be

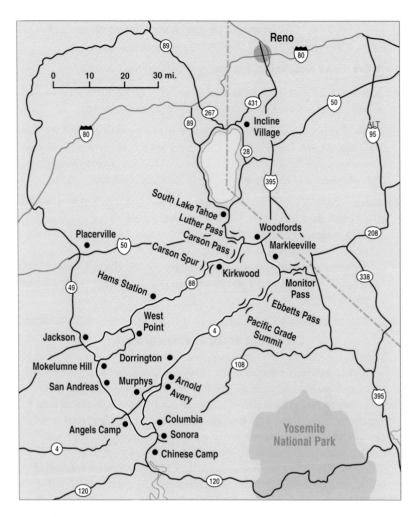

just beyond that. If you are in the sidecar, have the driver stop so you can sample a pint of their Snowweizen.

32 Miles Calavaras Big Trees State Park, on your right, is worth a visit. Back in the 1850s, this grove of giant sequoias was considered one of the wonders of the world, and people would come from San Francisco to view them. Since then, we've become too jaded, and today's pilgrims tend to say, "Is that all? We came all this way just to see that?" before returning to their video games.

36 Miles Dorrington, and the **Dorrington Hotel,** built circa 1860, used to be on the Big Trees-Carson Valley Toll Road, which charged users a stiff fee between 1862 and 1910. Now it is a long, easy, sometimes four-lane, uphill run through the woods.

59 Miles Enter **Bear Valley,** a ski resort with beds, food, and gas.

61 Miles CA 207 (a/k/a Mt. Reba Road) goes off to the left to the ski area. CA 4 narrows as it continues eastward, and it is closed in the winter.

63 Miles Drop down to **Lake Alpine** and loiter in the sunlight at 7,400 feet. The **Lake Alpine Lodge** will have all amenities during the June to September season—or whenever the road is opened and closed. The landscape at this altitude consists of rock, sparse fir trees, lakes, and distance.

71 Miles A mildly ferocious climb brings you to **Mosquito Lake** on the **Pacific Grade Summit** (8,050 feet). Why water comes out of mountain-tops rather than emerging in the valleys has always been, for me, one of those inexplicable bits of geology.

A seriously twisted descent will take you down into **Hermit Valley** (7,060 feet); I don't know if a hermit ever lived there, but it certainly must have been

Columbia State Historical Park

This place is very much worth a stop, or even an overnight stay. The brick town of **Columbia** flourished in the 1850s, continued on for a good many years, and then fell into disrepair. The state has since salvaged the place, from jail to livery to saloon, and it now offers a pleasant, although somewhat commercialized view of the Gold Rush past. If you stay at the **City Hotel** or the nearby **Fallon Hotel,** you will get an even better appreciation of the past; I must recommend the top-of-the-line $105 balcony rooms in the City (209-532-1479; 800-532-1479). And dinner at the **City Hotel Restaurant,** staffed by trainees from the nearby **Columbia College,** is to be commended. Less formal food is served at the **Columbia House Restaurant.**   ❋

The old mining town of Columbia is the best preserved example of life in the gold-rush days; only horses, pedestrians, and bicyclists are allowed on the streets.

a remote spot before the age of the motorcycle and motorcar. From here, you will begin a torturous climb to the actual pass.

76 Miles After cresting **Ebbetts Pass,** at 8,780 feet, you will begin another entertaining descent that has been known to knock the brakes out of many a motorhome. Thankfully, we have less than a half a ton to slow and three disc brakes to do the job.

87 Miles Continue straight as CA 4 vanishes after merging with CA 89 going north (CA 89 South, the turn to the right, goes over Monitor Pass). This road will go north along the **East Fork Carson River,** where you will usually spot a lot of hopefuls casting their lines. Pass the **East Fork Resort,** where the fishermen will be getting photographed with their catch.

Into Murphys

If you took a left onto Main Street and went downtown, you could visit the **Murphys Hotel,** first opened in 1856. A lot of well-known 19th-century personalities have stayed there, from **Mark Twain** to **Ulysses S. Grant.** The current owners bought the place in 1963, after the local sheriff came in one night and closed the place down because he felt the crowd was too rowdy. The alleged rowdies, a group of **University of the Pacific** students, were outraged at the insolence of this public servant, so they purchased the hotel and proceeded to drink at will. "Historic" hotel rooms and much newer (and quieter) motel-type rooms are available ($70+; 209-728-3244; 800-532-7684). The **Nugget Restaurant,** closer to CA 4, is where you'd find all the pick-up trucks parked early in the morning.   ✳

92 Miles Enter **Markleeville,** seat of **Alpine County,** named for one **Jacob Marklee,** who built a bridge across what is now known as **Markleeville Creek** and collected tolls back in the early 1860s. Who needed investment bankers and stock brokers when you could build a small wooden bridge and make good? However, Jacob was shot dead during an argument in 1863, and it might just have been someone disputing the toll charges. The **Alpine Inn** serves a delicious breakfast, lunch, and dinner); the inn was originally called the **Hot Springs Hotel,** and if you want to soak your tired bones, go west of town four miles to **Grovers Hot Springs State Park** (open 2 to 9 Monday through Friday, 9 to 9 on the weekends). If you want to stay in town, the **J. Marklee Toll Station Motel** ($50; 530-694-2507) will gladly put you up.

99 Miles STOP sign and turn left (west) onto CA 89/88 at the **Woodfords Junction.**

105 Miles Go straight on CA 88 at **Picketts Junction,** as CA 89 goes off to the right (north) to Lake Tahoe. From here, CA 88 doubles as US 50 Alternate, should something happen at **Echo Summit** (7,382 feet) on US 50, which parallels CA 88 some ten miles to the north (see Lake Tahoe sidebar).

The Alpine Hotel in Markleeville, the seat of Alpine county, has been serving good grub to hungry travelers for a very long time.

114 Miles After going through the valley, ride over **Carson Pass** (8,573 feet), past **Red Lake,** and up the hill; **Kit Carson** crossed over the Sierras here in 1843, while scouting for John Fremont's **U.S. Army Topographical Corps.** I wonder when the army dismantled that useful corps? It is probably all done by satellite now.

From that point, head down to **Caples Lake** and past **Kirkwood,** where the **Kirkwood Inn** serves breakfast from 8 o'clock on.

122 Miles You will reach **Carson Spur** (7,900 feet), with great views over the wilderness to the north. Pass **Silver Lake** and **Tragedy Springs**—there could be a good story behind that name.

132 Miles Stay straight as US 50A goes off to the northwest on Mormon Emigrant Road, to rejoin US 50 at **Pollock Pines.**

Lake Tahoe

If you are of a mind, you could go up over **Luther Pass** (7,740 feet) to **Tahoe Valley** and do a 72-mile loop of **Lake Tahoe.** I would recommend a clockwise loop, so you will be on the side of the road nearest the water. The riding is not very good, since traffic can be a bit much, as tourists flock here by the thousands, as do golfers who play the ten courses adjacent to the lake. **Emerald Bay State Park** is one of the nicer places, but it is usually crowded. As you loop around **Crystal Bay,** you will cross into Nevada, and then the ski resort of **Incline Village,** before connecting with US 50 at **Glenbrook,** to arrive in the hellish gambling paradise of **South Lake Tahoe.** From there, follow 89 back into California and back down to **Picketts Junction.** ✸

148 Miles Ham's Station has food and spirits for breakfast, lunch, and supper. Roads with names like Cat Crossing and Panther Creek indicate that there is, or was, a fair amount of wildlife around here.

152 Miles Shake Ridge Road goes off to the right, which could take you to Fiddletown and Plymouth on CA 49, or you could turn at Lockwood Junction to go through Daffodil Hill and Volcano, and then return to CA 88; they're all great rides, no matter which way you go. **Volcano** has an impressive B&B, and weekend restaurant, called the **St. George Hotel** ($60+; 209-296-4458).

162 Miles Entering **Pioneer,** a sign will point off to the right reading DE-FENDER GRADE RD, WEST POINT.

Alternate Route

Going via **West Point** provides a very countrified alternative to the hurly-burly of Jackson and CA 49. If you take this route, you will meet up with CA 26 in less than two miles. From there, take a left to the lazy town of West Point, and then continue on another 16 miles to **Mokelumne Hill** on CA 49.   ✹

While in Mokulemne Hill, an old gold-rush town right along CA 49, a trip to the Adams & Co. Saloon is very worthwhile.

Jackson

Turn right, following the sign for "Old Town," and you will be in a sinister neighborhood—or so it was a mere 45 years ago.

During the early gold-rush days, Jackson was the scene of placer mining, but that washed out, and by the late 1860s, hardrock mining was the word, with deep tunnels going down into the center of the earth. A lot of relics from that era are very much visible, especially the apparatus of the **Kennedy Mine,** which lasted well into the 20th century. During World War II, however, the mines were closed to aid the war effort, the miners went off to fight, and the chemicals used in extracting the gold from the ore were used elsewhere.

After WWII, the price of gold was frozen at $35 an ounce, but the cost of production was well above that. To support itself, Jackson turned to sin, and became a well-known gambling and red-light center. It was so well-known that in the later 1950s, the state had to crack down. So phase three in the town's economic development has become the tourist industry.

Down at the south end of Main Street, you'll find the **National Hotel,** dating from 1862; it has 30 rooms ($50+, cheaper ones without bath; 209-223-0500), but my preferred accommodation is the **Bordello Suite,** for a mere $80 a night . . . a deal. More conventional lodging can be found at the **Best Western Amador Inn** on CA 49, with 112 rooms ($50+; 209-223-0211; 800-543-0221).

Food will be everywhere. For a snack, try **Fat Freddy's** on Main, kitty-corner to the National Hotel; Fred turns out a fine hot hound for a reasonable price. **Magdaleno's** on Main is good for breakfast, and **Teresa's Place** and **Buscaglia's** on Jackson Gate Road serve lunch and dinner.   ✹

165 Miles CA 26 will go off to your left, toward West Point, while Pioneer Road, to your right, leads to Volcano.

177 Miles Turn left on CA 49, after CA 88 meets this road at **Jackson;** named after one **Colonel Alden Jackson,** this thriving town, once fallen on hard times, is now making its way back by the dint of hard labor (see Jackson sidebar).

Leaving town, go south on CA 49.

185 Miles Arrive at **Moke Hill,** which is more easily pronounced than Mokelumne Hill. CA 49 just skims the town, but do turn left, go in, and take a look. The fanciest place is the **Hotel Leger,** on top of the hill, a white, two-storied affair, claiming to be "in continuous operation since 1852." They have a dozen rooms done up in 19th-century Martha Stewart, some with private baths, as well as a restaurant and a saloon ($55–$100; 209-286-1401). Half a block along, the **Adams & Co. Saloon,** in the old **Odd Fellows Hall,** an interesting place to knock back half a dozen whiskeys . . . as long as you are staying at the Leger.

191 Miles A sign will say that Old CA 49 (a/k/a Gold Strike Road) goes off to the left; I recommend your taking it to San Andreas, where it will rejoin the new CA 49.

192 Miles **San Andreas** has a small old section, and the **Black Bart Saloon,** which serves up sarsaparilla and whiskey, though not mixed.

205 Miles Enter **Altaville,** which is sort of a suburb of **Angels Camp.** At the traffic light, a left turn would put you on Murphys Grade Road, the back way to Murphys.

206 Miles Enter **Angels Camp,** named after one **George Angel** in 1849 (so much for the ethereal ones). The place was made famous by **Mark Twain's** story, "The Celebrated Jumping Frog of Calaveras County," and a frog-jumping competition, the high-point of the year, is still held every summer. Otherwise, there's not much there, really. If you want to stay, the **Gold Country Inn Motel** has 40 rooms ($50; 209-736-4611), and is right next to **Rodz Grill,** and opposite the **Angels Camp Museum.** Downtown, a quarter-mile south, is **Sue's Angel Creek Cafe,** serving from 5 to 2, and for dinner you can go down the sidewalk to the **Bistro of Angels.**

Pass the intersection where CA 4 goes east to Ebbetts. CA 49 will cross **Angels Creek** to go straight toward Sonora. The road goes through **Frogtown** (not much there), winds down past a large quarry, down to the bridge over **New Melones Lake,** and up the other side.

214 Miles A sign will tell you that the **Mark Twain cabin** is off to the left—a very, very sharp left, about 300 degrees. Go for a mile up the little road and you will find a replica of the cabin that Mark Twain is said to have stayed at in 1864 and 1865. It is behind a black, wrought-iron fence, and was definitely in great need of repair when I last saw it. Twain buffs will love it, however.

217 Miles At a sharp left-hand corner, Rawhide Road, a shortcut to Jamestown, goes off to your right; it is a good way to avoid the Sonora traffic if you are headed south or west.

220 Miles Parrotts Ferry Road goes off the left; from this point, you will be backtracking.

223 Miles Arrive back at the **Sonora Inn.**

Trip 21 Sonora Pass & Tioga Pass

Distance *244 miles*

Highlights *This is pass-bagging at its best, two gorgeous High Sierra runs that will take you all darn day. Get an early start.*

0 Miles Go east on Stockton Street, following CA 108 Business toward **Wilma's Cafe.**

0+ Miles Turn left at the traffic light, where a big sign says RESTANO WAY. And immediately after 100 feet, turn right onto Mono Way, following CA 108 Business.

1+ Miles Turn left at the traffic light, where 108B joins CA 108, and head east over **Sonora Pass** to meet US 395. The clutter of expanding businesses boxes in the four-lane road, but that is the price of progress.

9 Miles The four-laner continues, but the sign will point to the left for a detour along the old road through **Twain Harte.**

Detour

Twain Harte is named for the 19th-century writers **Mark Twain** and **Bret Harte,** who passed this way. The old Route 108, now Twain Harte Drive, curves into town. On the outskirts, the very old-fashioned **Gables Cedar Creek Inn** backs onto a nine-hole golf course, with seven cabins to rent ($63; 209-586-3008). The town announces itself with a gloriously unattractive framework over the entrance to **Joaquin Gully** that reads TWAIN HARTE, where old 108/Twain Harte Drive veers off to the right. On Joaquin Gully Road, you'll find the **Sportsman's Coffeeshop** on your left, and the **Cottage Cafe & Espresso** on your right; different menus for different palates. A hundred feet up from Joaquin Gully you'll find the **Erickson House & Tivoli Beer Garden,** a touch of Garmisch in Tuolumne County. Twain Harte Drive meets CA 108 about a mile farther on.   ❋

---

16 Miles Come into **Sierra Village,** where all the pickup trucks will be parked outside **Wens Donuts & Stuff** during breakfast and lunch.

19 Miles The village of **Long Barn** will be down to your right, and you could go through by paralleling the new 108 for a couple of miles. Having a big four-laner bypass your town is great for cats, dogs, and children, but less good for business.

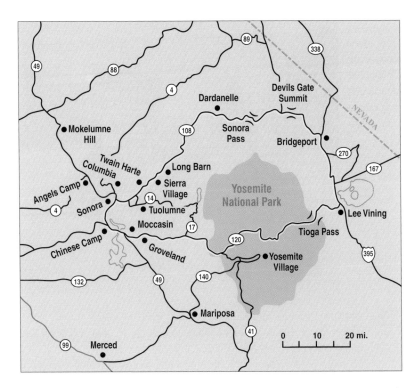

25 Miles The four-laner ends and you will be going back on the narrow road, which is much more fun.

29 Miles If you should have any enquiries, you can stop at the **Summit Ranger Station.**

31 Miles After you cross over the **Stanislaus River,** the **Strawberry Inn** will be on your left, wining, dining, and lodging travelers since 1939 ($75+; 209-965-3662; 800-985-3662).

38 Miles The sign reads NOT PLOWED; for you Sunbelt folk, that means the road is not open in the winter. It can shut and reopen a couple of times in late fall, but once the first big snow comes, that is it for wheeled traffic (though not for snowmobiles).

46 Miles The **Donnell Vista** looks down on **Donnell Reservoir** and northeast to **Dardanelles Cone.**

49 Miles The Clark Fork Road heads northeast to a dead end.

51 Miles Arrive in **Dardanelle** (pop. 2), with gas, a store, and cabins. In my mind, this is the place to stay on this road, but you will need to bring your own food and be prepared to cook it. **Joann Cheney** is half of the population and a permanent resident. A number of summer people also have little houses in the

A view of me, my motorcycle, and Sonora Pass in the fall, all captured by balancing my self-timing camera on a rock.

area, but none live there all year. In the winter, when the road is closed, snow-mobilers come in. Joann has eight cabins to rent ($70+, with kitchens) and four motel units ($55; 209-965-4355).

The road will leave the valley and start some serious climbing. Way back in the early 1860s, some enterprising types tried to build a toll road between Mono Lake and Sonora. Try to imagine going over this in a stagecoach.

67 Miles Crest **Sonora Pass,** at 8,624 feet. It will be even more precipitous on the east side.

Go down, down, down into **Pichel Meadows,** where that large resort-looking structure on the far mountain turns out to be the headquarters for the **U.S. Marine Corps Mountain Warfare Training Center.**

82 Miles STOP sign—turn right at the junction with US 395; the elevation here will be 6,950 feet.

Go over **Devil's Gate Summit** (7,510 feet) on 395, and down into the valley of **Bridgeport Lake.**

99 Miles **Bridgeport,** the seat of **Mono County,** will greet you (see Bridgeport sidebar).

106 Miles The road to the right goes to **Bodie,** probably the most interesting ghost town left, since it has been preserved as a California State Park (see Bodie sidebar).

113 Miles Stay on US 395 to **Conway Summit** (8,138 feet). After that, a great elongated S-curve will take you down to the valley, and **Mono Lake** will be spread out in all its geologic grandeur in front of you.

118 Miles CA 167 goes off to the east to Hawthorne, Nevada.

126 Miles Enter **Lee Vining,** a small town that operates off of the tourist trade, much of which depends on whether or not **Tioga Pass** is open. Half a dozen motels cater to the passers-by. At the north end of town, you'll find **Murphey's Motel,** with 44 units ($60; 760-647-6316; 800-334-6316), as well as the **Best Western Lake View Lodge** ($80; 760-647-6543) with 46 units.

In between, there will be several places to eat, including the **Yosemite Trails Inn** and **Nicely's** (open 6 a.m. to 10 p.m.).

126+ Miles Turn right onto CA 120, heading for Tioga Pass and Yosemite National Park, a positively grand ride that climbs to 3,000 feet in 11 miles along the walls of the **Lee Vining River,** through the **Inyo National Forest.** Not that there are a lot of trees along the road—a "forest" can encompass many different landscapes.

Bridgeport

Bridgeport consists of one wide street which is awash with motorcycles during the annual motorcycle jamboree every summer. Don't even think about getting a room in town that weekend, as everything will be booked solid as soon as the previous event is over. At any other time, the **Bridgeport Inn,** established in 1877, will welcome you, and they have motel units out behind ($50), as well as hotel rooms with genuine 19th-century hospitality (i.e. no phone, TV, or bathroom— that being down the hall; $45); the trick is to get the **Mark Twain Suite,** which does have a bathroom ($75; 760-932-7380). Up Main Street a hundred yards, you'll find the more conventional **Best Western Ruby Inn** with 30 rooms ($65; 760-932-7241).

Food can be found at the Bridgeport Inn, the **Hay Street Cafe, Rhino's Bar & Grill,** or any number of other places. Justice is meted out in the 1880 courthouse. ✸

Bridgeport is the seat of Mono county, and the courthouse has been dispensing justice for well over a hundred years.

Bodie

You really should make this side trip. Who knows how many more times you will have the opportunity to get a proper appreciation for a real ghost town. The road out to Bodie will be ten miles of pavement and three of graded dirt, which might be a touch washboardy, but still an easy traverse.

Come up on the rise of a hill, and before you will be the remains of Bodie. Although it will look big, only five percent of the original town remains. Ghost towns, before they become ghostly, are often quite large until their precious metals give out, and then people would walk, ride, or drive off, leaving the buildings behind. Then scavengers would come along and tear down structures to use the wood elsewhere, or a fire would burn everything up—which explains why there are so few ghost towns remaining.

Bodie may be a State Historic Park, but it has been left to preserve itself, weathering away at a natural rate. Two bucks will get you past the gate guard. Bodie boomed in the 1870s, with some 10,000 people living here by 1880. Summer temperatures here at 8,300 feet were well over 100 degrees and the winter temps went to 20 below zero. It was a rough place to live, so the boys drank a bit, shot each other when provoked, and generally carried on. It wasn't your average God-fearing community, although a number of churches tried to remedy that.

The town folded up when the Depression hit, the buildings happily crumbled away, and 30 years later (1962) the state stepped in to prevent the "souvenir hunters" from destroying the place. It's a beaut. Take it in.

When you leave, you can either retrace the entry road, or angle off from the toll-booth on Cottonwood Canyon Road, which will run for 11 mildly rough miles down to Mono Lake and CA 167. ✹

The ghost town of Bodie is just as we imagine a ghost town should look, thanks to its being protected by the California State Park system.

Tioga Pass, at 9,945 feet, is the highest roadable pass in the Sierra Nevadas. From this point, Uncle Sam wants $10 to defray the costs of running Yosemite National Park. (Photo by Somer Hooker)

Connector

If you've had enough of these mountains and want to see the wide open spaces of **Death Valley,** head south on US 395 for another 122 miles. You will go through **Bishop, Big Pine, Independence,** and **Lone Pine,** and at the south end of Lone Pine you will turn left onto CA 136, clearly marked DEATH VALLEY. From here, see Chapter 13. ✹

136 Miles **Tioga Pass Resort** will be on your right, the last genuinely free enterprise for the next 60 miles, with gas, food, lodging, and a small store. **Tioga Lake** and the **Ansel Adams Wilderness** will be to your left.

138 Miles At the top of **Tioga Pass** (9,945 feet), a motorcycle rider will pay $10 to get into the park; $5 would be okay, but $10 is a bit much for a two-hour ride-through.

The Tioga saddle is a longish one, traveling across the top of the world, descending a little to **Tuolumne Meadows,** where many backpackers hike off to confront Mother Nature on terms established by REI and North Face (two of the major purveyors of camping goods).

The scenery will be dramatic, with clean granite bluffs all over the horizon. To quote **Charles Frazier,** author of *Cold Mountain,* "Earth has not anything to show more fair. Dull would be the soul who could pass by the sight so touching in its majesty."

And there you'll see **Tenaya Lake,** also ringed with granite. From here, the road will get into heavy fir, and the vistas will become tunnels. You will go down and down and down, past **Porcupine Flat,** all the way to **Crane Flat** (6,200 feet), where you will find a small store with very limited food.

The town of Groveland, on CA 120 heading into Yosemite, is doing a good job of attracting those who want to experience a piece of California history.

184 miles STOP sign, and turn right at Crane Flat, following CA 120. If you went left, you would be on Big Oak Flat Road going into **Yosemite Valley** (see Yosemite Valley sidebar).

Connector
To get down to **Kings Canyon** and **Sequoia National Parks** (see Chapter 11), take CA 41 93 miles south to Fresno, and then take the Van Ness/Civic Center/CA 180 exit and head east. ✳

192 Miles At **Hodgdon Meadow** and the **West Gate of Yosemite,** you must show that you have paid your money before heading west on the North Yosemite Hwy./CA 120.

201 Miles On your right, you'll see the turn for Cherry Lake, just before crossing the bridge over the **Tuolumne River.**

Alternate Route
This is officially U.S. Forest Service Primary Route 17, and it provides a great ride, if a trifle bumpy and twisty. At **Cherry Lake,** about 13 miles along, turn left onto USFS 14 (Cottonwood Road) going west to **Tuolumne,** a superb and completely unused road built for the convenience of the workers at the **Cherry Valley Dam.** From Tuolumne, a run down County Road E17 will take you back to **Sonora.** ✳

217 Miles Enter **Groveland.** The **Groveland Motel & Indian Village** will allow you to sleep in a cabin or mobile home ($65), a three-bedroom Victorian house ($150), or a pseudo-teepee with communal bathroom ($30; 209-962-

7865). I prefer going along half a mile to the **Groveland Hotel,** circa 1849, which has 12 elegant rooms and an excellent restaurant ($115–$195; 209-962-4000; 800-273-3314). Just up the street, you'll find the **Iron Door Saloon,** dating from 1852, as well as the **Iron Door Grill.** Breakfast should be taken at **P.J.'s Cafe,** at the east end of town; the a.m. sourdough sandwich, with sausage, cheese, and egg, is truly tasteful.

223 Miles   At the top of the hill, called **Priest Grade,** the road will split three ways. The **Priest Station Motel** ($35–$185; 209-962-4181; 800-300-4181), a pleasantly ramshackle place with 16 very different rooms/cabins, is a great

Yosemite Valley

Since you've paid your $10 to get in, you might as well see the rest of **Yosemite Valley.** And it will be worth it. I first rode over Tioga in 1965, coming from Massachusetts on my Velocette Venom, and when I got to the valley I was so taken by its beauty that I got a job and stayed for a month. Unfortunately, it is a lot more crowded now.

Descend toward the valley and go through two tunnels, with glimpses of **Half Dome** in the distance. Remember to stop at the vista points. Down on the valley floor, CA 140 will cut back to Mariposa, but you should stay with the road, going upstream along the **Merced River.** After it crosses over, the road will become one-way going east. Pass the CA 41 turn that goes south to Wawona and Oakhurst, and go all the way into the valley, a west-bound one-way on the north side of the river . . . the result of much too much traffic.

The valley is a gorgeous, stunning, beautiful, incredible place, if you can just lift your eyes above the crowd. If you want to stay in the valley and money is flush, go to the **Ahwahnee Hotel** ($200+; 209-252-4848). That phone number could also get you reservations at the **Yosemite Lodge** or **Camp Curry,** which are considerably cheaper, but not nearly as nice.   ✳

Although it's a hazy day, Half Dome, at the east end of Yosemite Valley, is visible over my front wheel.

The small town of Jamestown attracts a fair number of morbidly inclined tourists who like to see an effigy hanging from the gibbet on Main Street.

place to sleep. Just sitting on the deck with a Tecate beer in hand, looking down on **Don Pedro Reservoir** will be a charm. You can rent one of the three cabins on stilts that look as though they are about to slide down the hill—but they won't . . . or at least haven't so far. Sandy, the manager, is well-accustomed to motorcyclists. All three of the roads that go down the hill from there offer great riding. The little restaurant serves dinner from 7 p.m., but if you get hungry you could go back up the road a couple of miles to **Big Oak Flats,** where the food is cooked from morning 'til night.

226 Miles As you cross the bridge at **Moccasin,** CA 49 will come in from the left, and 120/49 will continue together alongside **Don Pedro Reservoir.**

235 Miles Stay right on CA 49 at **Chinese Camp,** while CA 120 goes off to the left. There's not much in Chinese Camp except for a few shabby houses and a couple of brick buildings from the Gold Rush days.

238 Miles Stay right as CA 49 merges with CA 108, heading east into Sonora.

241 Miles Enter **Jamestown,** with CA 49 skirting the town, past the Harley-Davidson dealership; if you want a genuine Harley experience, stay at their "motel," a nice studio behind and separate from the shop ($45 winter, $55 summer; 209-984-4888). If you took the well-marked turn to the Business District, you would find an interesting street about a half-mile long, with lots of food and trinkets available, as well as the restored **National Hotel** at which to eat and sleep ($80+; 9 rooms; 209-984-3446). In Jamestown, you'll also find the **Railtown State Historical Park,** with old steamers chuffing about on a six-mile run.

243 Miles Exit right of the CA 108 road that bypasses Sonora, taking CA 49 into Sonora.

244 Miles Arrive back in downtown **Sonora.**

Kings Canyon & Sequoia

Headquarters *Being a linear trip, there isn't one, but I list a number of watering spots and rentable mattresses along the way.*

Information *Since the focus of this chapter will be on two national parks, I will give the park info number, where relevant.*

Best Time to Visit *April through November, though check to make sure that the road through the park will be open, and call Ponderosa Lodge (559-542-2579) to check the condition of the Western Divide Highway*

Getting There *The logical place to start would be in Fresno (the Spanish word for "ash tree"), a big city on the east side of the San Joaquin Valley. These days, urban problems have given Fresno a bad rap, but the town has a positive place in history. In 1910, Fresno became the site of the first state college in California, the same year the Industrial Workers of the World made their first effort to organize unskilled farm labor. Anyway, CA 99, a main north-south route, goes right through Fresno, and CA 41, running from Morro Bay to Yosemite National Park, cuts a diagonal through town, while CA 180 goes east to west. From either CA 99 or CA 41, find CA 180, Kings Canyon Road, and head east.*

This will be a high country delight, taking in two national parks (**Kings Canyon** and **Sequoia**), some magnificent foothill riding, and a trip along the western crest of the **Sierra Nevadas.**

To simplify map-orientation, we will start in **Fresno** and end in **Kernville,** covering 212 miles. Side trips, such as the one down into Kings Canyon, will add a good deal more mileage to the route.

The old road into the south end of Sequoia National Park used to run underneath this rock, before lawyers got into the act and bypassed the tunnel completely.

CHAPTER
11

Trip 22   A Linear Route through the Parks

0 Miles   Ground Zero, such that it is, will be in **Fresno** at East Kings Canyon Road and Cedar Street, heading east on CA 180. Unfortunately, Fresno signage is not the best in the world, but all you really need to do is find CA 180; in central Fresno it is on Ventura Street, which leads onto Kings Canyon Road. My own personal theory is that Fresno does not like its unofficial status as the **Gateway to Kings Canyon** and secretly wants to get tourists lost in town so they will stay the night and spend money.

Leaving Fresno (elev. 294 feet) the road will be straight and boring— merely a way to get out of the valley. Go through **Centerville** and across the **Kings River;** life will start to improve as you get into the Sierra Nevada foothills. After passing **Squaw Valley** (1,700 feet) and **Clingans Junction,** you will enter the **Sequoia National Forest** and begin switch-backing up to **Snowline Lodge.**

50 Miles   CA 245 will go off to the left to provide an alternate route south, should **Sequoia National Park** happen to be closed for any reason, like a sudden snowstorm blocking the highway.

Alternate Route

Go 11 miles down CA 245 to **Badger,** and just past the **Badger Motel & Store** you will see a road to the left signed HARTLAND 10; do not take it. Instead, go on another mile, where CA 245 makes a major curve to the right in front of the **Mountain House Bar & General Store,** and another road will go to the left, also marked HARTLAND 10. Take that road, officially known as County Road J21, but locally called Dry Creek Road. Eighteen miles later, J21 will end at CA 216, alongside the **Kaweah River.** Turn left, go over the river, and half a mile farther on, 216 will end at CA 198 at a Texaco station in **Lemoncove.**   ✴

Keep going east on 180.

53 Miles   When you arrive at **Kings Canyon Big Stump Park** entrance, the attendant will charge you $5 for a seven-day pass, which will also be good for **Sequoia National Park** (so don't lose the receipt).

54 Miles   Stop and think at the three-way intersection in the middle of the woods. Straight will go to Sequoia NP, and eventually become CA 198, left on CA 180 will go to Kings Canyon NP (see Kings Canyon sidebar).

Back at that three-way intersection, continue east . . .

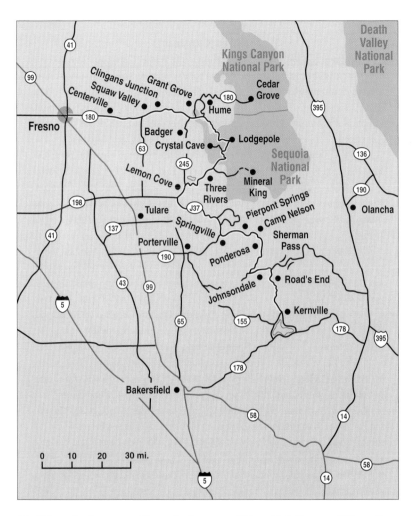

57 Miles At the turn to **Hume Lake,** you will be officially out of Kings Canyon National Park and in the Sequoia National Forest. There are two lodges in the next ten miles, but they're nothing to rave about.

61 Miles Enter **Sequoia National Park,** created in 1890 and dedicated to the Big Trees, or *Sequoia gigantea* in proper Latin. Giant sequoias are bigger cousins of redwoods *(Sequoia sempervirens)* that one finds near the coast of California. The giant sequoia can grow to more than 300 feet tall, with a diameter at the base of 40 feet, and may live 3,000 years. I'd say that is definitely worthy of a national park. For the botanically inclined, there are another 1,400 plant species in these two contiguous parks.

There is not much point to my going into detailed descriptions of the park; you'll just have to go and see it for yourself.

Kings Canyon

Do—and this is good advice—do go down into **Kings Canyon;** lots of people give it a miss because they don't want to go 35 miles, and then have to turn around and come back the same way. Those folk are not bright. First, how many times in your life will you have the opportunity to visit Kings Canyon, which is truly an awe-inspiring spectacle? And second, it's a hell of a good ride. So go.

A little more than a mile down the road on the right is **Grant Grove Village** (6,555 feet), with a store, rustic cabins to rent (559-335-5500; $35+ without bath, $80 with bath), and information; that one phone number will secure reservations at any of four places in the Kings Canyon/Sequoia National Parks. Lodging is open here the year around, but elsewhere is usually closed from November through April.

On the left as you leave the village, you'll see the turn to go see the **General Grant Tree,** a seriously big hunk of lumber which is a little larger than the **General Lee Tree** (as you might guess, this place became popular right after the Civil War).

Seven miles farther on, after going through **Cherry Gap** at 6,897 feet, note the left turn to **Hume Lake,** as that's the way we'll go to get to Sequoia NP. Straight north of you will be **Spanish Peak,** just over 10,000 feet high.

Continue on, and soon you will get a huge view of the canyon below, where the **Middle Fork** and **South Fork of the Kings River** meet. You will be going down there—more than 2,000 feet down, in case you were wondering.

Down toward the bottom, you will cross over **Ten Mile Creek.** The privately owned **Kings Canyon Lodge** is a nicely funky place where you can get drinks, food, and lodging in eight cabins ($70+; 559-335-2405). You can also get expensive gas out of old circa 1938 gravity-feed pumps, probably the last active pair in the nation—at least until the EPA-crats find out about them.

From there it will be another 22 magnificent miles up along the **Kings River** to the end of the road, which runs along the bottom of an impressive canyon that is 3,500 feet deep. About four miles before the end of the road, **Cedar Grove** has food and a small 18-room lodge ($82.50; 559-335-5500), but no gas.

Now head back 27 miles to the Hume Lake turn-off, and turn left. After a little more than four miles you will come to the lake, with a store and gas, and from there it is another five and a half miles up to the **Generals Highway** (Civil War again) that leads into **Sequoia National Park.**   ✱

Dropping steeply down to Kings Canyon from Grant Grove Village, the road affords some spectacular views.

At the Kings Canyon Lodge, a private lodge on the western end of Kings Canyon, they still sell gas out of gravity-feed pumps—or at least they were late in 1999. Who knows what the latest EPA restrictions have done to this old-fashioned system.

78 Miles **Lodgepole** has a visitor center, and commercial enterprises such as a store and laundry, but no lodging. Lodgepole, by the way, refers to the lodgepole pine, a very tall, slender tree.

80 Miles The **General Sherman Tree** will be off to your left, where all the tourists are; it is said to be the biggest tree (by bulk) in the world. Or put another way, one of the biggest living things in the world.

82 Miles On top of the hill, the **Giant Forest** complex has a store, motel-style lodge ($96.50; 559-335-5500), and other trappings. You will be at more than 6,600 feet here, as you start the descent to the south, which drops off more than a mile.

The General Sherman Tree, in Sequoia National Park, is said to be the largest living thing on earth; I'm surprised the lumber company executives aren't lobbying Congress for permission to cut it down.

84 Miles On your right, you will see the turn to **Crystal Cave,** a steep, six-mile road which descends some 2,000 feet. If you like hiking, caving and a 48-degree temperature (very nice on a hot day), try this one, but remember to get your ticket at either the Lodgepole or Foothills (to the south) visitor center.

98 Miles After a very exhilarating descent down to the **Kaweah River,** you will come to the **Foothills Visitor Center** and the park headquarters, at 1,300 feet. Exit the park at **Ash Mountain** . . . and pick up CA 198. For whatever legal and territorial reasoning, the state highway number does not go into the national park.

99 Miles Several small lodges and a restaurant will appear, just before the **Pumpkin Hollow Bridge** (1922) that crosses over the Kaweah River. For a place to stay, I recommend the **Buckeye Tree Lodge** ($50+; 559-561-5900). Next to the Buckeye is the **Gateway Restaurant & Lodge** ($55+; 559-561-4133); the restaurant opens at 11 a.m., 8 on Sundays).

101 Miles A sign will indicate that a forest service fire station will be coming up, and a green sign, pointing to the left, will say MINERAL KING 25 (see Mineral King sidebar).

103 Miles The **White Horse Inn,** a steak joint which toasts the meat properly, will be on your right.

104 Miles Enter the community of **Three Rivers; the Big 3 Bakery & Restaurant** will be on your left, open for hearty breakfasts and lunches Wednesday through Sunday.

105 Miles A Chevron gas station will be on your right, next to **Angelina's Family Dining;** I haven't tried it, but the fellow taking my gas money said it beats his wife's cooking.

107 Miles If you are in need of a room, watch for the **Best Western Holiday Lodge** on your right; it's easy to miss the entrance if you are going fast. This is a conventional place, close to the river, with 54 rooms (559-561-3427, 800-528-1234; $65+, but you'll want a "riverview" room, which will cost more).

Now the road, CA 198, whisks around the southern side of man-made **Lake Kaweah.**

116 Miles Stay straight at the intersection where CA 216 goes off to the right, as mentioned in the Badger Alternative at the beginning of this chapter; pass the Texaco station on the corner.

From here, you will be entering **Lemoncove,** where lemon trees are grown, and several small stores still have enough business to stay open.

122 Miles Turn left. You will be passing a large grove of trees on your right, which the owner has conveniently signed OLIVES. He was probably tired of having city-folk stop and ask what sort of trees they were. A green sign pointing left says BALCH PARK 42, with the road, Yokohl Drive, cutting off just before you get to the bridge over the **Yokohl River.**

125 Miles Turn left. A sign pointing left reads BALCH PARK 41 (even though you've just come three miles from the last sign). Turn left, continuing on Yokohl Drive, a nice, little-used country road along the **Yokohl Valley** that passes a ranch or two, as well as the **Milo**

My wife, Sue, stops for a Kodak moment on the bridge over the Kaweah River, next to the Gateway Restaurant & Lodge.

Mineral King

If you like serious twists, turns, and climbing, this is the road for you. Take a sharp turn to the left, and after a hundred yards a sign says that it takes 90 minutes to go 25 miles. "Ha!" you say; "Ha, ha!" I say—it *will* take you a while. The road climbs from about 1,000 to more than 7,000 feet in those 25 miles, and while a Gold Wing towing a trailer could do it with ease, the rider would have to be good. Halfway up, a park ranger will greet you as you re-enter **Sequoia National Park.**

There are a couple of short dirt stretches near the top, several government campgrounds, and a small commercial enterprise at **Silver City** which has a little store, cafe, and a dozen rustic cabins to rent ($60+; 559-561-2223).

At the end of the road is **Mineral King Valley,** a beautiful place that the Disney Corporation tried to buy and turn into a ski resort; the **National Park Service** got a hold of it instead, for which I am quite grateful.

But I remain bemused at the thought of the men who came up here in the 1870s looking for silver—the trip up would have taken a lot more than 90 minutes. More like 90 hours.   ✱

The store up on top of Mineral King, in the tiny community of Silver City, sells canned tomatoes and excellent hamburgers, but no gas. (Photo by Jeff Haynes)

A lot of labor went into building the road up to Mineral King, which included the construction of a lot of bridges. (Photo by Craig Erion)

125 Miles Turn left. A sign pointing left reads BALCH PARK 41 (even though you've just come three miles from the last sign). Turn left, continuing on Yokohl Drive, a nice, little-used country road along the **Yokohl Valley** that passes a ranch or two, as well as the **Milo** forest service fire station. From here, you will zig-zag over a low rise and drop into the **Tule River Valley.**

145 Miles STOP sign—turn right following County Road J37 (Balch Park Road) down to **Springville;** go right, unless you want to take the left and have an extra pleasant, 30-mile detour through **Balch Park** itself and the **Mountain Home State Forest,** as the Balch Park loop will come right back to J37.

152 Miles STOP sign—turn left by a big red barn, J37 intersecting with CA 190. If you went right, in less than a mile you would be in downtown **Springville,** with gas, food, stores, and the ten-room **Springville Inn** ($75+; 559-539-7501). Leaving Springville, CA 190 will go east along the **Middle Fork Tule River** into the **Sequoia National Forest,** to climb and twist a whole lot as it hauls itself up over 3,500 feet.

166 Miles Come into **Pierpont Springs,** whose 4,500-foot elevation makes it a lot cooler than Springville in the summer. The business center is taken up by a combined market, post office, restaurant, bar and five-room motel called the **Pierpont Springs Resort** ($70+; 559-542-2423). The larger adjoining community, just off the main road and more often found on the map, is **Camp Nelson.**

CHAPTER
11

Leaving town, a sign will read QUAKING ASPEN, which refers to a national forest campground ten miles along. And those ten miles are gnarly indeed, the road getting even tighter and twistier. It's great fun for a motorcyclist who likes that sort of thing. Now, if you are a Freeway Rider, you might not be so enchanted.

From this point, you will be on the **Western Divide Highway,** which means the **Kern River** has divided the **Sierra Nevada Mountains** down the middle, and you are on the west side, running along the divide that sends creeks either east into the Kern, or west into the **Tule River** (see California Highway Numerology sidebar).

168 Miles The **Ponderosa Lodge** will be on your left, at 7,250 feet, with gas, food, a bar, and lodging ($50+; 559-542-2579); if it is a weekend, and you don't like cheerful music, ask for a cabin away from the lodge, so you can stagger back for a quiet sleep after a night of carousing. Try the grilled trout and scrambled eggs for breakfast.

At the Ponderosa Lodge, on the Western Divide Highway, trout and scrambled eggs are a breakfast specialty; Craig "Fireball" Stein prepares to dig in, as Craig Erion looks on.

Beyond the Ponderosa, the Western Divide Highway is not cleared after the snow-season starts. But we motorcyclists are not likely to be going up there in the winter. The Divide is a great ride in the other three seasons, however, a smooth road running south along that western ridge of the Sierras.

181 Miles STOP sign—turn left; the road is now weaving tightly, heading downhill. After a few miles, you can see a small lake and a lot of RVs way down below to the right.

187 Miles Curve right, with sign indicating JOHNSONDALE 1, KERNVILLE 27. The left turn deadends 20 miles later up along the Kern River.

188 Miles Note the sign for R-RANCH IN THE SEQUOIAS to the right. This used to be an old logging community, **Johsondale,** until some slightly befogged or shysterish types figured they could sell time-shares in this denuded valley. The sign says the restaurant is open to the public, but the hours are often moot.

California Highway Numerology

Technically, the numerical designation CA 190 disappears soon after you leave **Pierpont Springs,** vanishes completely in the national forest, and reappears miraculously 35 crow-flying miles later on the east side of the Sierra Nevada Mountains, in **Olancha.** It is almost as though in some long-gone day an engineer sitting at a desk in some sterile office penned a line that would go from Pierpont Springs to Olancha—without bothering to check the feasibility, or practicability, of building such a road.

CalTrans does mystifying things with its enumerations, as though some autistic child prodigy is responsible. Don't fret yourself about this, as CA 190 does eventually become the **Western Divide Highway.** ✸

192 Miles After more downhill, go over the **Johnsondale Bridge** spanning the **Kern River,** and you will see a road going off to the left, with a sign saying SHERMAN PASS, BLACKROCK STATION—more on that in Chapter 12. For now, stay straight.

From here, the road runs right along the east side of the Kern River luring lots of RVs and 4x4s on the weekends. Pass a small dam put up by **California Edison,** as well as several resorts, such as **River's End** and **McNally's,** but we are headed into Kernville. Boogie on.

212 Miles Kernville, we have arrived. Now go on to the next chapter to see where to stay.

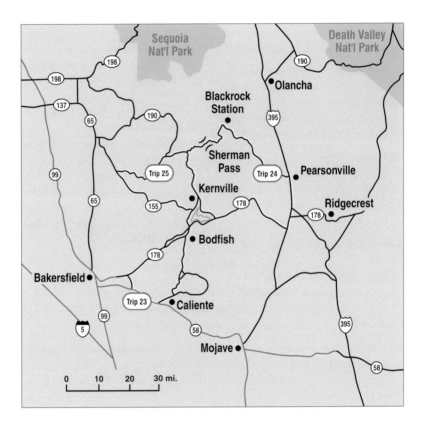

The Southern Sierras

Headquarters *Kernville*

Chamber of Commerce/Tourist Bureau *800-350-7393*

Best Time to Visit *March through November, though Sherman Pass may well be closed until later, and perhaps Parker Pass, out of the Hot Springs Ranger Station (661-548-6503), might be closed until April*

Getting There *The easiest way is to take CA 178 east from Bakersfield, or west from CA 14 near Ridgecrest in the Mojave Desert, get to Isabella Lake, and go north a few miles.*

Ground Zero *Start in front of Circle Park, opposite Cheryl's Diner.*

This little trio of Trips takes place way down at the southern end of the **Sierra Nevadas,** that 430-mile long range of mountains that stretch from **Lassen Peak** to **Tehachapi Valley.** The roads we will be on go from 9,200 feet on **Sherman Pass** in the mountains down to 800 feet in the **San Joaquin Valley.** The loops I have planned are not for the cruise-control set. In fact, the roads will be 90 percent crooked, the views, magnificent, and the countryside, superb.

Sherman Pass stands 9,200 feet above the level of the far-off Pacific Ocean, 130 miles away. (Photo by Craig Erion)

You can't complain about stashing your bags in **Kernville** for a night or two or three. Unless it is on Labor Day weekend when half of the San Joaquin Valley is trying to escape the heat.

Kernville sits astride the **Kern River** at the north edge of Isabella Lake. For the historically impaired, **Edward Kern** was a topographer (early sort of mapmaker), who came to the area with **John Fremont's** expedition of 1846. **Isabella Lake** (which was very small at the time) was named by Spaniards who passed this way for the same queen of Spain who sent Columbus across the ocean blue. When the dam on the Kern River was completed in 1953, all of the original Kernville got drowned, except for a few houses that were hauled up to the new location at the north end of the lake. The new site used to be called **Whiskey Flats** in the bad old days, and one small part of town still retains that moniker.

The Kern River area was reasonably quiet until gold was discovered in 1854, and then the usual rush took place. After the gold panned out, lumbering and ranching took over, and now the main source of revenue is that mysterious migratory animal, the tourist.

There are lots of places to stay. Right down in the middle of town, which is quite small, opposite Whiskey Flats (or **Circle Park,** as maps refer to the place), is the **Kernville Inn,** with a swimming pool, a two-minute walk to the river, and 26 units ($60+; 760-376-2206). Next door, try **Cheryl's Diner** for an outside breakfast. Across the road, the serious come to drink at the **Sportman's Bar.**

For upper-scale accommodation, seek out the **Whispering Pines Lodge,** a B&B right on the east side of the Kern River just north of the main part of town,

At the only general store in the area, Craig Erion awaits the return of those who have gone to purchase the fixings for supper and breakfast.

That $2.98 cooler holds a steak for supper, a pint of milk for breakfast coffee, and a six-pack of Sam Adams. (Photo by Craig Erion)

with 18 rooms ($100+; 760-376-3733). They have a very good breakfast and a nice swimming pool, in case you do not wish to immerse yourself in the cool mountain waters of the river.

A mile farther up the river, at a wide spot in the road that calls itself **Riverkern,** there is a delightful old motel, the **Sequoia Motor Lodge,** with some 20 units ($60; 760-376-2535); ask for #17, which overhangs the river. Right across the road, **Cheyenne's Stage Stop & Dining Hall** serves up dead cow just the way it should be.

In addition to establishments for eating and sleeping, Kernville has a good museum just up the street from **Whiskey Flats,** on Big Blue Road. And there will be the ubiquitous antique stores, of course. And fishing. Yes, fishing. There is a fish hatchery you can visit, and for the price of a fishing license you can catch your own trout, put it in a skillet with some olive oil and tarragon, and have yourself a superb meal.

Trip 23 Bodfish-Caliente Road & Kern Canyon

Distance *91 miles*

Highlights *This is a great half-day, which could be turned into a full day at the slightest inclination. The distance will be short, but the speed will be leisurely: you won't even average 30 mph for most of the trip.*

0 Miles **Cheryl's** diner will be on your left as you head south on the west side of the Kern River, past the golf course. Soon the river will turn into **Isabella Lake.**

4 Miles Enter the strung-out (physically, not emotionally) town of **Wofford Heights** and pick up CA 155 going south; 155 West will be covered in Trip 25.

   Several campgrounds and recreation areas will be along the lakefront, and on the right you'll see the turn to **Keyesville,** the site of the original gold mining claims. One has to ride a bit of dirt road to get there, however.

11 Miles CA 155 crosses over CA 178, a freeway at this point, and officially ends. But the road goes on for another 300 yards.

11+ Miles STOP sign—turn right, onto Lake Isabella Boulevard; you have just entered the town of **Lake Isabella,** which tries to separate itself from Isabella Lake by transposing the words. Like the town of Kernville, the original Lake Isabella was also drowned in the mid-fifties, and this long strip of commercial enterprises is the result.

14 Miles When Lake Isabella Boulevard turns into the Caliente-Bodfish Road, you will see the **Country Korner Market** on the right, and the left turn onto Kern River Canyon Road, on which we will return later. For now, you go straight, but you'll be back at this corner in two to six hours, depending how you hustle.

   From this point, you will start a hard charge up the hill, with two long switchbacks carrying you over the summit and down into a small valley.

21 Miles Arrive in the community of **Havilah,** with a restored courthouse and schoolhouse. Gold was found here in 1864, and when **Kern County** was organized in 1866, this town became the county seat—hard to imagine now, because it is such a tiny place. Its bureaucratic glory lasted only until 1872, when the job went to Bakersfield, and the gold began petering out in the early 1880s. Some people still look for it in the hills, but nobody has made a real strike in the last 100 years.

24 Miles The Breckenridge Road goes off to the right, with a steep climb out of the valley, and a long, long descent into the **San Joaquin Valley** east of **Bakersfield,** to meet up with Comanche Drive after 36 miles. It is a nice road,

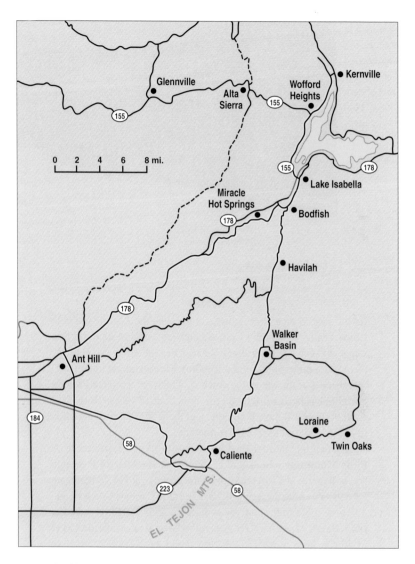

much of it through national forest, but stay straight, as the views from west to east will be better.

25 Miles At the top of a rise, a **Trading Post** will be on your right, a general store where cold sodas can be appreciated on a hot day.

From there, you will drop down into **Walker Basin. Joe Walker** was a busy man back in the 1830s, hiking over much of this territory. His name appears a dozen times on any map of California, from **Walker Pass** east of Isabella Lake, to the town of **Walker** on US 395 just north of Yosemite. Those were days of true adventuring.

It is hard to believe today, but the tiny town of Havilah was the seat of Kern county from 1866 to 1872.

29 Miles STOP sign—turn right.

Detour

If you want to do a 28-mile loop, rather than the 12-mile run over **Lions Trail,** you could go left, zig and zag east and south for two miles, and catch Walker Basin Road. After traveling straight for three more miles you find the **Cowboy Memorial,** an interesting little tribute to the life of the cowboy, which ex-cowpoke **Paul de Fonville** has been working on for more than 17 years; "Just $500,000 and I'll have it all done and there won't be anything like it." True. Call 661-867-2410 for details.

After cutting through the **Piute Mountains** you will come to the **Piute Mountain School,** and 13 miles from the Mile 29 STOP sign, you will arrive at **Twin Oaks,** with the promise of gas, lodging, and food. By this time the road will have become Caliente Creek Road.

Three more miles and you will come upon **Loraine,** with **Karen's Bar & Grill.** Twelve more miles west along **Caliente Creek** (if it has been a bad winter you could be travelling more on creekbed than asphalt) and you will arrive at the intersection with Lion Trail, a/k/a the Caliente-Bodfish Road. ✹

If you turned right at the STOP sign, you would be hustling down the west side of **Walker Basin Creek,** past the west end of Walker Basin Road and the **Rankin Ranch,** where the dudes and dudettes come to stay, ride horses, and punch a few cows. Then you would climb gently up on **Lions Trail,** as the locals refer to that stretch, come over the top, and descend steeply to **Caliente Creek,** with four switchbacks. Good fun.

31 Miles Bear right at the intersection with Caliente Creek Road, a natural turn. A sharp left would take you up to Loraine and Twin Oaks.

34 Miles Enter the almost defunct community of **Caliente,** now reduced to a post office and lots of railroad track belonging to **Union Pacific.** Bounce over the track; past the P.O., the road curves right and then heads under the railroad, the sign reading BAKERSFIELD, HWY 58.

Alternate Route

Right in **Caliente** there will be a small intersection where Bealville Road goes straight to CA 58, but Caliente-Bodfish Road goes off to the right, right past the **Caliente Disposal Site** on the corner. You could take this road, which is a country delight, but generally it seems to be closed for repairs about five miles along; a sign to that effect will be posted as Cal-Bod Road ends at Bena Road, forcing you to go back to CA 58.

If the road is not closed, take a right on Bena, which turns into the **Edison Union Highway,** which crosses Comanche Drive after 12 miles. ✹

Be nice to those people in the Day-Glo orange vests; they are the CalTrans workers who maintain most of California's roads, keeping them in rather good condition.

Whiskey Flats, in Kernville, is not nearly as raucous as it was during the gold mining boom of the previous century.

36 Miles STOP sign—turn right onto CA 58 West toward Bakersfield. The highway will soon turn into a freeway, climbing up and over the **Kern Mesa.**

50 Miles Exit freeway to STOP sign—turn right at Comanche Drive. If you are in need of gas, food, or a bed, continue on CA 58 another four miles and exit at Weed Patch Hwy./CA 186; everything a motorcyclist could want is there, short of a dealer (those are in Bakersfield). From there, you would go north on CA 186 for five miles to connect with CA 178, where you'd be headed if you'd gotten on Comanche Drive.

Comanche Drive goes north, with another STOP sign at the **Edison Highway.** Go straight through the orange groves.

52 Miles Comanche Drive crosses the aforementioned Breckenridge Road, if you care to head back to **Havilah.** This is the best direction in which to take Breckenridge Road, as the drop from **Breckenridge Mountain** down into **Havilah Canyon** is spectacular. Comanche continues through the aged **Ant Hill** oil field, where rather decrepit equipment will be peacefully pumping away.

55 Miles STOP sign—turn right onto CA 178, the **Kern Canyon Highway.** The road is wide and straightish for the first several miles, but when it gets into the canyon proper it gets appreciably narrower and much more curvaceous. It will be a great road if there is no traffic, merely a good road if you get caught behind a freight-train of ten cars and RVs. Ah, well . . .

The **Kern River** will be rushing along beside you to the left, and numerous signs advise against swimming; a goodly number of lives have been lost in that turbulent water.

64 Miles Bear right after the sign says KERN CANYON ROAD 1/4 M. The main road, CA 178, goes more or less straight, and turns into a four-laner after crossing the river; Kern Canyon Road will be much more fun as it winds along on the south side of the river, high up and farther and farther away from the water.

As it gets back closer to the river, a sign on the left, just as you come on a bridge, will direct you to **Miracle Hot Springs,** open from six in the morning to ten at night, $5 a person (760-379-4407, for more information). The springs are right down by the river, and on one side of a small wall the water will be 102 to 105 degrees, on the other, 54 degrees or less.

Continue on, past Borel Road.

77 Miles STOP sign—turn left; Kern Canyon Road ends at the **Country Korner Market,** and from there you will be retracing your steps to **Lake Isabella.**

80 Miles Turn left where the sign reads KERNVILLE, heading up CA 155 to **Wofford Heights.**

91 Miles Arrive back at **Whiskey Flats** and have a beer or a sarsaparilla at the **Sportsman's Inn.**

Trip 24 Sherman Pass & Walker Pass

Distance *161 miles*

Highlights *These are the last two passes in the southern Sierras. Sherman, though paved, is not often visited by street motorcyclists. Off-road motorcyclists by the dozens congregate up on top of these mountains, however, as there are hundreds of miles of ORV trails to follow.*

0 Miles Start with **Cheryl's** on your right, and head over the bridge toward Sierra Way.

0+ Miles STOP sign—turn left, heading north on Sierra Way, past the **Jame's Store** on your right, a full-service market. A dozen pillow-stops will be on your left, including the **McCambridge Motel, Whispering Pines B&B,** et cetera.

3 Miles Enter **Riverkern,** with **Cheyenne's** and a general store on the right, and **Sequoia Motor Lodge** on the left.

15 Miles You will pass **Fairview Lodge** and **McNally's Restaurant,** "Home of the 40 oz. Steak." No thanks, I'm big enough.

Pass **Road's End Resort,** then the inlet for the **California Edison** turbine powerplant, and swoop around a very large, half-acre turn-off area where people can get out and put their toes in the water.

Thanks to the thoughtfulness of our government, the national forests have excellent campgrounds, such as this one at Horse Meadows, about 15 miles from Sherman Pass.

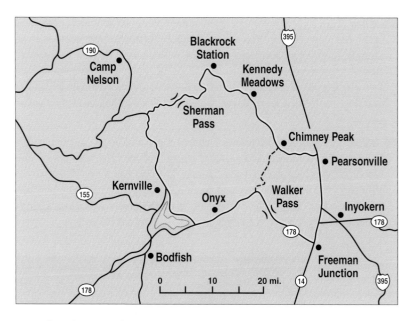

20 Miles At a very sharp turn to the right at a well concealed intersection, cutting back about 300 degrees; the sign reads BLACKROCK STA 36, US 395 67. This will be the road to **Sherman Pass.**

Make the turn, and climb, climb, climb. Do watch out for debris on the road for the next 67 miles; this forest service road is neither kept open in the winter, nor swept in the summer. When sand or dirt is washed onto the pavement, it will stay there until the few passing vehicles blow it off. I talked with a ranger who said that at least once a year some motorcyclist will go too fast, ride beyond his line of sight, hit a skiddy bit, and wrap himself around a tree. You have been warned, and my lawyers do have a copy of this book.

The pavement, however, is quite good, and there is nary a straight stretch on the way up. The last logging trucks came down in 1998, and you will generally see few vehicles save the occasional 4x4 or RV.

26 Miles Pass the turn to **Horse Meadows Campground,** with six miles of asphalt, four of dirt. The campground has running water and pit toilets. I camp up there at least once a year because it is both accessible and remote.

36 Miles From the viewing area at the top of **Sherman Pass** (9,200 feet), you can see **Mt. Whitney** (14,494 feet) some 40 miles to the north-northeast. On a personal note, the gent who calculated its height, geologist **Josiah Dwight Whitney,** was raised in my hometown of Northampton, Massachusetts.

The next 20 miles will run along a ridge of the mountains and stay above 8,000 feet; it's very nice riding through clear forest and the occasional meadow.

229

53 Miles Turn right at the intersection in the middle of the woods, onto Kennedy Meadows Road; **Blackrock Ranger Station** (8,150 feet) will be straight ahead a hundred yards, complete with a ranger to give out information.

After ten miles, the road will start to descend toward **Kennedy Meadows** and the **South Fork Kern River,** with a scattering of houses in the far distance.

76 Miles The **Kennedy Meadows General Store** will be on your left, with a pot-bellied stove inside and gasoline pumps outside. The road up to here, County J21, is kept open all year around. The area has about 35 permanent residents (and no telephones), and about 350 property owners who have vacation homes. The left turn dead-ends at the **Kennedy Meadows Campground**—but you want to go straight southeast toward US 395.

Since the U.S. Forest Service hates for people to get lost, the signage is usually quite good, as it is here in the Sequoia National Forest.

Visible right above the motorcycle, Mt. Whitney, at 14,494 feet, is the highest peak in the contiguous United States; you can hike to the top if you are so inclined.

78 Miles **Grumpy Bears Restaurant & Tavern** will be on your right, opening at 11 o'clock summer and winter. His three-egg sandwich is a serious brunch.

87 Miles You will come up to the **Chimney Peak fire station** and **Chimney Meadow;** if you have a d-p bike, or are adept on your K1200LT, you could take a 15-mile dirt road south to join CA 178 eight miles west of **Walker Pass.**

From this point you can see the **Mojave Desert** down to the east of you, as the road starts a steepish descent through **Nine-Mile Canyon.** Keep your eyes on the road, please, and stop when you want to admire the view. There is no guardrail on your right, and it would be a hell of a bumpy ride to the bottom.

97 Miles STOP sign—turn right at the junction with US 395.

Connector

To head into **Death Valley** from here, take a left and head north on US 395. In 32 miles you will be in **Olancha** at the intersection with CA 190—which you last saw east of **Pierpont Springs** in Chapter 11. And that road will lead into Death Valley.　✹

Heading south on 395, you will be cruising along a four-laner at 2,500 feet above the western edge of **Indian Wells Valley.** If you need gas, there will be a big Shell station three miles south on the east side of the highway at **Pearsonville,** right next to the **Pearson Speedway,** where they run stock cars most weekends. And that is about all there is to Pearsonville.

107 Miles Stay straight on CA 14, heading for Los Angeles at a well-marked Y in the road. US 395 goes southeast toward Inyokern and San Bernardino.

109 Miles A big sign on the right reads MOJAVE RED, INDIAN WELLS BREWING CO.; out there in the middle of roughly nowhere is a brewery, and the **Indian Wells Lodge,** which serves dinner. The brewery grew out of a bottled water company, as the old wells have served a lot of people over the years. This is part of the **Joseph Walker Trail,** as that mountain man traipsed along here around 1834, making use of this very watering hole.

111 Miles CA 178 goes east toward Inyokern and Ridgecrest, but you should ignore it.

The store at Onyx claims to have been doing business since 1851, but there have likely been a few rebuilds in the last 150 years.

114 Miles Turn right onto CA 178, heading west toward **Isabella Lake** and **Bakersfield;** if you read the historical plaque, you would learn that this intersection is called **Freeman Junction,** though who Freeman was, I have no idea.

CA 178 ascends up **Freeman Canyon,** although it does not look like a canyon at all, being quite open on both sides of the road.

123 Miles Arrive at **Walker Pass** (5,250 feet); it's not a high pass, but that made it all the more useful in the days of wagons drawn by horses and oxen. Back in the 1850s, this was the communications route between those on the east side of the southern Sierras, and those on the west.

From here, the road starts a nice curving descent to **Canebrake Creek.**

131 Miles The dirt road down from **Chimney Peak** goes off to the right.

CA 178 weaves around a number of curves, and a valley of green trees will appear in front of you as Canebrake Creek merges with the **South Fork Kern River.**

143 Miles You will have just passed downtown **Onyx,** with several stores and a gas station. You will want to stop at the original **Onyx Store** for a grilled sausage. There it is! A raggedy old building with a huge tree stump out front, run by **Six-Shot Sharon,** one-time mayor of Whiskey Flats (an honorary title). The store claims to have been around since 1851, but whether or not any of the original boards are still in use is moot.

148 Miles Turn right where the sign points to Kernville, to head northish on the **Sierra Highway.** The road goes north for a mile, crossing over the **South Fork Kern River,** then west about seven miles, then north again, and it is all a good ride. After ten miles, you will pass the little **Kern Valley Airport** and continue straight on into town.

161 Miles Arrive back in **Kernville.**

Trip 25 California Hot Springs & Parker Pass

Distance *110 miles*

Highlights *Not much traffic, lots of twisties, and even the opportunity to soak in a warm swimming pool*

0 Miles Start with **Cheryl's** on your left.

4 Miles Turn right in the middle of **Wofford Heights,** following CA 155 to the west, up the hill, toward Glennville and Delano. This stretch is officially called Evans Road, though I have never heard anybody refer to it as such.

11 Miles You will be at **Greenhorn Summit** (6,102 feet), which is just west of the mountain resort community of **Alta Sierra.** At the summit, roads go left and right.

Detour

If you want some dirty options, go left onto Rancheria Road, which begins with pavement and degenerates to gnarly dirt as it goes for 35 miles south along the ridge of the **Greenhorn Mountains** and drops down 5,000 feet to CA 178 near the Comanche Road intersection.

To the right, the road is also called Rancheria Road, and it is seven dirt miles (usually in good condition) to **Portugese Pass** at 7,280 feet. From Portagee you can either go north on some seriously bad pavement to meet good pavement near **Johnsondale,** or go west down to **Posey**—where you'll join the regular route. ✱

In Glennville, on CA 155, the Crazy Horse is the only eating and drinking game in town.

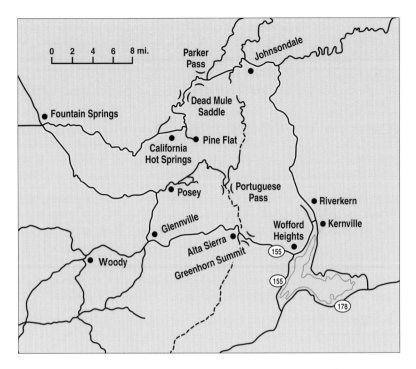

24 Miles Stay straight (a bit to the right, maybe) in Glennville, while CA 155 curves off to the right. As you entered **Glennville** (pop. 130 or thereabouts, elev. 3,150 feet), a fire station was on your right, followed by the **Crazy Horse Restaurant & Saloon** (breakfast from 7:00 on weekdays, 8:00 on weekends) and then a green-and-white sign indicating that Delano is off to the left along CA 155, but you want to head straight for **Porterville** and the **Poso Creek Recreation Area,** along White River Road.

25 Miles STOP sign—turn right onto Jack Ranch Road, where the sign reads FOUNTAIN SPRINGS 18, and the road winds pleasantly through ranch country until it T-bones into Old Stage Road.

30 Miles Turn left onto Old Stage Road, which parallels **Arrastre Creek,** running nice and twisty past the **White River Cemetery.** If you went right, you'd get to Posey and Portuguese Pass.

47 Miles STOP sign—turn right at **Fountain Springs** (elev. 800 feet) onto M56, a/k/a Hot Springs Drive, a sign reading CA HOT SPRINGS 18. The intersection has only a fire station and the **Fountain Springs Saloon** (since 1858); around 1858, Fountain Springs was a way-station for the **Butterfield Overland Stagecoach Company,** but it is doubtful that that is the original building. From 9:00 a.m. to closing, the barkeeper doubles as cook. There is no gas here, and the next gas will be in **Kernville,** more than 60 miles away; if you are in need, go west seven miles to **Ducor.** If you are riding late in the season, a sign at Fountain Springs will tell you if **Parker Pass** is closed or not.

The ride out to the **Hot Springs** is a delight, and you will hardly be aware that you are climbing (unless you are two-up on a 125 Vespa). As you come over a ridge, you can look down, way down, to the community of Hot Springs.

65 Miles **California Hot Springs** (3,040 feet) will be on your right, with food and drink 9 to 5 daily. The big pool will be about 90 degrees, but the two smaller, hotter tubs will be an invigorating 100 and 105 degrees; inside the big building there is a large dance floor (805-548-6582, for details).

68 Miles Turn left where Hot Springs Drive butts into another road; **Hot Springs Ranger Station** will be a hundred yards up the hill. If you went right, you would be in **Pine Flat** in half a mile, where the **Rabbit Foot Trail Inn** has eight rooms, a bar, and haphazard dining hours ($53+; 661-548-6813). If you are headed back to Kernville, the best way is over Parker Pass, with a nice nine-mile climb over **Dead Mule Saddle** and **Cold Springs Saddle** to the pass itself (6,400 feet); from here, it will be all downhill.

79 Miles Stay straight at the four-way intersection, where Western Divide Highway goes off to your left, and there is a trailhead to your right.

The western slopes of the Sierras are ranching county, and this homestead is on Old Stage Road between Glennville and Fountain Springs.

The sign at Fountain Springs will tell you whether the road over Parker Pass is open or not.

82 Miles The road down from **Portuguese Pass** will be on your right.

85 Miles Bend right at the three-way intersection. A road off to your left eventually dead-ends after going up along the **Kern River** for some 20 miles.

Pass **Johnsondale,** the remains of a logging community, now better known by the large sign which reads R-RANCH IN THE SEQUOIAS.

110 Miles Arrive back at Ground Zero in **Kernville.**

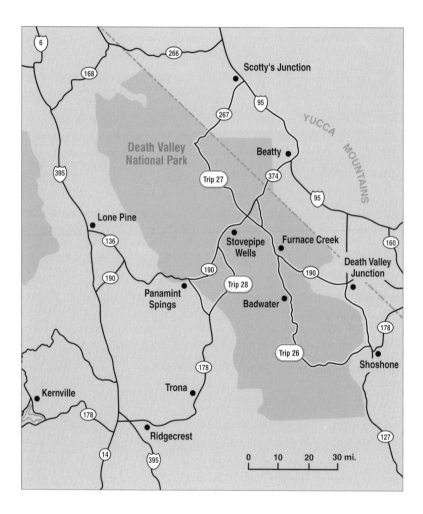

Death Valley

Headquarters *Furnace Creek Ranch*

Park Service Headquarters *760-786-2331*

Best Time to Visit *All year, although it can get powerful hot down there, and you might not want to be riding between 10 a.m. and 5 p.m. during the summer months*

Getting There *It's a snap. You can come north along US 395, which parallels Death Valley on the western side, and take CA 178 via Ridgecrest and Trona, or CA 190 from Olancha. Or, if you are coming south on 395, you could take CA 136 from Lone Pine. Also, I-15 is to the south, and you could take CA 127 from Baker to Shoshone, to meet with CA 178. From the east, US 95 runs up from Las Vegas through Nevada, and you could cut off at Beatty or, if you're coming down from the north, at Scotty's Junction.*

Ground Zero *Pull out of Furnace Creek Ranch onto CA 178/190.*

This is one of my favorite places, except maybe in July and August: smooth roads, lots of interesting places (both geological and historical), and superb night skies. **Death Valley National Park** covers some 5,300 square miles (bigger than the state of Connecticut), the altitude goes from **279.8 feet below sea level** (Badwater) to **11,049 above** (Telescope Peak)—though you can only ride a bike up to 8,133 feet, at **Mahogany Flat.**

Furnace Creek is roughly smack dab in the middle of the Valley of Death. That name is a misnomer really. More on that in a bit.

Stunning place, Death Valley. I first went there in 1967, to attend the last official **Death Valley Motorcycle Rally** on a Triumph TR6R, and have been going back ever since. Even after 30 or more trips, I always find something new. On April 15th, 1998, I ran into snow on **Salsberry Pass** at eight o'clock in the morning . . . and that was something new.

Some soulless people come to the valley, pass through, spend a night at **Furnace Creek,** see **Zabriskie Point** and **Badwater,** yawn, and move on. "Been there, done that, bye." But for anybody who has an appreciation for the desert and for desolation, Death Valley will be an endless variety show.

There are hundreds of miles of paved two-lane road within the park, often smooth and unblemished by the passage of heavy trucks. The biggest hazards are, of course, the recreational vehicles, huge, slow-moving tortoises with sightseers, rather than drivers, at the steering wheels.

I remember coming in with a small group of bikes, and as we rode from Stovepipe Wells to Furnace Creek there was a 30-footer trundling along at a

Abbreviated Valley History

The Indians who cheerfully lived in and around the valley for thousands of years had the good sense to stay away during the summer; a number of reliable springs otherwise provided water for man and beast. In December of 1849, some California-bound emigrants tried to take a short-cut through the valley, and 27 wagons came down **Furnace Creek Wash** with several families and a group of bachelors who called themselves **Jayhawkers.** When camp was made, a discussion was held, and they figured they were well and truly lost. The group began to split up, some going west, some south, and some just stayed to wait for help to come. Eventually everybody made it safely away from the valley, except for one Jayhawker who died while walking out.

According to undocumented lore, one of the emigrant women, as her group climbed up toward **Emigrant Pass,** turned and shook her fist at the innocuous landscape, shouting, "Goodbye, Valley of Death!" Maybe, maybe not.

One of the Jayhawkers had picked up an odd rock, and much later he found that it was nearly pure silver—and the rush was on. Prospectors headed to the area, soon to be followed by saloons and prostitutes, and many mining towns appeared and vanished.

However, the real money was in **borax;** this unromantic mineral was used in everything from cleansing agents to making glass, and the image of 20-mule teams hauling wagonloads of borax off to the railhead at Mojave is seared in the minds of today's Boomer generation, thanks to a television show called "Death Valley Days," which featured a B-movie actor named **Ronald Reagan.**

The borax era lasted roughly from the mid-1870s to the 1920s, and then the **Harmony Borax Company** made a gift of Death Valley to the **National Park Service.** Now its main business is tourism, and lots of tourists come all year around. It is amazing what air-conditioning can do to counteract an outside temperature of 120 degrees. **Furnace Creek** has always been considered the epicenter of the valley, as it has a constant and prodigious supply of water. ✳

These are the 20-mule-team wagons that made history, hauling borax from Death Valley to the refining plant at Mojave; that last wagon was a water tanker, to keep the men and mules from dying of thirst along the way.

stately 35 mph, a "Cruise America" sign on the back indicating it was a rental. As we went by, a small dog was frantically trying to bash its brains out on the windshield, and the red-faced man at the wheel was fighting hard to keep from leaving the road and driving across the desert (a definite no-no by park rules). As we were gassing up at Furnace Creek, he pulled in, got out, and started imprecating against us, calling us dangerous, irresponsible, and some rather less choice words. We calmed him down by pointing out that with his obviously limited skills at steering his mobile bathtub, it was he who was the more hazardous.

Other than the sheriff and CHP officer who might take note of the excessively throttle-happy, there is not much risk to a motorcyclist in Death Valley (see Abbreviated Valley History sidebar).

Death Valley is a national park, and their haphazard system of collecting an entry fee might set you back $5. If they don't catch you at the entrance just south of Scotty's Castle, you are supposed to present yourself at the museum at Furnace Creek and pay up.

National parks lease out concession rights to various organizations, and the one at Furnace Creek is called AmFac Parks & Resorts. **Furnace Creek Ranch,** some 200 feet below sea level, used to be a real ranch, raising cattle to feed the miners; that's all gone. Now there is a big hotel/motel called the **Ranch Resort,** along with a store, cafeteria, restaurant, saloon, tennis courts, golf course, airstrip, date palms, horses to rent, et cetera.

At the Ranch (760-786-2345), rooms go for a low of $90 for one of the old cabins, to $130 for one of the reconditioned parkside bungalows (my own preference). Or you could go a mile away to the **Furnace Creek Inn** (same phone), where a view of the hillside will cost you $145 in the low season, and a "luxury" view will cost $290 in the high season. There is a "dress code" at the Inn, but only for dinner, and that merely requires a jacket; a good Hein Gericke Ventura jacket will do fine against the next table's Brooks Bros. blazer.

The Ranch is far more rowdy than the Inn, and preferable to my tastes. The saloon used to be a delightfully dark and gloomy place, very Old West, but a couple of years back some dolt decided that the new design should be light and airy; I'm surprised he didn't use ferns to enhance the decor. It's too bad, but fortunately the beer is still cold. The Ranch has great grassy swards to stroll across, palm trees to walk under, and a swimming pool to dive into.

The paved roads in the park are very definitely an entertaining ride, from the high-speed sweepers coming down from **Scotty's Castle** to the twisty stuff between **Wildrose Canyon** and **Emigrant Pass.** Plus there are miles and miles of dirt roads for dual-purpose riders.

Motorcycle Notes: there's not much in the way of dealers in Death Valley. However, there is an excellent Honda/Yamaha shop, **Desert Sport Center,** in **Ridgecrest** (760-375-2540), 125 miles west of Furnace Creek Ranch. Also, in about the same distance to the east, Las Vegas will have every possible dealer.

Trip 26   Badwater, Shoshone & Death Valley Jct.

Distance   *127 miles*

Highlights   *If you want to get on the throttle, you could do this in less than two hours, but most people who have never been here before will take all day.*

0 Miles   Turn right coming out of **Furnace Creek Ranch** to head east on CA 190/178.

0+ Miles   Turn right as you come on a rise, with the **Furnace Creek Inn** up on your left. A well-marked road, CA 178/Badwater, will cut sharply to the right; that will be the one you want. CA 190 will go straight ahead to Death Valley Junction.

3+ Miles   At the entrance to **Mosaic Canyon,** there is a left turn up a short dirt road to a parking area where you could start a very pretty, very geological

---

West Side Road

If you take the **West Side Road,** you'll see a couple of smaller roads shooting off to the west which are good for dual-purpose bikes. After 5+ miles, you'll spot Trail Canyon Road, which used to climb up to **Aguereberry Point** some 20 years or so ago, but a big slide took out a big chunk of the road and left nothing but a steep mountainside. In another 5 miles, **Hanaupah Canyon** will go off to the left and dead-end after a few miles. And in another 10 miles, after passing the grave of **Shorty Harris** and the remains of the **Eagle Borax works, Johnson Canyon** will go off to its own dead end, becoming impassable long before you get to the ruins of **Hungry Bill's** ranch. Yet another 5 miles farther on, by some old tanks, **Galena Canyon** goes west a short way to an old talc mine.

Seven more miles beyond Galena Canyon, Warm Spring Canyon Road will cut back to the west; if you were to follow it for about 33 miles, it would take you right out of Death Valley and into **Panamint Valley.** I'd advise you to reset your tripmeter to 0 at the turn. From there, you would beat up a long, rocky wash and come into **Striped Butte Valley.** At 15+ miles, keep to your left; in another 5+, also keep left. The only possible problem you might have would be climbing the little cliff right at **Mengel Pass** (4,326 feet); it's not for the faint of heart, but *lots* of people do it. That will lead you into **Goler Wash,** which runs out to Panamint Valley and Wingate Road, going north to **Ballarat.** Good d-p exercise.

If you are staying strictly on the West Side Road, you will be back on CA 178 just three miles beyond the turn-off to Warm Spring Canyon Road. ✳

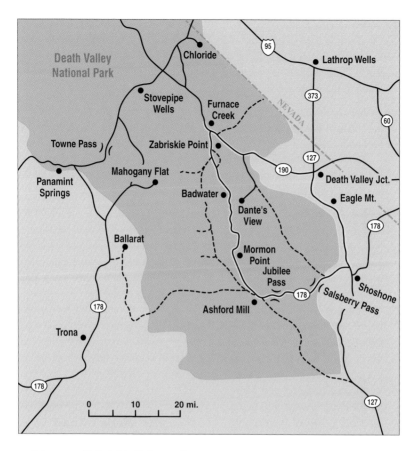

hike up to **Zabriskie Point.** Being a lazy cuss, I recommend you ride two-up to Zabriskie and walk back downhill to where you left the other bike. It is one of the more popular hikettes in the park, and you will pass lots of people.

5 Miles On your left, you will see the north end of one-way Artists Palette Drive; this is the end not to enter.

7 Miles On your right will be the northern entrance to the **West Side Road,** 35+ miles of sometimes good, sometimes bad dirt road, depending on the past winter and the amount of repairs done. If it has been raining, forget it, unless you have a d-p and are willing to get dirty. If it's dry, however, a Gold Wing could go through (see West Side Road sidebar).

10 Miles On your left, you'll see the entrance to Artist Drive, which is a very pleasant one-lane, one-way jaunt for 9 miles through the foothills of the **Black Mountains,** one of the many smaller groups that make up the **Amargosa Range.** There's lots of attractive geology to see out there, especially in the afternoon when the western sun is striking the rocks.

CHAPTER

13

12 Miles To the right will be the turn to the **Devil's Golf Course,** which is located a mile down a good dirt road. Over a couple of million years, the wind and rain have left neatly formed stacks of salt and gravel scattered all along the old lake bottom. If you will be needing salt for your picnic, just take a pinch of the white stuff.

14 Miles To the left will be a turn up a two-mile dirt road to the parking area for the **Natural Bridge.** A short quarter-mile hike will bring you beneath the 50-foot arch.

The road develops a few twists and turns along about now, as it hunkers in under the steep cliffs to the left (east), avoiding the potentially marshy bits of the **Salt Creek Basin.**

17 Miles You can park your bike at **Badwater,** 270 feet below sea level, where a white sign up on the cliffs will remind you of where you would be if somebody dug a 200-mile trench from the **Pacific Ocean**—if you put some turbines along there you could generate some real electricity as the ocean rushed in. If you want to get the full impact, you could walk out onto the saline flats about three miles and stand at –279.8 feet.

South of Badwater, the quality of the road deteriorates a bit, as it is not heavily used and the USNPS has only limited funds. But it is still a good road, although it has a lot of patches, and it swoops around the edges of the slag that has come off the hills—great honking curves of a mile or more, where the last guy can see the first in a chain of 20 fast-moving sportbikes.

As you come around **Mormon Point,** the road will begin a gentle, barely perceptible climb.

43 Miles You will have reached the southern junction of the West Side Road.

45 Miles Enter **Ashford Mill,** or better put, the small remains of the old borax mill. It's not the sort of place you'd want to vacation in, although I have slept on the picnic tables there, much against park regulations, and the place has a pleasantly eery aura about it.

47 Miles Hwy. 178 makes a sharp left to the east, to take you

Mr. Wade's Road

You could go straight on Henry Wade Road, a dirt and sand track that ties into CA 127 after 33 miles. The sign recommends high clearance and four-wheel drive; I recommend a dual-purpose bike, although I watched **Jim Wolcott** run a Sportster over it years ago. The road runs along the **Amargosa River,** which flows (?!) north into Death Valley; the river is usually dry unless very heavy rains have fallen, but at one point the road crosses the river and there is a stretch of soft sand. It's not a real problem for a d-p bike or a well-ridden naked motorcycle, however. Gold Wings and TL1000Rs might find it a bit much. ✱

Badwater is more than 270 feet below sea level. If I could just dig a ditch from the Pacific Ocean to Death Valley and stick in a couple of water turbines to generate electricity, I could let gravity make me rich. (Photo by Craig Erion)

up over **Jubilee Mountain,** while Henry Wade Road goes straight (see Mr. Wade's Road sidebar).

51 Miles The road gets right twisty as you come up on **Jubilee Pass,** cut deep through the mountain at a modest 1,290 feet. The road will then slip down into a valley and immediately start to climb again.

56 Miles Once you are up at **Salsberry Pass,** at a somewhat more lofty 3,315 feet, you will drop down into **Greenwater Valley** (I'll leave you to figure out where that name came from) and leave the park.

62 Miles Off to your left will be a small collection of unmarked dirt roads heading north into Greenwater Valley. They all more or less congeal into one 28-mile dirt road that goes up the valley and connects with the road to **Dante's View.** More on that from the other end.

72 Miles STOP sign—turn left, as CA 178 connects with CA 127. Our route goes left, but a short trip to the right, to Shoshone, might be in order (see Shoshone sidebar).

Connector

If you are interested in heading to **Palm Springs,** you can take CA 127 South to Baker, then continue straight across I-15 onto Kelbaker Road, going through **Kelso** and on to **Amboy** on old US 66. From there, the Amboy Road will go south to 29 Palms, and you could turn to Chapter 14 to figure out what to do next. ✸

Shoshone

Go right one mile into the tiny town of **Shoshone** if you are interested in gas, food, information, or a place to sleep. Shoshone, which flourished briefly as a mining center, has become a small stop on the back way into Death Valley. You can get a room at the **Shoshone Inn,** an old-fashioned motel with 16 units; prices start at $50 (760-852-4335). Next door, you'll find the **Charles Brown General Store;** Mr. Brown, a local politician, basically owned the town, and he passed the whole thing along to his grand-daughter Susan when he died. Across the road, you'll see the **Red Buggy Cafe & Crowbar Lounge,** otherwise known as **Brown's Bar,** serving solid food seven days a week from 7:00 in the morning to 9:30 at night. Don't miss the **Shoshone Museum,** which has a bit of everything that has withstood the ravages of a hundred years of use and exposure to the elements. ✳

While cruising north on CA 127, you will be riding beside the **Amargosa River,** which flows (when it flows, which is very, very, very rarely) south past Shoshone to the **Dumont Dunes.** The 25-mile stretch from Shoshone to **Death Valley Junction** is known for its flatness and fast curves. Ahead of you will be **Eagle Mountain,** a great hunk of stone sticking up some 2,500 feet from the desert floor, out in the middle of nowhere. In the distance, you'll see a cluster of buildings; it will take a few minutes to get there, although it will seem as if they are just a mile away.

97 Miles **Death Valley Junction,** you have arrived (see Death Valley Junction sidebar).

90+ Miles Just north of the Opera House, CA 190 turns to the left, back to Death Valley.

Alternate Route

If you wanted to skirt the east edge of the national park, you could go north on CA 127 to the Nevada state line and continue on to Beatty, Nevada.

Seven miles along, at the state line, where CA 127 morphs into NV 373, you will find the new **Longstreet's Inn & Casino,** with food, 60 rooms starting at $60 (702-372-1777), and some ordinary gambling. They also offer "Camel Rides," $45 for an hour's ride and breakfast, $75 for a ride and dinner; you could not pay me $45 to ride one of those blessed dromedaries for an hour. Across the road you'll find the old **Stateline Saloon & Gambling Hall,** right next to **Mom's Place,** which offers beer, gas, and packaged food.

Continuing north, you will come into **Amargosa Valley,** where Mecca Road goes off to the west. Here, you'll find **Rosa's Mexican**

Restaurant, open 8 to 8 every day except Monday, and a hundred yards behind the restaurant, the **Desert Village Motel,** a two-story affair with 17 units starting at $45 (702-372-1405). Curious place, this valley, with good and plentiful well water right here in the middle of the **Amargosa Desert.** There is even a turf farm and a 5,000-cow dairy nearby.

After 23 miles, NV 373 ends where it butts into US 95 at **Lathrop Wells,** where a really ugly, cheap, fake-front joint called the **Amargosa Saloon & Casino** will try to take your money. Take a left, and you will be headed toward Beatty, Nevada. The road is quite open and straight, going through the Amargosa Desert. Other than the **Yucca Mountains** to your right, the **Funeral Mountains** to your left, and lots of dirt roads disappearing into the mountains, there is not much here. A monstrous sand dune will be off to your left.

After 52 miles you will arrive in **Beatty.** More on that metropolis in Trip 27.   ✸

Back at **Death Valley Junction,** head west on CA 190, a long, straight road with a slight climb.

Death Valley Junction

Death Valley Junction began as the town of **Amargosa** in 1907, but after the **Tonopah & Tidewater** and the **Las Vegas & Tonopah** railroads arrived about 1914, it became DV Junction. Population then soared to 300. The railroad was used to haul borax out of nearby mines until 1928, and then things went into a slow decline. When World War II came along, the railway tracks were torn up to help the war effort.

In the middle of town, you'll see the large, one-story, U-shaped complex which used to house railroad workers, but is now owned by **Marta Becket,** the ballet dancer. At one end of the U, you'll find the **Amargosa Opera House,** where Marta has been putting on superb performances since 1968, always on Saturday night, and sometimes on Mondays, depending on the season. It's a cultural event you should not miss; call (760-852-4441) for full information. She also has a dozen rooms available in her **Amargosa Hotel,** which is in the complex, with prices starting at $45. For food, you could go to the **Serenity Ice Cream Parlor,** located at the other end of the U, open at 10 a.m. on most days. And that will be it for businesses in DV Junction. For serious food, you will have to go seven miles north to the Nevada state line, where the casino serves 24 hours a day.   ✸

Those Ducatis just did the last 25 miles in twelve minutes flat, to meet up with the fast boys and girls who gather at Death Valley Junction.

Ah, yes, Dante's View, at 5,475 feet, is the best view in California, with Badwater below at −279.8 feet, and snow-capped Telescope Peak in the distance, at 11,049 feet.

107 Miles You will cross the nameless saddle (3,040 feet) between the **Funeral Mountains** and the **Greenwater Range,** to begin the long, 20-mile descent to Furnace Creek Ranch. It would be right easy to pick up a serious head of speed along here.

115 Miles There will be a turn to the left which will take you 13 miles up to **Dante's View**—and it is a must-do (see Dante's View sidebar).

119 Miles Pass the east (NO ENTRY) end of the one-way road through **Twenty Mule Team Canyon.**

121 Miles To your left will be the start of the Twenty Mule Team Canyon Drive, a well-maintained dirt road a little less than three miles in length which weaves through the hills; any good rider can do it. They say that if you are there in the evening as the land cools off, you can hear some sort of snap, crackle, and pop. By the way, the old 20-mule borax hauling wagons never came through here—it's just a catchy name.

122 Miles Ah, **Zabriskie Point.** Old man Zabriskie happened to be a superintendent at the borax mines a long time ago, and now his name lives on, attracting mobs of tourists. The huge buses in the parking lot are likely full of French and German tourists (though never in the same bus). Park your bike, climb the hill, and look out over the other-worldly scene. I'd suggest you skip

---

Dante's View

Right after the turn, you will notice an operating borax mine off to your left, the **Ryan Mine,** just outside the somewhat gerrymandered national park boundaries. The road will continue up **Furnace Creek Wash** into **Greenwater Valley.** After seven miles, the road will turn sharply to the right, with a parking area for trailers, and off to the left will be the Greenwater Valley Road, 28 miles of dual-purpose dirt that will connect you with CA 178 just east of **Salsberry Pass.** It is an entertaining dual-purpose ride, climbing gradually to 4,050 feet, and then dropping slowly down to about 2,000 feet by the time you see pavement again.

The paved road starts a serious climb to **Dante's View,** first straight, and then winding through a delightful little canyon, followed by some serious squiggles to get to the top and the view. Of course, you know that Dante wrote *The Divine Comedy,* in which he describes visiting Heaven, Purgatory, and Hell—and this, according to some well-read namer of places, would be his view of Hell. You will be at 5,475 feet, directly above **Badwater,** right across from 11,049-foot **Telescope Peak** only 20 miles to the west, with Death Valley spread out to your left and right. It is a superior view, especially if you can catch it at dusk on a full moon, the sun setting in the west, and the moon rising in the east. Perfect. Just watch out on your way down. ✹

Serious Dual-Purpose Rides

The 9+ mile **Echo Canyon Road** is a fun, but serious, dual-purpose ride. A skid plate should be considered essential equipment. I knocked a hole in the sump of a V65 Sabre years ago trying to get there, and once crunched, twice shy. Otherwise, it is a great ride, but not for the faint of heart. You'll go about five rough miles up to the canyon, then have a twisty trundle over a lot of smooth loose rocks as you go through the narrow, winding canyon.

As you clear the canyon and come out into a small valley, a significant (i.e. you can't miss it) dirt road goes off to the left. Twelve years ago, I found an old map of Death Valley dating from 1951, and it showed a road going off from **Echo Canyon** and crossing over the **Funeral Mountains,** coming out at **Amargosa Valley** on the Nevada side. Of course, I took my KLR 650, with my bride-to-be on the back, and went exploring. The only real problem, other than finding ourselves up a few dead-ends, was an eight-foot dry waterfall, but previous passers had built a loose-rock ramp which we negotiated with a good deal of care. Then we climbed to the top of the mountains and came down a long, long dry wash into the Amargosa Desert, with a far-off view of **Big Dune.** It was the best 20-mile trip I've ever taken.

If you wish to try it, do take a friend along on another bike, as well as some water, just in case . . .

Back in Echo Canyon, keep on going until you come to the site of the old **Inyo Mine,** very isolated and romantic, with a few decrepit old buildings slowly falling apart. Half a mile beyond the mine the road will be barricaded as it disappears into the mountains. ✸

Occasionally I do Death Valley on a dual-purpose bike; that is Kurt "Baja" Grife and myself, taking our ease in Rhyolite.

it during the day when the crowds are around, and come up late at night instead. It will be purely ethereal.

123 Miles Look for a small sign off to your right indicating ECHO CANYON, with a dirt road running off from **Furnace Creek Wash** toward the Funeral Mountains (see the Serious Dual-Purpose Rides sidebar).

126 Miles The road will swoop around a couple of curves, and **Furnace Creek Inn** will appear on your right. The building to your left used to be a garage that could actually do repairs, but that closed up about ten years ago. Just beyond the defunct garage will be the left turn down CA 178 to Badwater.

127 Miles You'll be back at **Furnace Creek Ranch.**

Twenty Mule Team Canyon is five miles of good dirt road that any bike can deal with—presuming the rider is competent.

Trip 27 Beatty, Scotty's Junction & Scotty's Castle

Distance *155 miles*

Highlights *This loop will take you out of Death Valley via Hell's Gate and into western Nevada, as the park does cross state lines. From Beatty, a working town with a little bit of gambling and a smidgen of prostitution, the road goes north across high desert, then west back to Death Valley.*

0 Miles Turn left coming out of **Furnace Creek Ranch** and go 11 miles on the fine, paved road that runs through the center of the valley.

11 Miles Turn right at **Beatty Junction** (190 feet below sea level) and roll up-hill along Daylight Pass Cut-Off Road.

16 Miles At a well-marked turn to the right, a well-maintained dirt road goes 2+ miles up to the parking area at the **Keane Wonder Mine.** Begun in 1903, the Keane was worked into the 1930s, and now there are a lot of remains. This was no hole-in-the-ground operation, but a big-bucks investment.

21 Miles STOP sign—turn right as you come to the **Hells Gate** intersection, going up Daylight Pass Road. It will have a few serious curves, and some RVers will find the downhill a trifle steep for their smoking brakes.

24 Miles A dirt road to the right goes up to **Chloride,** where you'll find some good views of the valley. They mined silver there up until World War I.

Titus Canyon

The approach to **Titus Canyon** is a one-way dirt road of some 24 miles, usually kept in pretty good repair as many small motorhomes go through. It is a beaut trip, but a bit rough on an Electra Glide or a Buell, or for anybody who is fearful of riding on bumpy, rutted dirt; whether you are on a DR or a GL, you had better know your way around dirt.

The first five miles go straight across the **Amargosa Desert,** then the road starts to wind upward to the 5,250-foot summit, before dropping down to the remains of **Leadfield.** For a few brief months in 1920, gullible suckers arrived from all over the country, conned by a promotor who had convinced them that there was lead in these hills.

After leaving Leadfield, the surface of the road into Titus Canyon is made up of small, water-washed rocks. It is quite navigable on a bike if you are familiar with such terrain. At the end of the canyon, the road suddenly opens out into Death Valley, and there will be less than two miles of good, two-way dirt back to the pavement 20 miles south of **Scotty's Castle.** ❋

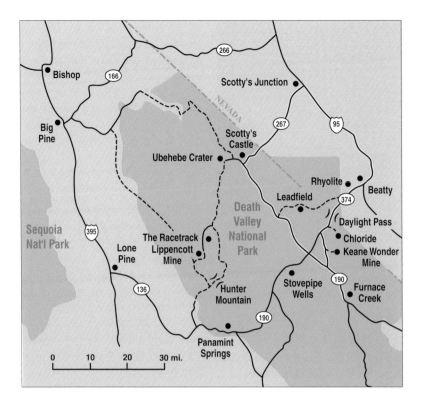

27 Miles Cross **Daylight Pass,** at 4,317 feet, site of the annual ride to Death Valley begun back in the late Seventies by some Young Urban Professionals from Los Angeles. On a Saturday night, everyone tears up to Beatty for lots of red meat at the **Burro Inn,** and on the way back everybody stops at the top of the pass, kills their engines, and begins a coasting race. The hotshots put 70 pounds of air in their tires, and sewing-machine oil in their wheel bearings. Drafting someone with a dead engine can be fun, especially when you can grab the other fellow's rear turn signal and pull yourself up alongside.

Soon you will be entering **Nevada.**

31 Miles Leave the park boundaries.

34 Miles The road to **Titus Canyon** starts on your left (see Titus Canyon sidebar).

36 Miles A left turn would take you up to **Rhyolite,** where some 6,000 people once lived while digging for the gold which was first discovered here in 1904; although the road dead-ends in two miles, it is very much worth the trip. At the intersection, you will see the remains of a large, modern, semi-mining operation that is being closed down in early 2000. Modern technology had made it possible to extract more gold from the old mine tailings (the

The Keane Wonder Mine produced a lot of gold from 1903 to 1916. It was occasionally mined after that, but hasn't seen any activity since the Thirties.

tailings being what was left after the gold was separated by the rather crude methods of the early 20th century), and this place opened for business in the late Eighties. However, they have run through all the old tailings and there is nothing left to do. This operation was a major employer in the Beatty area.

Stay on the highway, wind over the hills, and drop into **Beatty.**

40 Miles At the intersection with US 95, the **Exchange Club,** with gambling and rooms ($44; 702-563-2333), will be directly across the street. If you went right on US 95 for a half a mile, you'd discover one of my favorites, the **Burro Inn,** with casino and motel ($42; 800-843-2078), as well as the Burro's restaurant, another favorite. It's nothing fancy, but they offer good grub cooked well.

If you were to go straight, hooking into US 95 North, you'd pass the only two gas stations in town.

43 Miles On your left, a few hundred yards off the road, you will spot **Angel's Ladies,** a brilliant pink, temporary home to some women of the world's second oldest profession. There is an airstrip out front, for the fly-in crowd, decorated with a wrecked twin-engine plane (see Prostitution sidebar).

50 Miles All that is left of **Springdale** is a small house surrounded by a lot of valuable antiquities—or junk, depending on your point of view. But I did run out of gas there once and a fellow cheerfully sold me a gallon.

From here, you will have a straight, fast ride across the **Sarcobatus Flats.**

72 Miles At a bright yellow collection of trailers off to your right; a sign at the gate reads SHADY LADY. They're the competition for Angel's Ladies.

75 Miles Turn left at **Scotty's Junction,** where there is a little store with bits of this and that decorating the front. Although it advertises rooms, it has none. However, they do have "emergency" gas in five-gallon cans, though I did not ask the price. After the left turn, you will be on NV 267 heading across the flats, past the ruins of a smelter.

86 Miles If you have ever wondered what it would be like to tear across such a piece of uncluttered, unpoliced terrain at any speed, just turn off to your right, onto **Claire Dry Lake**—unless, of course, it has rained recently.

After leaving the flats, the road will go deceptively downhill, and you could pick up a head of speed without quite being aware of it. Just as you enter the park boundaries, the road seriously twists along the long-gone creek that created **Grapevine Canyon.** Be gentle, as there are big boulders right off the road which would bring an errant motorcycle to a swift and sure stop.

100 Miles On your right will be **Scotty's Castle,** an appealing place that is worth a visit—as long as the wait is not too long (see Scotty's Castle sidebar).

103 Miles A paved road off to the right goes to **Ubehebe Crater** (see Ubehebe Crater and The Racetrack sidebar).

104 Miles The ranger station will lighten your wallet by a five-dollar bill, but the admission ticket will be good for seven days.

Prostitution

Nevada, a sensible state which understands the need for a sound tax base, has decided to take financial advantage of the inevitability of prostitution. The Houses of Joy are closely regulated on a county-by-county basis, by both the taxman and the medical profession. There are now 36 licensed cathouses in the state, which accommodate everyone from truck drivers, to tourists, to bisexual housewives. In these little compounds, you'll find none of the glamour of the bawdy houses we see in movies, but rather more of a Motel 6 approach to sex. Since the introduction of Viagra, the number of elderly gents visiting these establishments has greatly enhanced their profitability.   ✳

Angel's Ladies, a house of ill repute in Beatty, Nevada, has its own airstrip for the use of its patrons. Obviously the pilot of this plane was a little too excited at the thought of what was in store for him.

You will begin a long descent, dropping more than 2,500 feet in 25 miles. The road is good, the curves are gradual, and the view down the valley will be marvelous, with the **Mesquite Flat** sand dunes in the far distance.

122 Miles A sign pointing to the left reads TITUS CANYON. It is a two-mile, two-way dirt road leading to the mouth of the canyon and the start of the one-way road. If you don't care to take your Nomad all the way down the canyon, you could ride up to the parking area and walk into the canyon for half a mile. It is impressive.

Scotty's Castle

Walter Scott was a cheerful braggart, rodeo rider, prospector—you name it—who befriended a wealthy Chicago man, **Albert Johnson,** who wanted to bring his wife to the dry climate of Death Valley. Being a bit on the shy side, Johnson let Scotty be the front man for the house that he built at **Grapevine Springs.** Officially, it was known as the **Death Valley Ranch,** but Scotty had no objection to having the place known as "his" castle.

The construction started in 1924, and when it was done the elaborate house had 18 fireplaces, a many-piped organ, and a 260-foot swimming pool. Actually, the house was never completely finished; when Johnson died in 1948, the flow of money ceased, and Scotty carried on for another six years, telling everyone who cared to listen that he had a secret gold mine. He died in 1954 and was buried on a hill overlooking "the shack," as he self-deprecatingly referred to the mansion.

Among the castle's many curiosities is a huge stack of 120,000 railroad ties that were bought when the **Tonopah & Tidewater Railroad** was torn up; unfortunately, back then nobody thought to ask if the creosoted wood would burn well in a fireplace . . . it doesn't.   ✳

The Antelope Valley (California) HOG chapter was out for a look at Scotty's castle.

Ubehebe Crater and The Racetrack

Take the left turn toward **Ubehebe Crater.** After 2+ miles, another dirt road, known as Death Valley Road, goes off to the right toward **Big Pine.** It will be 35 miles of good dirt, with about four miles of pavement in the middle, in **Hanging Rock Canyon.** A Voyager could get through with no problem—if the rider is familiar with loose-surface riding.

If you were to continue another two paved miles to the left, you would arrive at the parking area for the crater, which was created by a volcanic explosion a few thousand years ago. It is half a mile across and 500 feet deep. The athletically inclined can walk to the bottom.

Right by the parking area will be a sign indicating a (bad) dirt road to the **Racetrack.** This is a helluva good ride for a good dual-sporter, but do get a good map, as what I am saying here is not intended as a guide, just a titillation. First, you will have to battle your way up **Racetrack Valley** along a dry wash with lots of stones. After 19+ miles you will arrive at **Teakettle Junction**— and yes, there are a lot of tea-kettles hanging from the sign.

Keep straight, and in five more miles you will be at the Racetrack, a dry lake on your left. More than forty years ago, there were big rocks on the lake bed, often weighing more than 100 pounds each. These rocks would actually move and leave trails behind—a rather bizarre geological sleight-of-hand attributed to extremely slick mud and very high winds. However, tourists have since liberated all these rocks and taken them away, so you shouldn't expect to see anything now.

In another five miles, you will be at the old **Lippencott lead mine,** and if you are really, really good on your d-p bike, you could ride down a very steep, rocky road for three miles, which comes out on Saline Valley Road four miles beyond that. From there, you could go north 40 miles on good dirt to meet up with Death Valley Road, or south 30 miles on dirt to meet up with CA 190.

But, back to Teakettle: if you were to turn left and go through **Lost Burro Gap** and **Hidden Valley,** you'd pass a couple of old mine sites, then climb up over **Hunter Mountain,** before dropping down to meet with Saline Valley Road. It is a great ride, and not terribly difficult.   ❋

133 Miles A very good dirt road to the right will lead down to the sand dunes, which are the perfect place to take a walk at dawn.

135 Miles Daylight Pass Road will go off to the left, toward Beatty.

136 Miles STOP sign—turn left onto CA 190/178.

155 Miles Arrive back at **Furnace Creek Ranch.**

Trip 28   Towne Pass & Wildrose Canyon

Distance *126 miles*

Highlights *Warning: there will be a little bit of good dirt road on this loop, close to Wildrose Canyon itself, but this ride is a beaut, running you over the Panamint Range, through the Panamint Valley paralleling Death Valley, then back over the Panamints on another road.*

0 Miles Turn left leaving **Furnace Creek Ranch** and stay on CA 190/178.

25 Miles **Stovepipe Wells Village** has a store, gas, restaurant, bar, and 83-unit motel ($60+; 760-786-2387) that is a bit cheaper than the Ranch, but there is not much to do there. The actual **Stovepipe Well,** five miles northwest of here across the dunes, was long identified by an old bit of stovepipe travelers had used to prevent the hole from filling up with sand.

As you make the long run up and over the **Panamint Range,** you'll see lots of signs warning car drivers to turn off air-conditioners, lest their engines overheat. We motorcyclists don't need no stinking air conditioning.

34 Miles As you pass **Emigrant Campground,** a sign points off to **Emigrant Pass;** you will be coming back this way.

40 Miles After cresting **Towne Pass,** at 4,956 feet (Wowzer!) you will start a beaut descent, the road swooping down through the mountains until suddenly the **Panamint Valley** will be spread out before you. There will be sand dunes to the north, a large dry lake in front of you, and off in the distance, the sun will be glinting off some buildings. Although it all looks as though it is right in front of you, it will take forever to get down to the lake—the distances are big.

59 Miles Turn left onto CA 178/Panamint Valley Road, where the sign reads TRONA, having just crossed the lake (see Panamint Springs sidebar).

Panamint Valley Rd./CA 178 heads south, exits the park in a couple of miles, and rolls on over undulating desert.

61 Miles STOP sign—turn left onto the Trona-Wildrose Road (CA 178 goes to the right, but you want that left).

Panamint Springs

Less than two miles ahead on CA 190, you'll find the pleasantly rustic **Panamint Springs Resort** (760-482-7680), a privately owned motel, campground, restaurant, et cetera. When federal funding turned Death Valley National Monument into a national park a few years ago, the boundaries were extended to include **Panamint Springs,** though it was left in private hands. It has 14 rooms, with prices starting at $56. It is a nice place to stay and the food is good, too. ✳

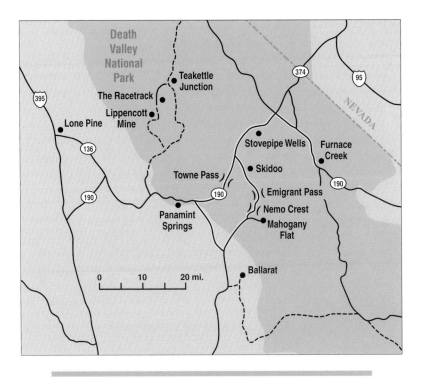

Connector

If you went left, following CA 178, you would be in **Trona** in 33 miles, and from there, CA 178 passes through **Ridgecrest, China Lake,** and **Inyokern,** eventually cresting **Walker Pass** on the way to **Isabella Lake** (Chapter 12). ✸

As you climb a bit, you'll see the park's limits denoted by a large sign. After seven miles, the road will begin to deteriorate, becoming dirt. Years ago, the park used to keep this stretch paved, but every few winters the water rushing down the canyon would tear up the asphalt and leave a righteous mess. Finally, some brilliant administrator decided to leave things as they were and just run a dozer over the road in the spring if it were needed. You will go through **Wildrose Canyon** proper on the dirt.

71 Miles STOP sign—turn left; to the right will be **Mahogany Flat** and **Telescope Peak** (see Mahogany Flat sidebar).

From the STOP sign, the road will wind through a narrow canyon, break out into a small valley, and then climb again, crossing **Nemo Crest** at 5,547 feet, before descending to **Emigrant Pass** (5,318 feet); this is the route on which the **Jayhawkers** emerged back in 1849. It's great fun on a bike, but with ox-drawn wagons . . .?

Mahogany Flat

The road out to **Mahogany Flat** is a mild roller-coaster; should you ever get six or eight bikes rolling along here, the sweep rider will get a delightful view as the motorcycles are constantly topping hillocks, disappearing, others appearing—grand video stuff. After five miles the road will turn to dirt, and these great beehives will appear on your left.

The beehive affairs are charcoal kilns. Few people today understand the importance of charcoal but, essentially, charcoal is far more transportable than wood and it turns out a higher heat. Historically, charcoal was important for smelting ore and extracting gold and silver, since the gold and silver was a long way from where the trees were up on the mountainsides.

A scrabbly dirt road leads up to Mahogany Flats, the highest place in Death Valley accessible by motorcycle (at least legally). From here, at 8,133 feet, you could walk up to the top of **Telescope Peak** (11,049 feet) via a seven-mile trail; I've never done it, but I invite those of you who do to write and tell me about it.   ✹

Behind me is old Dinah, a steam-powered tractor that used to haul wagons around in the valley in the early years of the 20th century; the spokes on those wheels did not bend easily.

The Death Valley Railroad did not actually run into Death Valley, but to the mines up toward Death Valley Junction; this steam engine was hauled down to serve as an exhibit at Furnace Creek Ranch.

81 Miles The road will level out on the **Harrisburg Flats,** and a dirt road goes off to the right, six miles out to **Aguerreberry Point.** The view from the point will be superb, looking down on **Furnace Creek** 6,500 feet below. About a mile back down the dirt road, you will see a locked gate on your left, at the beginning of what was once the road going down to **Trail Canyon** and the West Side Road. Park the bike, take a short walk, and you will see why the road is no longer usable.

83 Miles A seven-mile dirt road goes off to the right to the remnants of the boom-and-bust town of **Skidoo,** abandoned in 1917. Not much remains.

   The paved road starts dropping down through **Emigrant Canyon,** a pleasantly curvy stretch for the next nine miles.

92 Miles STOP sign—turn right; you will be back at the intersection by the **Emigrant Campground.** For some stunning views, turn right and head down the hill toward **Stovepipe Wells.**

126 Miles Arrive back at **Furnace Creek.**

CHAPTER
13

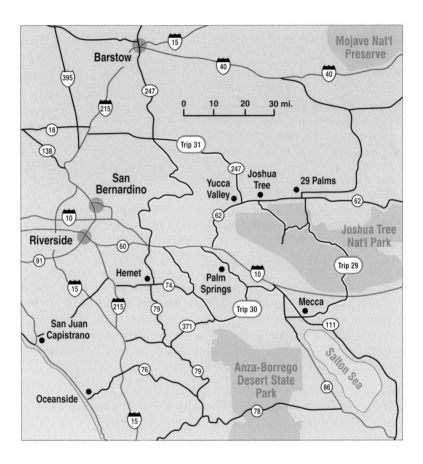

Palm Springs Alternatives

Headquarters *Palm Springs*

Palm Springs Tourism Office *760-778-8415, 800-347-7746*

Best Time to Visit *All year, although you can find ice and snow in the mountains in the winter. Be wary if you want to haul over the San Bernardino Mountains or San Jacinto Mountains in January.*

Getting There *Easiest way is just to head east out of the Los Angeles Basin on I-10. Or you might be coming in from Phoenix, Arizona, on I-10.*

Ground Zero *The following trips will start where Ramon Road crosses between Indian Canyon and Palm Canyon, a convenient spot, as Indian Canyon goes straight north to I-10 going west, Ramon goes due east to I-10 going east. And this is also the IHOP corner, so you can have breakfast there and plan the day.*

In the curious geology that is most of California, desert and mountains sit side by side, and you could be swimming down below and skiing up above. We've all heard of **Palm Springs,** where the rich come to play golf and die, the middle class come to party and leave, and the poor commute to work from **Indio.** Not many people might think of Palm Springs as a focal point for great riding, but it is.

Nice town, thanks to a phenomenal amount of water deep down in the desert. Through the miracles of modern technology, the local authorities pump it out at a great rate and keep the 20-some golf courses green and healthy. **Palm Springs** very much has a live-for-today attitude, as nobody really wants to think about the

It's a long, lonely road coming into Joshua Tree National Park from 29 Palms.

inevitable day when the water will give out. The **Coachella Valley,** the long strip running from Palm Springs east to Indio, averages less than three inches of rain a year. In contrast, the date farmers need at least ten feet of water for their trees.

"Take the cash and let the credit go, nor heed the rumble of the distant drum."

Downtown **Palm Springs** is real nice on a quiet Monday afternoon. There are two wide, parallel, one-way streets, Indian Canyon Drive going north, and Palm Canyon Drive going south. The two miles between Alejo Road and Ramon Road is the place to be, with a multitude of good open-air restaurants, shops and shopping centers, and a few museums thrown in for good measure. **Palm Canyon** is more the strolling side. For post office purposes, everything north of **Tahquitz Canyon,** a major east-west cross street, is referred to as North, and south of . . . etc.

If you like Southwest cooking, go to the **Blue Coyote Grill** (445 North Palm Canyon; 760-327-1196). For French cuisine, try the **Elan Brasserie** (415 North Palm Canyon; 760-323-5554). For all-American show, try the **Burger Factory**

Somehow Paul Bunyan got moved from Minnesota to Idyllwild, California. If you wish to change the pink flamingo decor in your front yard, you may purchase this statue from its creator (shipping will be extra).

If you are up in Big Bear City, high (6,700 feet) in the San Bernardino Mountains, and feeling peckish, Thelma will fill you up.

(333 South Indian Canyon; 760-322-7678), where the one-pound "Kong Burger" is good for two people. Breakfast, in this land of food franchises, is best eaten at the previously mentioned **IHOP** (International House of Pancakes, for those who have forgotten).

There will be almost an infinite number of places to sleep, as greater Palm Springs has about 10,000 pillows to offer. The pricing structure also will be quasi-infinite, ranging from mid-week low-season to weekend high-season. You'll find the high end of the scale at the **Hyatt Regency,** at 285 North Palm Canyon Drive, and the middle at the **Best Western Las Brisas** ($70–$150; 222 South Indian Canyon; 760-325-4372; 800-346-5714). Just south of the tourist area, the family-owned **Desert Lodge,** managed by the estimable **Genevieve Stokes** ($45–$90; 1177 South Palm Canyon; 760-325-1356; 800-385-6343) is a favorite of the cost-conscious biking crowd.

For local entertainment, there are museums (such as the **Air Museum,** with all the WWII fighter planes), shows (**Liberace** wannabes are popular on the circuit), exertions (like rock-climbing and tandem sky-diving), and the great American pastime, shopping. But I prefer to get on the road . . .

Joshua Tree National Park & Mecca

Distance *150 miles*

Highlights *This trip goes through open, flattish country, from low to high desert and back, with lots of curvy pavement.*

0 Miles Head north on Indian Canyon Drive, a very straight road.

6 Miles Cross over I-10 and Indian Canyon Drive becomes Indian Avenue.

9 Miles Pass the entrance to **Two Springs Resort** (Members Only—but it is easy to become a member) on your right. This very fine and expensive place to soak your bones was built back in the 1930s.

11 Miles A gentle curve, angling off to the left—the first curve in 11 miles!

14 Miles STOP sign—turn right at the intersection with CA 62. You will be gaining altitude, going over a hill, and dropping into the **Morongo Valley.**

25 Miles You will have gained even more altitude and entered the town of **Yucca Valley** (3,256 feet) on the edge of the **Mojave Desert.** On your right, you'll see **Dick Hutchin's Harley + HYKS** (Honda, Yamaha, Kawasaki, Suzuki) and the **Harley Cafe,** open from 7 to 2 every day except Monday. Good food.

29 Palms

If you are in no hurry, keep straight on Park Boulevard, and after four miles you will come to the **North Entrance Station** to the park. In another five miles, the **Oasis Visitor Center,** the park's headquarters, will be on your left, in the **Oasis of Mara,** in the town of **29 Palms,** just a few hundred yards south of CA 62.

Take a left immediately after the visitor center, and at 73950 Inn Avenue (don't ask me how they got to 73,000 on a very short street) will be the **29 Palms Inn** ($45–$225; 760-367-3505), offering hospitality since 1928. The place has more than a dozen separate little residences, either adobe cottages or wood cabins, and a restaurant beside the swimming pool that serves lunch and dinner seven days a week, brunch on Sunday. It is a very nice place to lay back.

29 Palms itself does not have too much too offer, being an old Marine Corps town that has steadily been losing inhabitants, except that it has decided to revamp itself into the **City of Murals,** and consequently, lots of buildings have their sides painted.

When it is time, head back south into the park—your ticket will be good for seven days—back to the intersection of Park Blvd. and Pinto Basin Rd. ✴

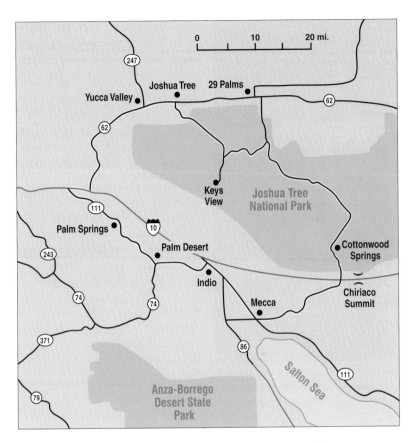

26 Miles Go straight where the sign to Pioneertown points left.

26+ Miles Note **Johnny's Restaurant** on your right, in case you are in Yucca Valley on Monday, when the Harley Cafe is closed.

27 Miles Stay straight on CA 62, a/k/a 29 Palms Highway, as CA 247 goes off to the left.

33+ Miles Turn right onto Park Boulevard, where a sign indicates the way to Joshua Tree National Park. You will be in the middle of the small town of **Joshua Tree.**

38 Miles At the **West Entrance Station** to the park, an attendant will take $5 and give you a map. The high desert into which you will be heading is a pretty spectacular place.

    The park covers some 800,000 acres, and while there are jackrabbits, bobcats, and golden eagles in residence, what you will see most of are cacti, be they Joshua trees, ocotillo, cholla, or whatever. And a lot of rocks, often adorned with rock-climbers wearing bright shirts and shorts; geologists have

CHAPTER
14

Something like 90 percent of the dates grown in the United States come from the Coachella Valley; Shields, one of the growers, will gladly sell you a box of the fruit, or a date shake, one of the sweetest concoctions known to man.

identified these odd and other-worldly formations as **monzogranite intrusions.** The road will be good, and quite curvy.

48 Miles Stay on the main road, Park Boulevard, as it goes leftish; if you want to get a fine view of the desert, take the right turn, which dead-ends after 6+ miles at **Key View** (5,185 feet).

59 Miles Turn right onto Pinto Basin Road (see 29 Palms sidebar).

Riding along Pinto Basin Road, you'll find yourself dropping down from the high **Mojave Desert** to the low **Colorado Desert** . . . you will be able to see for miles and miles into the basin. Go gently, as the road is a tad more than twisty, and tourists tend to clutter up the narrow asphalt. And you do not want to impale yourself on a cactus.

82 Miles A dirt road, immediately splitting into two dirt roads, goes off to the left, for you adventuresome dual-purpose types.

89 Miles You will arrive at the ranger station and visitor center at **Cottonwood Springs;** the springs and campground are a mile east of the visitor center.

From here, you will go over **Cottonwood Pass** (2,800 feet) and down **Cottonwood Canyon,** leaving the park on a delightful stretch of road.

96 Miles Arrive at I-10 (see The General Patton Museum sidebar).

Back at the 96-Mile mark, cross over the Interstate and turn right onto Box Canyon Road. The road will go through **Shavers Valley** before dropping down into **Box Canyon,** between the **Mecca Hills** and **Orocopia Mountains,** an excellent piece of riding.

111 Miles Cross over the **Coachella Canal** into a sea of green. You will be going below sea level as you enter the southern end of the **Coachella Valley.** This is very fertile land, as long as you have water to make things grow.

114 Miles Enter the small town of **Mecca** (elev. –189 feet), now home to several thousand farm workers, where the American date industry started about

100 years ago. Nobody seems to know precisely how the town got its name, but presumably it's because of its many date palms, which came from the Middle East.

115 Miles Traffic light, and turn right on CA 111, right after crossing over the **Southern Pacific** railroad tracks.

117 Miles If you have a very sweet tooth, stop at the **Date Garden Oasis** for a date shake; there's an awful lot of sugar in one of those babies.

Stay on CA 111 through the town of **Thermal.**

125 Miles Turn left onto Avenue 52—not a very romantic name, but a useful identifier.

Staying on Avenue 52, cross over CA 86 and head straight as the proverbial arrow toward **Indio Mountain.** Major farming here, but specialized, with dates and grapes abounding. From there, you will enter a new development town called **La Quinta,** its semi-expensive houses all looking just alike. The cross-streets all have presidential names: Van Buren, Jackson, Monroe, Madison, Jefferson. No Clinton, yet.

The General Patton Museum

For an interesting deviation, go four miles west on I-10 to **Chiriaco Summit** (1,705 feet), exit, and visit the **General George Patton Museum.** Back in 1940, when **President Roosevelt** knew that entering the European conflict was inevitable, he had the army set up training bases in the desert to prepare for battling the Germans in North Africa. Every sort of World War II tank imaginable is parked outside the museum, and inside you'll find an eclectic display of the equipment used by Patton and his troops.

Up on the Chiriaco Summit of I-10, east of Palm Springs, you can view World War II artifacts at the General George Patton Museum. As you can see here, many of the bigger items are left out in the dry desert air.

133 Miles Turn right (north) onto Washington Avenue.

136 Miles Traffic light—turn left onto CA 111; this little jog along Avenue 52 avoids downtown **Indio,** a thoroughly avoidable place.

138 Miles Stay straight on CA 111, as CA 74 goes off to the left.

146 Miles Stay straight on East Palm Canyon Drive, as CA 111 goes right onto Gene Autry Trail.

150 Miles Arrive back at **Ramon** and **Indian Canyon.**

Trip 30 The San Jacinto Mountains & Idyllwild

Distance *103 miles*

Highlights *Right above Palm Springs you'll see Mt. San Jacinto. You could take an aerial tramway up, but it is much more fun to circle around the peak on a motorcycle. Even if it is hot down in Palm Springs, take some warm clothes, as you will be going more than 5,000 feet above the town, and it can be cool.*

0 Miles Go south on Palm Canyon Drive.

1 Mile Curve left, keeping to the obvious main road, East Palm Canyon Drive.

4 Miles Cross the southern terminus (love that word!) of the Gene Autry Trail, and East Palm Canyon becomes CA 111.

12 Miles Traffic light, and turn right onto well-marked CA 74, where there is a SHELL gas station on the corner. This stretch is called the **Pines to Palms Highway.** It will be dead straight for the first five miles—then it will turn into Racer Road, known locally as **Seven Level Hill.** A beaut! It will turn back and forth for the next five miles, and you could go slow and admire the vistas, or fast and scrape excess metal from your bike.

The riding up CA 74 to the look-out on Seven Level Hill above Palm Desert is superb, as is the view over the Coachella Valley.

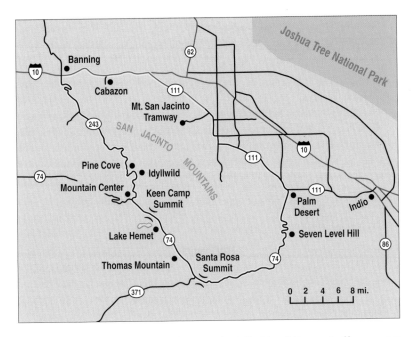

21 Miles A big pullout and lookout on the left side of the road offers a great view of the **Coachella Valley,** and on any weekend there will be motorcyclists there.

26 Miles A fire station will be on your right and the **Sugarloaf Cafe** will be on your left, open 7 a.m. to 9 p.m. daily, except Mondays; they feed a lot of tourists, but working folk frequent the place daily, so the food has to be good.

35 Miles The road flattens out and you will pass the **Pacific Crest Trail,** a hiking trail that runs from the Mexican border to Canada; myself, I'd rather ride.

36 Miles Crest the **Santa Rosa Summit,** at 4,919 feet.

37 Miles Go straight at the intersection with CA 371, which drops down to **Aguanga** (see Chapter 15). The cafe at the intersection is open on the weekends 7:30 a.m. to 6 p.m., 11 a.m. to 5 p.m. Monday, Thursday, and Friday.

Continue on CA 74, dropping gently into **Garner Valley,** the road reasonably straight past the growing community of **Thomas Mountain.**

45 Miles The general store at **Lake Hemet** (4,334 feet) will have all the resources that the campers and fishermen at the lake might need, including bait.

46 Miles After cresting **Keen Camp Summit** (4,917 feet), you will drop down twistily into **Mountain Center.**

48 Miles Turn right at Mountain Center, onto CA 243, while CA 74 goes straight. In the center of the intersection, you'll see the **Mountain Center**

General Store, with gas, and across the road, the sometimes-functioning **Mountain Center Cafe,** right next to the functioning post office. At the STOP sign, turn right.

51 Miles Enter the center of **Idyllwild,** a pleasant resort community (see Idyllwild sidebar).

CA 243 winds on to **Pine Cove,** sort of an adjunct to Idyllwild, climbing to more than 5,800 feet as it passes **Pine Cove Park.** This will be excellent riding, through a landscape of pine trees—unless there is a lot of traffic on the road, as 243 is a twisty, double-yellow byway that has little opportunity for legal overtaking. Ah well, if you don't have to go up in front of Ken Starr . . .

68 Miles Stay on CA 243 as Poppet Flat Road goes off to the left.

Idyllwild

Idyllwild is a great escape from the heat of Palm Springs. The **Idyllwild Cafe,** on your right (26600 Hwy. 243), serves an honest breakfast and lunch (7 a.m. to 2 p.m.) seven days a week. Smack in the very center of town is **Jo'An's Restaurant** (25070 North Village Center Dr.), open for lunch and dinner

This totem pole sits on Village Center Drive in Idyllwild, right next to Jo'An's Restaurant, which is a good place to break one's fast.

through the week, as well as breakfast on the weekend. For a really fine seafood dinner, try **Antonelli's Ristorante** (26345 Hwy 243), open at five in the afternoon Wednesday through Sunday. Lodging will be everywhere (key into http://www.idyl.com), from the funky fifties **Bluebird Hill Lodge** with 26 redwood cabins (26905 Hwy 243; 909-659-2696; $45 for a motel-type room to $100 for a two-bedroom cabin), to the **Idyllwild Inn** ($55 and up; 54300 Village Center Dr.; 888-659-2552), owned by the same family since 1904. If you want absolute silence, a mile from town you'll find the **Quiet Creek Inn** ($75 and up; 909-659-6110; 800-450-6110); from here, you could walk to any of the 15 restaurants in town to work up an appetite. ✱

75 Miles From here, the descent to Banning will begin in earnest, dropping more than 2,000 feet in five miles. Good fun. The road curves down into the valley, beyond which are the impressive **San Bernardino Mountains.**

76+ Miles Turn left as you approach the Interstate, a sign indicating that this is the way to get to I-10.

77 Miles Turn right, following Interstate signs, and in a quarter-mile you will get on I-10 going east. Go past the huge **Desert Hills Factory Stores** on the north side of I-10 (unless, of course, you are in a buying mood).

84 Miles Go through **San Gorgonio Pass,** the dividing point between the **San Bernardino Valley** and **Palm Springs.** If you wish to see a concrete Jurassic Park, take the **Cabazon** exit, go under the Interstate, and behind **The Wheel Inn** (which serves a much, much better hamburger than the adjacent fast-food joint) you'll find a very large and temptingly photogenic brontosaurus and tyrannosaurus rex.

This fossilized dinosaur is part of a concrete Jurassic Park behind the Wheel Inn at the Cabazon exit off I-10, west of Palm Springs.

89 Miles Exit right onto CA 111, which will follow the south side of the dry **Whitewater River** (no connection to the Clintons' problems).

97 Miles A large sign will indicate that the **Palm Springs Aerial Tramway** is to your left. If you went 3+ miles up that road, climbing steeply to 2,643 feet, you could get in the gondola, and in 15 minutes you would be up at **Mountain Station,** at 8,516 feet. After which an hour's serious hike could have you on the top of **Mt. San Jacinto** at 10,804 feet.

99 Miles **Palm Canyon** curves south, and right afterwards CA 111 will cut off to the left. You stay straight on Palm Canyon.

103 Miles Arrive back at **Ramon Road,** Ground Zero.

Trip 31 Over the San Bernardino Mountains

Distance *181 miles*

Highlights *You can look forward to a lot of desert, a good deal of mountain, and a good ride which will last you the better part of a day. This trip has the same beginning as Trip 29.*

0 Miles Go north on Indian Canyon, and follow the Trip 29 instructions for the first 26 miles—about the only thing to remember is to turn left at the STOP sign after 14 miles—and continue on into **Yucca Valley.**

26 Miles Turn left onto Pioneertown Road, going up through rocky, brushy country.

30 Miles Arrive at **Pioneertown,** a collection of old buildings and wagons, with some newer additions, such as a motel, to attract the tourists.

32+ Miles Turn right at a four-way, middle-of-nowhere intersection to follow Pipes Canyon Road, a winding stretch along **Pipes Wash** with a few scattered houses and a lot of horse activity.

Alternate Route

A dual-purpose rider might opt to go straight at the intersection. The pavement ends in a little over a mile, at **Rimrock,** then a rough dirt road continues past the **Farrington Observatory** for 17 miles (shortest version) to connect with CA 38 on top of the **San Bernardino Mountains.**

If you went left at the intersection, another dirt road would go for 16 miles to meet up with CA 38 at **Onyx Summit.** Although both versions have about a 4,000-foot climb, neither are terribly difficult. ✸

---

39 Miles STOP sign—turn left as **Pipes Canyon** ends at CA 247, also known as Old Woman Springs Road.

45 Miles You will see signs for **Landers,** a desert community off to the right, where local residents have twice spotted the mysterious **Big Tread,** or Goldeman, a legendary, never-photographed creature that leaves Kenda tracks in the desert. On your left, you will see what appears to be a row of statuary lining the road; that is **Moby Dick's** place. Dick moved out of The Big City (Los Angeles) in the late eighties, and has found happiness here in the high desert. He makes his mildly bizarre sculptures out of anything he can find, but his main source of inspiration is old motorcycle parts. With a hundred or more decrepit and cannibalized bikes neatly lined up, and boxes of

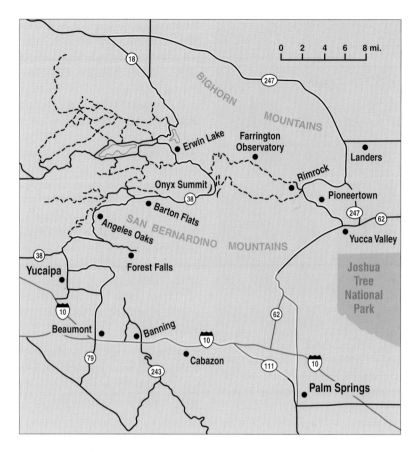

nuts and bolts under a protective roof, he could probably find you a carburetor for a DT1, though it might be a little corroded.

CA 247 will be entering **Johnson Valley,** which looks rather barren, spread out between the **Big Horn Mountains** and **Iron Ridge.** People do live out here, but not many, and civilization as we know it has been left behind. **Old Woman Springs** will be off to your left.

79 Miles Turn left onto Rock Camp Road at this remote intersection, with hardly a house or car to be seen.

84 Miles STOP sign—turn left as Rock Camp slides into CA 18, where there is a huge Mitsubishi cement plant stuck in the hillside in front of you. What are the Japanese doing making cement in the California mountains? Obviously the global economy is beyond my comprehension. But CA 18 otherwise provides a great ride up the mountainside as you climb into the **San Bernardino National Forest.** For trivia collectors, this was the second designated national forest in the country, signed into being by **Prez Ben Harrison** in 1892.

In Landers, Moby Dick creates sculptures from old motorcycle bits; look for a retrospective of his work at the Guggenheim sometime soon.

89 Miles As you arrive in **Cactus Flats,** a dirt road goes off to the right; had you come up from Rimrock you might have ended up here. From here, you will start a gentle descent down the **Johnston Grade** to shallow **Baldwin Lake,** whose surface sits at 6,698 feet above sea level. The San Berdoo Mountains are pretty high, and they stretch for more than 50 miles east to west . . . though we are just going to cut across the eastern end.

In the middle of the mountains are several lakes, **Big Bear** and **Arrowhead** being the best known. Not only is the whole area a resort so people can escape the heat of the Los Angeles basin, a lot of people have chosen to live up here year round, which means it is often crowded.

95 Miles Turn left as CA 18 enters a built-up area and meets head-on with CA 38, and both roads join to go to the right (south) on Greenway Drive.

96 Miles STOP sign—turn left at the end of Greenway, following CA 38; CA 18 goes to the right.

From here, CA 38 is known as the **Rim of the World National Forest Scenic Byway.** Follow CA 38 as it leaves civilization, angling right and going past the Big Bear suburbs of **Erwin Lake** and **Sugarloaf.** You will leave the forest, climbing slowly.

106 Miles Crest **Onyx Summit;** at 8,443 feet, it's the highest paved road in southern Southern California, which refers to that part of SoCal which begins just north of the Los Angeles basin. To your left will be the dirt road that could lead a d-p bike back down to **Pioneertown.** Up here high in the forest, it is hard to imagine that you are just 100 eagle-flying miles from the crowded heart of Los Angeles and the sun-soaked Pacific beaches.

From here, you will have a steep descent to Barton Flats and the stunning valley of the **Santa Ana River.** I promise you, once that river reaches the valley, the romance will be gone, but here in the wilderness it is a beauty. To the south will be **San Gorgonio Mountain,** the tallest peak in SoCal at 11,499 feet.

118 Miles After dropping 3,000 feet, you will be in the middle of **Barton Flats.** Glass Road goes off to the right, the pavement ending in a maze of dirt roads. Dozens of camps and private residences are scattered throughout Barton Flats, and in the summer it is virtually a city in the woods.

125 Miles You will be in the center of **Angelus Oaks,** which has a fire station, a general store, and a telephone, in case you want to reach out and touch someone.

130 Miles Turn right, following CA 38, as the road comes down into **Mill Creek Canyon,** with a wide riverbed in front of you. If you turned left, the road, Valley of the Falls Drive, dead-ends after 4+ miles in the community of **Forest Falls.** CA 38 goes down along **Mill Creek,** an impressive sight as it cuts down through the mountains.

And all of a sudden you will be out of the mountains with the **San Bernardino Valley** in front of you.

136 Miles Turn left onto Bryant Street at the **Mill Creek Ranger Station,** where a sign points left saying YUCAIPA 4.

141 Miles Traffic light—turn right on Avenue F after passing through downtown **Yucaipa,** following the road down **Wildwood Canyon** as it turns into Wildwood Canyon Road.

145 Miles STOP sign—turn right on Oak Glen Road, the road going alongside the **Little San Gorgonio Creek,** past the **Edward Dean Museum of Decorative Arts,** through **Cherry Valley,** and head due south to **Beaumont** ("Beautiful Mountain," in French).

151 Miles At the intersection with I-10, cross over and head east.

156 Miles After the Banning exit, pick up the last few miles from Trip 30, going past **Cabazon** and catching CA 111 back into **Palm Springs.**

181 Miles Arrive back at **Ramon** and **Palm Canyon.**

From Mill Creek Canyon, you can see San Gorgonio Mountain in the distance.

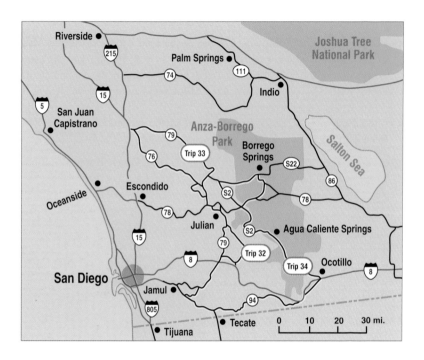

Eastern San Diego County

Headquarters *Julian*

Tourist Office *760-765-1857*

Best Time to Visit *All year. Except it can get downright nippy up in the Laguna Mountains in the winter.*

Getting There *Going north on I-15, take CA 78 East from Escondido; south on I-15, take CA 79 East from Temecula. If you are on I-8, take CA 79 North at Descanso.*

Ground Zero *The following loops will all start at the sole four-way STOP sign in the center of Julian, at the corner of Washington and Main Streets.*

With good mountainous country, desert to the east, and great roads all over, **San Diego** is home to a lot of serious motorcyclists—and they know that they have some lovely roads to ride. If the **King of the Alps, John Hermann,** author of *Motorcycle Journeys Through the Alps,* chooses to live here when he is not gallivanting over the Passo del Stelvio, you know there is some good motorcycling in the area.

Pleasant little town, **Julian,** which will probably end up on the cutesy side of nice by the time the year 2010 rolls around. But no matter—it is a good base for superlative riding.

There is essentially one main street in Julian, cunningly called Main Street, and everything can be located from that half-mile stretch. The town is on the list of **"State Registered Historical Places,"** whatever that means, and it tries very

In Julian, you can take a gentle one-horsepower ramble through the town, out to a bit of countryside, and back.

hard to maintain a hardscrabble attitude, even though B&Bs flourish and Benzes and Volvos clutter the streets every weekend.

The place was named after **Michael Julian,** a Confederate soldier from Georgia who originally came west with some cousins to try his luck at homesteading. But when gold was found in them thar hills in 1870, life changed drastically for a few years, until all the gold petered out. (Except for the gold in the tourists' pockets.) The **Eagle** and **High Peak** hard-rock mines, at the north side of town, are still open to visitors every day.

When the miners went away, people stayed to raise cattle and apples, and, in recent times, Julian has become known as **Apple Pie City.** In fact, when I first went there around 1981, my legendary riding buddy, **Fireball Stein,** bought an apple pie for $76.50—$4.50 for the pie, $72 for the speeding ticket. Yes, California's finest do enforce the laws, especially on the weekends.

The place had the fortune (misfortune?) to be "discovered" about 20 years ago and the population has been slowly growing. During the week, life is pretty quiet, but on a fall weekend it will be controlled chaos, with the flatlanders com-

Downtown Julian can get crowded on a nice weekend, what with all the tourists coming up to buy apple pie. (Photo by Jasmine Kimura)

ing up to eat apple pie, and buy apple pies to take home. A dozen pie shops line the main street to capitalize on just that, and I would bet that some of the pies are not even made in Julian.

Oh, never mind.

Julian's population is about 4,000, and it sits at 4,200 feet in the **Laguna Mountains.** About 30 hostelries offer a place to lay your head, from tiny B&Bs with just one cottage to rent, to middling-sized establishments that can sleep 50 or more. There will be nothing in the way of big resort accommodations in Julian, and certainly no chain motels.

At the high end of the financial spectrum, you'll find the **Orchard Hill Country Inn,** a newly-built hotel on top of, yes, Orchard Hill, two blocks east of the center of town on Washington Street. The owners, **Pat** and **Darrell Straube,** do have excellent taste. The lodge is all stone, with a lovely, great fireplace in the foyer, and large, well-lit rooms. There are also four cottages for larger parties; prices go from $132 to $225, including a large breakfast (2502 Washington St.; 760-765-1700; 800-716-7242). One note: there is a dirt drive up to the hotel, but the German motorcycle tour groups who use the inn frequently have no problem negotiating it.

For the historically inclined, the **Julian Hotel** on Main Street is "the oldest continuously operating hotel in Southern California." It has been around since 1897, when it was called the **Hotel Robinson,** and it is now a delightful B&B, with afternoon tea included. All the rooms are individually appointed with Victorian decor that is worth the price of admission—which ranges from $72 to $175 for the separate **Honeymoon House.** Although there is no private parking, the town is as safe a place to park your motorcycle as I know (2032 Main St.; 760-765-0201; 800-734-5854).

If you appreciate Fifties funky, check out the **Apple Tree Inn** (a motel by any other name) in **Wynola** about three miles west of Julian center on CA 78/79 (4360 Hwy 78; 760-765-0222; 800-410-8683). Sixteen units are spread around a pool in the best old motel tradition. Prices are quite good, ranging from $62 to $87 depending on the size of room and the time of the week. Next door, you'll find **Tom's Chicken Shack,** where the CHP meet to eat. And right across the road will be **Motorcycle Springs,** a large deli that does business seven days a week; owner **Tom Phillips** has quite an extensive motorcycle collection upstairs and hanging from the rafters, as well as an old BMW high on top of the sign by the road—definitely worth a visit.

For dinner, I prefer the **Julian Grille,** at 2224 Main Street, where they offer a 22-ounce porterhouse for $23. For breakfast, the **Julian Cafe & Bakery** at 2112 Main Street does the sausage and eggs just right. You could drink apple cider, but I recommend, instead, a very hearty cabernet sauvignon from the **Menghini Winery;** to get there, just take Main Street north, which turns into Farmers Road, which becomes Julian Orchards Drive.

Trip 32   One Lap Around Mt. Laguna

Distance *57 miles*

Highlights *This will be a half-day ride. Or stretch it out as long as you wish.*

0 Miles Head south on Main Street, past the Julian Hotel and the gas station.

1 Mile Turn right onto CA 79, where CA 78 goes straight. A long, smooth grade climbs into the wooded twisties, with quite a number of driveways going off to the left and right. Soon you will see Lake Cuyamaca in the distance in front of you.

6+ Miles Turn left onto County Road S1, marked MT LAGUNA 15, where CA 79 goes straight. This road is called the **Sunrise Scenic Byway,** as it runs along the east edge of the **Laguna Mountains,** 4,000 to 5,000 feet above the **Anza-Borrego Desert** visible to the east. **Lake Cuyamaca** will be off to your right.

14 Miles This is the turn-off to the **Kwaamii Point** overlook, a few hundred yards to your left. On a clear day, you can see the **Salton Sea** some 50 miles to the northeast. Stunning.

   Back on S1, you will be getting into nice pine woods, staying away from the eastern escarpment, the road swooping and leaning very pleasantly.

21 Miles You'll be coming into the mountain community of **Mt. Laguna,** at almost 6,000 feet, where you'll find several cafes, a store, and the **Laguna**

Anyone who wants to take a break from motorcycling can rent a boat and sit out in the middle of Lake Cuyamaca to contemplate the meaning of fishing.

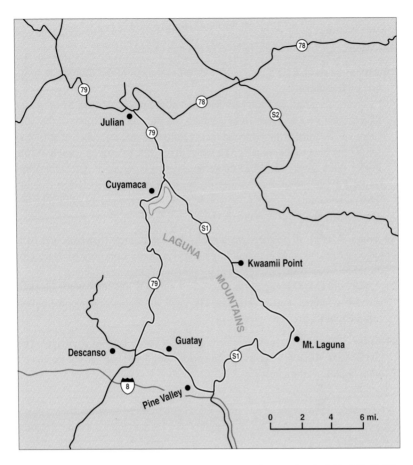

Mt. Lodge offering motel units and cabins at $40 to $100 (760-445-2342). An old garage sits on the left side of the road, but the owner allows that he does not have the expertise to work on motorcycles, preferring one-ton pickups with big V8s (he might be able to do something with a Boss Hoss).

S1 peaks a few feet above 6,000, then begins a descent toward **Laguna Summit** (4,055 ft.) on Interstate 8. The road is usually clean, lightly-trafficked, and double-lined, and as it breaks out of the high forest it clings to the west side of the mountains—with a long drop, should you get overly enthusiastic.

29+ Miles Turn right where the sign to the right reads OLD HWY 80 and PINE VALLEY 1. Interstate 8 will be straight ahead.

30 Miles Pine Valley, a main way-station before the Interstate appeared some 30 years ago, is a small but thriving community serving the traveler with gas and food.

Continue on Old Hwy. 80 through **Guatay.**

35+ Miles Turn right at the intersection with CA 79.

36 Miles Keep on CA 79 as a road goes off to the left to the farming community of **Descanso.**

From this point, you will be in **Green Valley,** irrigated by the **Sweetwater River,** where some smart folks heading via the southern route to the gold fields of California figured to get their gold by staying on, raising cattle, and selling the beef to the miners. The road will enter **Cuyamaca Rancho State Park,** which covers a hefty 25,000 acres. All this is part of the **Cleveland National Forest,** which has patches of forest all through San Diego County. "Why Cleveland?," you may be wondering. Grover signed the bill which began the national forest system in 1892.

42 Miles A road off to the right goes to the **Cuyamaca Museum** and park headquarters. The museum building itself is in an old stone ranch house, with information on Native Americans, local history, flora, and fauna.

Back on CA 79 going north, you'll be running through oak and pine on a woodsy, winding, well-paved road. The view will break as you come out on **Lake Cuyamaca.**

47 Miles The Lake Cuyamaca store and boat rental will be to your right. The lake covers 110 acres, and is stocked with trout, bass, catfish, sturgeon, and other aquatic vertebrates.

Residents up in the Laguna Mountains make a good bit of extra money selling healthy food to McBurger-eating city slickers.

CalTrans certainly does a good job with its signage in San Diego county . . . though road markers can be somewhat remiss in other parts of the state.

50 Miles You will have returned to the CA 79 and S1 intersection.

57 Miles Arrive back in the middle of **Julian.**

CHAPTER
15

Trip 33 Around Palomar Mountain and to the Top

Distance *121 miles*

Highlights *This is a fine country loop, and the climb up Palomar on S6 is one of the great short rides; this stretch has worn out a lot of footpegs—and even puts holes in the pannier bags of more enthusiastic riders.*

0 Miles Leave the **Julian** intersection and head south on CA 78/79.

3 Miles Past Wynola Road turn-off, where the **Red Apple Inn** and several large fruit barns lure the tourist, you will drop down the mountain, usually with a good bit of traffic. The **Inaya Memorial Park,** to your left, honors the firefighters who lost their lives in the great forest fire of 1956. Do be careful with flammables.

6+ Miles Turn right, following CA 79 to the north. You will have just dropped 1,200 feet and are now in the **Santa Ysabel Valley,** where CA 78 and 79 split. If you are hungry, or your bike needs gas, you could fill up here, in the ZIP-coded community of **Saint Isabelle.** Of most fame is **Dudley's Bakery,** a hundred yards east of the intersection, which offers some 20 varieties of bread, including White Regular, Irish Brown, German Black, and Danish Apple Nut. A loaf of Jalapeño is a meal unto itself.

The Chapel of San Francisco at Warner Springs has been around since 1830, and it still has services on Sunday.

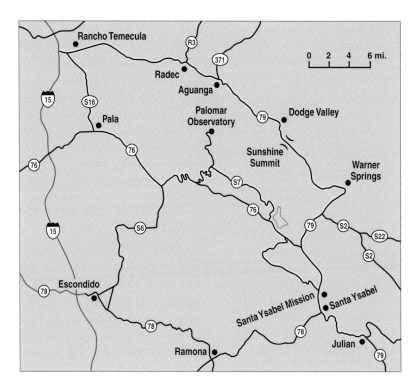

8 Miles Off to your right will be the small **Santa Ysabel Chapel.** The original chapel, built in 1818 as a mission outpost, made sure the local inhabitants got directions to Catholic heaven.

14 Miles Go straight on CA 79, ignoring the left turns to CA 76, curving to the right over the **Carriso, Matagual,** and **Buena Vista Creeks.** The flat land to the left is a broad valley that feeds **Lake Henshaw.**

18 Miles Ignore the right turn onto S2 and head straight up and over a ridge which leads down to **Warner Springs** and a large resort. The road will cross the **Pacific Crest Hiking Trail.**

22 Miles After crossing over the **Warner Springs Ranch Creek,** right ahead on the hill you'll see the old **Chapel of St. Francis,** a handsome building constructed in 1830. As an animal-lover, I appreciate old Saint Frank.

24 Miles CA 79 goes past the **Warner Springs glider port**—rides available any weekend, and often during the week if there happens to be a pilot and a tow-plane around. I recommend you take a glider ride at least once in your life; you will be surprised how much noise the wind makes.

From here, CA 79 winds through scrubby semi-desert. In a couple of hours, you'll be at the **Palomar Observatory** atop **Palomar Mountain,** which is currently visible ahead of you. The U.S. Navy runs a **mountain sur-**

vival school out here for pilots who happen to get downed over such inhospitable real estate. As you continue, you'll come to the community of **Sunshine Summit,** with a store, and just beyond that, the summit at 3,282 feet (see The Officials in Green sidebar).

31 Miles Dropping into **Dodge Valley,** the eponymous **Dodge Valley Inn,** with cafe and saloon, will be on your right. The cafe opens every morning at 7 a.m. and the kitchen closes at 7 p.m., a little later on Friday and Saturday.

The Officials in Green

There will be a U.S. Border Patrol station just a mile farther up, where you may be asked to stop by the boys and girls in drab green. You will see a lot of these Border Patrol types in SoCal, driving their green-and-white trucks, vans, and sport-utes. Very simply put, their job is to prevent "undocumented aliens" from entering the wage markets of Los Angeles and the San Joaquin Valley. They are usually pleasant enough, and have no direct authority to stop you for such mundane misdemeanors as speeding. However, if you are truly being irresponsible, "la migra" can stop you and discuss the weather until a California Highway Patrolman arrives to write you up. ✹

Determined to keep undocumented visitors at bay, the Border Patrol often sets up checkpoints on back roads in San Diego county.

Julia Flores, owner and cook, is assisted by her son **Jesus.** The **Dodge Valley Saloon,** right next door, will have rowdy music on Saturday nights.

CA 79 will go on briefly into **Riverside County.**

42 Miles At the **Aguanga** intersection, a right turn onto CA 371 would take you to Palm Springs.

45 Miles At the **Radec** intersection, a right turn onto County Road R3 will lead to Hemet. From here, CA 79 undulates through lightly civilized countryside until it crosses the **Temecula River** and enters **Pauba Valley.**

Oops! Lots of farming, lots of traffic, lots of construction . . . the road widens, traffic lights—but this stretch of suburbia is brief.

55 Miles Traffic light—turn left, with Pala Rd./S16 clearly marked, going toward the **Pala Indian Reservation.** The Riverside County part on either side of S16, romantically called **Wolf Valley,** is being highly developed, but as soon as you are back in **San Diego County** the build-up will be over. From here, the road will drop steeply and twistily down between **Mt. Olympus** and **Tourmaline Queen Mountain,** alongside **Pala Creek,** to the **Pala Indian Reservations.** Watch out, as there will be some tricky bits, including a 240-degree right-hand corner that refuses to quit.

64 Miles STOP sign—turn left at the little community of **Pala.** Right on the corner, you'll see the **Mission San Antonio de Pala,** built in 1816—which claims to be the only one of the old missions that still is dedicated to the spiritual well-being of Native Americans.

65 Miles STOP sign—turn left as S16 ends to merge with CA 76, which then rolls over hill and dale for some nine miles as it runs though **Pauma Valley.**

73 Miles Stay left on CA 76, where S6 comes in from the right—and from this point, the going will get really good. The road winds de-lightfully through some orange groves, flat and smooth, an easy ride or a peg-scraper. Then it climbs up steeply, with a few very tight corners to a mesa.

78 Miles Turn left onto the continu-ation of County Road S6, one of CalTrans' little offerings to the mo-torcycle community. It will be nearly seven miles and some 70 turns to the top, and on any week-end, the sport-riders will be out in considerable force. There is no need to go fast, but there is the op-portunity, should you be of the

The dome of the Mt. Palomar Observatory crowns the top of the mountain in the distance.

Palomar Observatory

If you stayed on S6 another four miles beyond Mother's, you would get to the Palomar Observatory parking lot. A short walk away, a smaller building houses a smaller telescope and gift shop; the big observatory with the 200-inch telescope is farther up the hill. Although the astronomers have been on Palomar for donkeys' years, the increasing light pollution from all the building that goes on around the mountain has pretty much ruined the place for any serious stellar observation. The tourists don't seem to mind, however.   ✱

knee-grinding persuasion. Note that several cattle-guards at inopportune mo-ments should keep you honest. This is a road that should be ridden with cau-tion until one has experienced it properly and noted all the seriously gnarly turns. I'll guarantee that your engine's temp gauge will go up. It is a great road, sure to rank high on anyone's list of the **1,000 Best Motorcycle Roads In The World.**

85 Miles Turn right at the intersection at the top (5,280 feet), and head down S7, East Grade Road.

But don't be too hasty, as you have your choices. Turn left, and immediately on your left will be **Mother's Kitchen.** On a bright Sunday morning, a hundred go-fasters of all marques can be found talking about aftermarket pipes, comparing the scrub marks on the edges of their tires, and telling lies. The Kitchen, a veggie joint, is not an exceptional cafe, but the omelets and coffee are fine (see Palomar Observatory sidebar).

Back at Mother's intersection, go right and head down the East Grade Road (S7).

85+ Miles After a quarter mile, you will see Crestline Avenue going off to the left. That is where most of the local community lives. If you were to go up Crestline to the end, you'd find the **Palomar Mountain Lodge,** based on a superbly retro log building built back in the 1920s. It has ten rooms, rates go

Joe and Chris Menne are the proprietors of the Palomar Mountain Lodge, which is a grand place to spend the night.

from $55 to $65, and the owners, **Joe** and **Chris Menne,** figure there is no way you cannot have a good time (note the double negative). It really is a great place to stay (760-742-8744).

Back on the East Grade Road, you'll be enjoying a long, smooth, softly curved (for the most part) 11 miles down through **Dyche Valley** to the **Lake Henshaw** intersection, dropping 2,500 feet along the way. After you go past the **Lake Henshaw Dam,** S7 will come to an end.

97 Miles STOP sign—turn left at the intersection with CA 78. The **Lake Henshaw Resort,** half a mile along on your right, caters mostly to the fisherfolk. Go past West Loop, a little bit of the old highway off to your right.

99+ Miles Turn right at the street sign marked CENTER LOOP, and you'll see a large sign denoting the biker-friendly **Hideout Saloon & Steakhouse,** open Thursday through Sunday (760-782-3656, for more info). Just before getting to the Hideout, you'll see the sign for Mesa Grande Road; turn right again, and you'll start to climb steeply through the woods on a very tight road which might have a few leaves on it in the fall.

Pop out on top of the mesa, and for the next few miles the asphalt will wend its way through farmland, so watch out for tractors. At the far end of the mesa, the road drops down to the **Santa Ysabel Valley,** but this time the curvaceous descent will be smooth and can be done at a goodly rate of speed.

112 Miles STOP sign—turn right, where Mesa Grande butts into CA 79, and head back on this previously traveled road to Santa Ysabel.

114 Miles STOP sign—turn left here at **Santa Ysabel,** and start heading back up the hill.

121 Miles Arrive back in **Julian.**

Trip 34 The Mexican Border & Anza-Borrego

Distance *217 miles*

Highlights *This long loop goes south to the Mexican border, runs along CA 94 to the east, swings north to Anza-Borrego Desert State Park and Borrego Springs, and returns up the Banner Grade.*

0 Miles Head south along Main Street.

0+ Miles Turn right onto CA 79, as you might have done in Trip 32. You'll be staying on CA 79 for the next 23 miles, past **Lake Cuyamaca** and **Cuyamaca Rancho State Park;** I covered this section, in reverse, on Trip 32.

23 Miles Cross under Interstate 8 and continue south on Japatul Road; you'll see a few houses on each side, sort of an ex-urban environment, as this is within commuting distance of San Diego.

28 Miles Turn left onto Lyons Valley Road, where a large green sign indicates the way to **Barrett Honor Camp,** where your delinquent second cousin might be staying. This superb, well-maintained road swoops down and around the edges of **Gaskill Peak** as it drops down from 3,300 to 1,700 feet.

36 Miles Turn left at a very country four-way junction, with trees, grass, fields, and an old water trough, onto Honey Springs Road, which offers some very rustic riding through lush ranchland.

43 Miles STOP sign—turn left, as Honey Springs butts into CA 94, the southernmost state highway in California.

47 Miles Come into the small town of **Dulzura,** where the **Dulzura Cafe** opens every morning at 8 a.m. to serve a good breakfast or lunch, suppers on the weekend. **Kathy Coffer** presides. Nobody seems to know quite when the original building was constructed, but learned commentary from the folk inside indicate it was probably in the late Teens. It has been added onto and altered over the last 70 years, and it is a small museum in itself. If you'd like to see a definitive collec-

Tecate, Mexico

If you want to pop into Mexico proper for a visit, take CA 188 for all of two miles, to the **U.S. Customs & Immigration** office on the border, just on the edge of the town of Tecate. It is a very easy, lightly-trafficked crossing, and three blocks south of the border, the town square, **Parque Hidalgo,** will be a good place to get your boots shined. You'll find sustenance at the **Restaurant Jardin TkT** ("TkT" is Spanish phonetics for "Tecate"). ✸

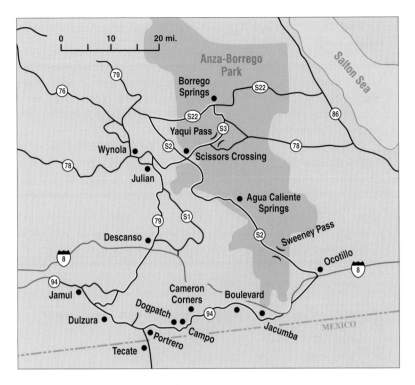

tion of manual eggbeaters, it is there. Dulzura, for the etymologically challenged, means "sweet" in Spanish, and the name apparently comes from the good-tasting water of the **Dulzura Creek.**

CA 94 will continue on through mildly mountainous countryside. You'll have a gorgeous view of the **Cottonwood Creek Valley** as you come around **White Mountain,** go over a ridge, and see the road drop down, cross the valley, and go up the other side, miles away.

53 Miles At **Barrett Junction** in the middle of the valley, the **Barrett Cafe & Fish Fry** hosts an all-you-can-eat extravaganza most evenings of the week. Once you climb back up into the hills, the narrow two-lane road will suddenly widen—but not for long.

57 Miles At the intersecton where CA 188 goes off to the right, you go straight, following CA 94, and the road will go back to being a narrow two-laner (see Tecate, Mexico sidebar).

60 Miles Staying on CA 94, you will pass through **Potrero,** with a general store and gas station.

65 Miles You will pass the almost non-existent community of **Dogpatch,** which was once a railway-workers stop along the **San Diego & Imperial**

Valley Railroad. Then you'll pass beneath the old rail line and head on along **Campo Creek.**

68 Miles Come into **Campo,** whose old depot is home to the **San Diego Railroad Museum.** A few miles of track have been retied, and a steam or, more often, a diesel locomotive hauls tourists around. The park operates most weekends and often during the week, but it's best to call and check (760-595-3030 or 760-478-9937).

Right alongside Campo Creek, you'll see the **Gaskill Stone Store.** In 1808, a merchant by the name of Gaskill built a typical store on that spot along the old wagon road, but when robbers burned the place in 1875, the merchant rebuilt the whole thing in highly-defensible stone.

70 Miles CA 94 goes up to **Cameron Corners,** where there is a gas station and a hamburger joint on the corner with the southern terminus of S1. Follow CA 94 over **Miller Creek** and under a high trestle for the SD & IV RR, on to the intersection at Boulevard.

The Desert View Tower was built in the early 1920s, with a splendid view over the Imperial Valley; it is off Interstate 8 west of Jacumba, just as it crosses from San Diego to Imperial county.

Desert View Tower

Cross under I-8 and turn right onto a sort of frontage road, which soon disappears around a corner and dead-ends in front of you at a very odd stone tower about 70 feet high. The ridge on the edge of the **Jacumba Mountains** where the **Desert View Tower** is situated is about 3,000 feet above sea level, and from the top floor of the tower, you'll have a superb view of the **Imperial Valley** all the way to the **Salton Sea.** It will cost a buck to go up to the top, but it will be a buck well spent. The tower was built between 1920 and 1922, but it never achieved any fame until I-8 was finished; now lots of tour buses stop there. ✱

It's eight o'clock in the morning, and I'm facing east from the Montezuma Grade just west of Borrego Springs; Borrego Springs and the Anza-Borrego Desert are spread out in the distance before me.

82 Miles   STOP sign—turn right as CA 94 ends and merges with Old Hwy. 80 going east.

90 Miles   Old Hwy. 80 will come into **Jacumba,** an old railroad town trying to figure out what to do in the 21st century. There is a very fine old spa in town, the **Jacumba Hot Springs Spa,** which has a faithful clientele of San Diegoites and bicyclists on a cross-country runs. The **Bachmeiers, Felix** and **Felix Jr.,** do a superb job of keeping the place quiet; noisy children are *not* tolerated. Room rates run from $32 to $50 (760-766-4333).

  Continue along Old Hwy 80.

95 Miles   Turn right onto Interstate 8 at the In-Ko-Pah entrance and head east on the Interstate (see Desert View Tower sidebar).

  Back on the Interstate, you'll cross into **Imperial County,** wind through the **In-Ko-Pah Gorge,** and then head out into the **Yuha Desert.**

107 Miles   Exit Interstate at the Ocotillo/Imperial Hwy./S2 exit, and turn left. The little town of **Ocotillo** does not offer much except gas and basic sustenance. Head north on S2, a/k/a **Imperial Highway,** going toward Anza-Borrego State Park. Go through town, such that it is, and watch out for that damn STOP sign (108.5 miles) set out in approximately nowhere.

115 Miles   You will be at the Imperial Highway monument, at the eastern edge of **Imperial County.** As you cross back into **San Diego County,** the name of the two-laner will change to Sweeney Pass Road; you will also be entering **Anza-Borrego Desert State Park,** the biggest state park in the country at 600,000 acres. It is a beaut ride, passing by the **Coyote Mountains,** past the

CHAPTER
15

Carrizo Badlands, and over **Sweeney Pass** (at a lofty 1,065 feet) and **Egg Mountain.** Great names. Just past the **Well of Eight Echoes,** S2 will change names again, becoming the **Old Overland Stage Route.**

131 Miles A road off to the left goes to **Agua Caliente Hot Springs** (a bilingual redundancy), a little county park inside a state park. The **Agua Caliente Regional Park** is open September through May (too hot in the summer), and campsites are available. The San Diego-based **Airhead BMW Club** can often be found out there parboiling their brain cells. The outdoor pool is kept at a natural 96 degrees, and the indoor pool is heated to 101. Enjoy.

S2 will continue on through **Vallecito Valley,** past the old **Butterfield Ranch,** a stopping point for the Butterfield stage of long, long ago. It then climbs past **Box Canyon** (pay attention here, as the turns get a little sharper than you might expect), and out into **Earthquake Valley,** where a small community has grown up.

154 Miles STOP sign—turn right at **Scissors Crossing,** where S2 crosses CA 78. You could go left to Julian if you are tired, but the right to Borrego Springs will finish this loop in a grand manner.

CA 78 East goes down through **Sentenac Canyon** and out onto **Yaqui Flats,** where, on a late winter's day, the wildflowers will be growing in glorious profusion.

The Gaskill Stone Store was constructed as a defensible building in 1885, after the previous store was destroyed by border marauders; it sits along Campo Creek, in Campo, down close to the border with Mexico.

Borrego Springs

If you want to stay in **Borrego Springs,** there will be upward of a dozen places to lay your head, ranging from $50 to $200 a night. If you arrive in wildflower season, you'd better have some reservations lined up, as horticultural enthusiasts will be flocking to this locale. For lodging, the simple **Hacienda del Sol,** on Palm Canyon Drive, has six rooms, four cottages, and ten duplexes ($55 to $80). Although they have no phones, there are coffee-makings in the room; this is as close to the middle of town as you'll find, not that the town has much of a middle (760-767-5442). Farther up **Palm Canyon,** the **Borrego Valley Inn,** a purpose-built B&B, has 14 rooms at $95 a night (760-767-0311). At the high end, the aforementioned **Casa del Zorro** is an old-fashioned place with 60 rooms and suites, and 19 separate cottages, along with six lighted tennis courts. The food is good and the price ranges from $75 mid-week in the low season, to $290 on the weekend in the high season (3845 Yaqui Pass Road; 800-824-1884).

The town does not offer much in the way of gastronomical delights. The locals hang out at **Bailey's Cafe** (previously known as Kendall's) on the "south side" of **The Mall** on Canyon Drive (which means around back); the place is open seven days a week, 6 a.m. to 8 p.m. If you want to watch traffic go by on Canyon Drive, eatables are available at **The Coffee & Book Store** from 6 a.m. to 4 p.m. daily. At **Carlee's Place,** on Christmas Circle, you can get all-American chicken, ribs, steaks, etc. for lunch and dinner. Fancier dining is available at **Le Pavilion** at **Rams Hill Country Club** (1682 Yaqui Pass Road), or at **Zorro's.** The sidewalks pretty much get rolled up in the evening, so you can plan on getting an early start the next morning. ✱

161 Miles Turn left onto S3 at the sign for Borrego Springs, go past the **Tamarisk Grove Campground,** and up over **Yaqui Pass** (1,750 feet). From this point, it will be a long, straightish, downhill shot into the desert town of Borrego Springs.

168 Miles Turn left at the intersection, which will be the most direct way to **Borrego Springs** proper, such that it is. **La Casa del Zorro** ("fox") **Desert Resort Hotel** will be on your right.

As you head west along Borrego Springs Road and curve north, the metropolis will be off in front of you.

173 Miles Enter **Christmas Circle,** the center of town, where several outdoor stands will be selling fruit. Palm Canyon Drive going due west is the main drag (see Borrego Springs sidebar).

Back on the road, head west on Palm Canyon Dr./S22.

175 Miles S22 turns left at the **Palm Canyon Resort.** If you went straight, you would end up in the parking lot of the **Visitor Center of Anza-Borrego Park Headquarters.** The nice museum, nice views, and a short stroll along the **Nature Path** will show you as much about desert botany as most people would care to know.

From here, S22 starts the climb up **Montezuma Grade,** a motorcycling road which rates two stars from my jaded soul. It is a spectacular ride, especially when taken early in the morning with the sun just coming up at your back. The road climbs more than 3,000 feet in about six miles, and the views back over the desert will definitely be worth a stop or two or three. Afterward, the road drops into **Montezuma Valley.**

193 Miles STOP sign—turn left, as S22 T-bones into S2; go south. The next 12 miles will go along **San Felipe Creek,** and they can be traveled at a great rate of speed—though the California Highway Patrol is aware of this, and often has a constable lurking in the bushes.

205 Miles STOP sign—turn right, back at **Scissors Crossing.** Go west on CA 78, 12 miles to Julian. The first five miles will be straightish until you reach the store and campground at **Banner,** and start up the **Banner Grade.** The next four miles will be very twisty, with a lot of downhill traffic taking more of the road than it should. Watch out.

213 Miles Wynola Road will go off to the right, which could provide an interesting back way into Julian. Just go up a little less than a mile, to the point where Farmers Road cuts to the left, and the **Menghini Winery** to the right. If you took the left, two miles later you would be back at the center of **Julian.**
Or continue along CA 78.

217 Miles Arrive back in the center of town.

One Lap of California

As I said in Chapter 3, the previous baker's dozen (that's 13, for those of you not familiar with baking terminology) of chapters have more or less circled the state of California. Now you will have an opportunity to put them all together in one Grand Tour.

While the other chapters have been "in depth," this one is "in breadth." It all depends whether you want to focus on an area and get to see everything, or nearly everything, or lots, or at least a good deal—or take one big swoop around the state in which you touch on nearly all the previous chapters.

The minimum "lap" is 2,500 miles—and we will start from LA. If time is of importance, or your Jawa Californian 350 seizes solid along the route, you can cut the trip short at any time by going back to the starting point in Los Angeles—or to any place else in the state, for that matter.

If you want to know more about places I touch on here, refer to the appropriate chapter(s). We will hit 11 out of our 13 designated touring sites, leaving out only the Kings Canyon/Sequoia route and the Kernville area.

Of course, since you readers have good imaginations and excellent geographic sensibilities, you may have already figured that the whole thing could be tied together in some haphazard way, so you could go home and say, "Been to California, done the whole state, nothing left to see." Ha!

Anyway, for the Grand Tour types, this version of a lap of the Golden State hits many of the high points.

If you care to swap saddles, most of the resorts offer horseback riding.

Trip 35 One Big Lap

Best Time to Visit *April through November*

Ground Zero *We will begin in Los Angeles, on CA 1 at Topanga Beach near Malibu (Chapter 3).*

0 Miles Turn right at the traffic light onto CA 27, Topanga Canyon Road.

5 Miles Turn left at the fork in **Topanga** village, onto Old Topanga Canyon Road.

10 Miles STOP sign—turn left onto **Mulholland Highway.** Follow Mulholland through the **Santa Monica Mountains,** past the **Rock Store,** until you reach the coast.

40 Miles STOP sign—turn right onto CA 1.

63 Miles Merge with US 101 going north.

71 Miles Exit US 101 onto CA 33 (Chapter 4).

84 Miles At the traffic light on the edge of **Ojai, turn left, following CA 33.**

142 Miles At the STOP sign at the junction with CA 166, turn left.

207 Miles Turn right onto US 101 going north.

235 Miles Exit US 101 onto CA 1, the Big Sur Highway, heading for **Morro Bay** and **Monterey** (Chapter 5).

371 Miles Arrive at **Monterey Peninsula;** continue on CA 1.

415 Miles Skirting the city of **Santa Cruz,** turn right onto CA 9 headed for **Felton** and **Boulder Creek** in the **Santa Cruz Mountains** (Chapter 6).

These Boy Scouts are getting set for a hike in the Joshua Tree National Park; that's a lot of gear they are carrying.

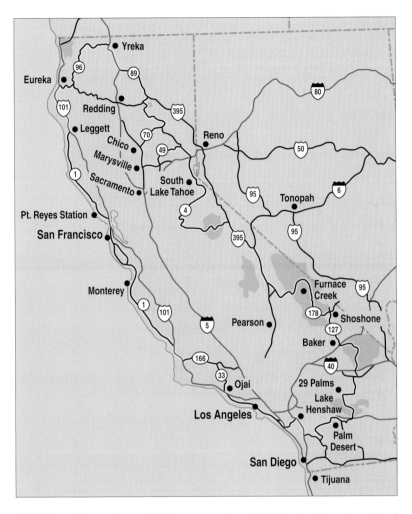

442 Miles Turn left onto CA 35 as you arrive at **Skyline Boulevard** and head toward **Alice's Restaurant.**

468 Miles STOP sign—turn left onto CA 92.

473 Miles Arrive in **Half Moon Bay** and turn right at the traffic light, onto CA 1 going north.

501 Miles Arrive at the **Golden Gate Bridge** on CA 1/US 101.

507 Miles Exit US 101 onto CA 1 headed for **Stinson Beach** (Chapter 7).

508 Miles Traffic light—turn left at **Mt. Tam Junction,** headed for Stinson Beach on CA 1—and just follow your front wheel for the next 200 miles.

708 Miles When CA 1 ends at **Leggett,** head north on US 101 . . . and after going north a few miles, take the well-marked **Avenue of the Giants** (CA 254) which parallels US 101 for 31 miles.

805 Miles Exit US 101 onto CA 299 going east toward **Willow Creek** (Chapter 8).

844 Miles Turn left onto CA 96, to go north and east along the **Klamath River.**

991 Miles Turn right onto CA 263 headed for **Yreka.**

999 Miles Turn left to get onto I-5 going south.

1,038 Miles Exit I-5, turn left and head east on CA 89.

1,129 Miles Pay $5 at the entrance to **Lassen Volcanic National Park** (Chapter 9).

1,220 Miles STOP sign—turn right onto CA 70, going down **Feather River Canyon.**

1,282 Miles Merge with the **Chico-Oroville Highway,** continuing on CA 70.

1,316 Miles Turn left onto CA 20 at **Marysville,** heading east to **Grass Valley.**

1,351 Miles CA 20 will merge with CA 49 heading north.

1,355 Miles Turn left at **Nevada City,** onto CA 49, heading for **Downieville,** for a stunning run up along the **Yuba River.**

1,428 Miles STOP sign—turn right, CA 49 merging with CA 89.

1,433 Miles Turn right, staying on CA 89 in the middle of downtown **Sierraville** (pop. 85).

1,456 Miles Turn right onto I-80 going west toward **Truckee.**

1,458 Miles Exit I-80, heading south of CA 89.

1,472 Miles STOP sign—turn right, following CA 89 as you enter **Tahoe City** (Chapter 10).

1,500 Miles Traffic light—turn right, following CA 89/US 50 in **South Lake Tahoe.**

1,505 Miles Turn left onto CA 89 just after the **California Agricultural Inspection Station.**

1,516 Miles At the STOP sign at **Picketts Junction,** turn left, following CA 88/89.

1,522 Miles Turn left to follow CA 89, in the little village of **Woodfords.**

The wind that funnels through the San Gorgonio Pass, west of Palm Springs, generates a lot of electric power with these windmills.

1,534 Miles Go straight, moving onto CA 4 (CA 89 goes off to the left), over **Ebbetts Pass** (8,730 feet).

1,616 Miles STOP sign—turn left onto CA 49 toward **Sonora.**

1,651 Miles Stay straight on CA 120, heading into **Yosemite National Park,** as CA 49 goes off to the right.

1,685 Miles Enter Yosemite and pay the $10 entrance fee.

1,694 Miles Turn left at **Crane Flat,** following CA 120, as it were, heading up to **Tioga Pass.** (Now, if you want to eat the whole jar of pickles, you could stay straight, going into **Yosemite Valley** before heading south on CA 41, pick up CA 180 going east out of **Fresno** (Chapter 11), then go south to **Kernville** (Chapter 12), and head east over **Sherman Pass** or **Walker Pass** and on to **Death Valley.**)

1,754 Miles STOP sign—turn right onto US 395.

1,876 Miles Turn right onto CA 136, at the south end of **Lone Pine,** heading for **Death Valley** (Chapter 13).

1,894 Miles Go straight as CA 136 becomes CA 190.

1,980 Miles Turn right onto CA 178, opposite the **Furnace Creek Inn,** the sign pointing to **Badwater.**

2,052 Miles STOP sign—turn right toward **Shoshone** on CA 127/178.

2,053 Miles Stay straight on CA 127, as CA 178 goes off to the left.

2,111 Miles At the STOP sign in **Baker,** stay straight, and go under I-15, onto Kelbaker Road, through **Kelso,** and under I-40.

2,179 Miles STOP sign—turn right onto Old Route 66, a/k/a **National Trails Highway.**

2,185 Miles Turn left onto Amboy Road, having passed the one cafe/gas station/motel that is **Amboy** and gone over the railroad tracks; the sign will point toward **29 Palms.**

2,233 Miles Turn left onto Utah Road, which could catch you by surprise, but if you go on a mile to the traffic light on Adobe Road, you will figure things out (Chapter 14).

2,240 Miles Pay $5 at the entrance to **Joshua Tree National Park.**

2,244 Miles Turn left at the three-way intersection, taking Pinto Basin Road toward Cottonwood Springs.

2,281 Miles Turn right onto Pinto Road after passing over I-10, heading for Mecca.

2,301 Miles Turn right onto CA 111, right after crossing over the railroad tracks.

2,324 Miles Traffic light, turn left onto CA 74; you will be right in the middle of the town of **Palm Desert.**

2,349 Miles Turn left onto CA 371, marked AGUANGA, while CA 74 continues on straight; CA 371 will drop 3,000 feet in the next 20 miles.

2,369 Miles STOP sign—turn left onto CA 79, as CA 371 ends at the **Aguanga** intersection (Chapter 15).

2,387 Miles Turn right onto CA 76.

2,391 Miles Turn right onto San Diego County Road S7, just past the **Lake Henshaw Resort.**

2,402 Miles Turn left onto County Road S6 at the **Palomar Mountain** intersection.

2,409 Miles STOP sign—turn right onto CA 76.

2,430 Miles Turn right onto I-15 going north.

2,459 Miles Exit Interstate onto CA 74 and turn left, going west over the **Ortega Highway** (Chapter 4).

2,492 Miles Turn right onto I-5 going north.

2,503 Miles Take I-405 North.

2,556 Miles Take I-10 West, toward **Malibu.**

2,559 Miles I-10 will turn into CA 1, heading north.

2,565 Miles Arrive back at **Topanga Beach.**

California Weather

The weather in California is generally very good. But on occasion it can be very bad. We get snow in the mountains, and the temperature can reach 120 degrees in the summer desert (we'll deal strictly in Fahrenheit here, as it sounds so much more impressive).

Since California is so big, the weather can vary a lot. At the beginning of each chapter I have put in a little line on Weather to indicate which months may be the best time to plan your trip to Eureka, or Julian, or wherever.

But *do not* take my word for it. You should not try to project a September weather pattern in June, even if you've brought up all the weather channels in the universe . . . the forecast might just be terribly wrong. If, say, you are sitting in San Francisco and are thinking of going up to Quincy, you'd be better off buying the *San Francisco Chronicle* and consulting its five-day forecast. Which will only be wrong half the time.

The best approach of all might be to call the telephone number of the local chamber of commerce or tourist bureau, also listed at the start of each chapter, and ask the person at the other end to look out the window. It would be a start, anyway.

If said person truly deserves the job of representing the town to foreigners, of promoting its scenic beauty and historical significance, of bringing in free-spending yokels from Los Angeles or Boston or Paris, then that person should also have scrutinized the local weather report that morning, and should be able to tell you whether a nor'wester is about to blow in and dump ten inches of rain, or

During summer in the Sierras, you can ride in a T-shirt to 6,000 feet. (Photo by Craig Erion)

a tropical high is expected to keep the temperature between 70 and 80, with humidity at 64 percent.

All in all, however, you just can't tell. I've gotten rained into Death Valley at Thanksgiving, all the passes closed due to mud-slides and snow. I've alternately roasted and frozen in Redding, which can be one hellaciously hot sumbich in summer, and one cold misery in winter—and you never know which way spring and fall are going to go. I've also found mountain passes closed with snow as late as July.

The Pacific Coast can be really foggy all through the summer, Los Angeles can be awash in rain more months of the year than not, and if you stay in Bear Valley in November, you might find a foot of snow on your motorcycle seat in the morning.

And if that's not enough to deter you, think of earthquakes opening up the road in front of you, forest fires sweeping through your campsite, hailstones battering you at Mono Lake, and extra-terrestrials kidnapping you for a few experiments. California has it all.

But mostly we have benign weather. Yes, it rains a lot up north, but that's what rainsuits are for. And the mercury can boil in Palm Springs, but that is why motels are air-conditioned. No guarantees on the weather, but anytime of year, somewhere in California, there will be better motorcycling weather than any you'd find in Massachusetts in the winter, or Florida in the summer.

And since my routes can take you anywhere from below sea level to nearly 10,000 feet, you should bring layers of clothing accordingly. Because, in truth, there is not much you can do about the weather, except to dress appropriately.

When spring comes, the wildflowers in California can be simply marvelous, especially the poppies.

Motorcycle Rentals

Quite a few companies are trying to make a buck renting bikes—which isn't that hard to do. If you were to buy a Harley Wide Glide for $13,000 and rent it out for $125 a day, it would be paid for in less than four months. However, the rental company does have to worry about insurance (which can be very expensive indeed), repairs, maintenance, et cetera.

There are some very reputable outfits which rent bikes in good condition. I've also heard that you can get real junkers. Unfortunately, I can't tell you which companies are the best ones, because I've never rented a bike in this state.

If you make a long-distance arrangement and have to put down a deposit, make sure that you get all the particulars in print, so you will have some recourse when the guy offers you a Bridgestone 350 GTR instead of the BMW R1100R you were expecting.

Here is a list of California-based rental outfits; I expect that several of these may have gone out of business by the time you read this, and new ones will have appeared. If you have a computer, run up www.motordirectory.com and see what the screen says.

American Rentals *(San Francisco)*

2715 Hyde Street, San Francisco, CA 94109
415-931-0234
Offers Harley-Davidson, Honda, and Yamaha.

Big Twin Adventure Rentals *(Santa Cruz)*

1144 Soquel Avenue, Santa Cruz, CA 95062
831-466-9836
Offers Harley-Davidson.

California Beemin' *(San Jose)*

1886 West San Carlos Street, San Jose, CA 95128
408-295-0205
rentals@sjbmw.com

California Motorcycle Rentals *(San Diego, LA, San Francisco)*

3304 Buena Vista Street, San Diego, CA 92109
619-581-6879
Offers Harley-Davidson and Kawasaki.

Cruise America Motorcycle Rentals *(Los Angeles, San Francisco)*
796 66th Avenue, Oakland, CA 94621
510-639-7124; 800-327-7799
Offers Harley-Davidson, Honda, and Buell.

Dubbelju Motorcycle Rentals *(San Francisco)*
271 Clara Street, San Francisco, CA 94107
415-495-2774
www.dubbelju.com
Offers Harley-Davidson and BMW.

EagleRider *(Los Angeles, San Francisco, San Diego, and Las Vegas)*
20917 Western Avenue, Torrance, CA 90501
800-501-8687
Offers Harley-Davidson.

Great American Motorcycle Rentals *(Redding)*
3202-B South Market, Redding, CA 96001
530-242-8715
Offers Harley-Davidson.

Harley Owners Group *(San Diego, San Bernardino, Los Angeles, San Francisco, Oakland, Las Vegas, and Reno)*
You have to be a HOG member to take advantage of this, but if you are, dial 411-343-4896 for all the particulars.

The Motorcycle Rental Company *(Los Angeles)*
141 East Santa Clara Street, Arcadia, CA 91006
877-437-3685
Offers Harley-Davidson.

Island Riders *(San Jose, Las Vegas)*
170 South Market Street, San Jose, CA 95112
408-277-0861
Offers Harley-Davidson.

Malibu Motorcycle Rentals *(Los Angeles)*
22853 Pacific Coast Highway, Malibu, CA 90265
310-456-1815

These editors from a German motorcycle magazine have come to see Death Valley up close and personal.

Moturis Motorcycle Rentals *(L As, San Francisco, Las Vegas)*
400 West Compton Blvd., Gardena, CA 90248
310-767-5988; 877-MOTURIS
Offers Harley-Davidson, Honda, and BMW.

North American Motorcycle Rentals *(Las Vegas)*
4625 East Tropicana, Las Vegas, NV 89121
702-434-7200
Offers Harley-Davidson.

Rebel USA *(San Diego)*
5600 Kearny Mesa Road, San Diego, CA
888-737-3235; 619-292-6200
Offers Harley-Davidson.

Recreation Unlimited *(Los Angeles)*
1021 West Taft Avenue, Orange, CA
714-998-8170

Route 66 Riders Motorcycle Rental *(Los Angeles, Palm Springs)*

4161 Lincoln Blvd., Marina del Rey, CA 90292

800-434-4473; 310-578-0112

Offers Harley-Davidson.

San Francisco Bay Area Motorcycle Rentals *(San Francisco)*

757 Lincoln Avenue #18, San Rafael, CA 94901

888-812-9253

www.motorbikeusa.com

Offers Harley-Davidson.

Tahoe Motorcycle Tour & Rental company *(Reno)*

P.O. Box 20188, Reno, NV 89515

877-348-0965

www.swbike.com/tahoemc

Offers Harley-Davidson.

Motorcycle Tours

Running tours to the Alps or the Andes is one thing, running tours in California is quite another. First, the roads in California tend to be well-marked (excepting those in Fresno), and two, it is generally not difficult to find a place to eat or sleep.

Pick up a copy of a German or Italian or Dutch magazine, and chances are you will find an ad or three for junkets to the US of A, rental bikes and chase vehicle included. That is understandable, as your average non-English-speaking rider might want the security of a guide. And British magazines offer their own ads, as well.

But there are also some companies that do tours for Americans, and here are a few that I have found. Give them a call to get the particulars. Or again, run up www.motodirectory.com on the insidious Internet.

Big Twin Adventure Tours

116 Alamo Street, Santa Cruz, CA 95060
831-426-4436

The Usal Road turn-off—would this be a good idea on a Gold Wing? No.

Classic Motorcycle Adventures
P.O. Box 2817, Truckee, CA 96160
818-339-4262

EagleRider Motorcycle Tours
20917 Western Avenue, Torrance, CA 90501
800-501-8687; 888- 900-9909
www.hogrent.com

Edelweiss Bike Travel
P.O. Box 1974, Wrightwood, CA 92397
800-582-2263
www.edelweissbiketravel.com

Lost Coast Motorcycle Expeditions
P.O. Box 1581, Laytonville, CA 95454
Offers dual-purpose trips in northwest California.

Tahoe Motorcycle Tour & Rental company
P.O. Box 20188, Reno, NV 89515
877-348-0965
www.swbike.com/tahoemc

Index

315

About the Author

A well-known name in motorcycle journalism, Clement Salvadori has written nearly 900 articles for several dozen motorcycle magazines during the past 21 years.

One of motorcycling's most erudite observers, Salvadori graduated from Harvard (where he rode an aged Indian Chief), served in the Army's Special Forces as a demolitions expert (a skill which he still occasionally applies to motorcycles), and became a Foreign Service Officer with the State Department after receiving his master's degree in foreign relations.

Following several overseas assignments, Salvadori realized he enjoyed traveling more as a motorcyclist than as a diplomat. So he resigned and spent the next three years riding around the world. Two decades later, he's still at it.

Perhaps the most well-traveled journalist in motorcycling today, Clement has ridden in 60 countries—from Afghanistan to Zimbabwe—on five continents. Which means, according to Salvadori, "There's still a lot of riding yet to do."

The only trouble with California riding is that eventually you can't go west any more.